ONE LAST JOB

TOM PETTIFOR/NICK SOMMERLAD

Mirror Books

D1419138

Published by Mirror Books,
an imprint of Trinity Mirror plc,
1 Canada Square,
London E14 5AP, England

www.mirrorbooks.com

twitter.com/themirrorbooks

Executive Editor: Jo Sollis
Editor: Robin Jarossi
Art Director: Julie Adams
Image Production: Paul Mason

ISBN 9781910335451

Second paperback edition

Printed and bound in Great Britain
by CPI Group (UK) Ltd, Croydon, CR0 4YY

About the Authors

TOM PETTIFOR is the Chief Crime Correspondent at the *Daily Mirror* where he has covered many of Britain's biggest cases, including the murders of Stephen Lawrence, Milly Dowler and Anni Dewani. He began his career reporting at the Old Bailey and specialises in investigating police corruption and organised crime. His work exposing the cover-up of child sexual abuse in Lambeth, south London, led to several Scotland Yard probes and formed part of a national public inquiry. This is his first book.

NICK SOMMERLAD is the Investigations Editor of the *Daily Mirror* where he has spent several years doorstepping crooks and conmen. He has worked undercover at an immigration detention centre, been attacked by a baseball bat-wielding fraudster and had tea with an illegal betting kingpin. He has been shortlisted five times at the British Press Awards, winning the Hugh Cudlipp Award in 2010. This is his first book.

CONTENTS

DEDICATIONS

Tom Pettifor dedicates this book to TC, DJ and TP.

Nick Sommerlad dedicates this book to DE, MJ, KR, IW and EA.

Prologue

The glittering steel and glass towers rose up from the banks of the River Thames like giant totems to the wealth that had created them. Canary Wharf's skyscrapers had been a fixture in the life of security guard Kelvin Stockwell as he made his way to work over the previous decade. Kelvin's home, almost in the shadows of the towers, was five miles east of his destination, the Hatton Garden Safe Deposit Ltd.

It was his first day back after the Easter Bank Holiday as the chief guard of the vault in the heart of the capital's jewellery district. Sharp-suited young bankers were sipping cafe lattes in the early spring sunshine while cleaners finishing their night shifts headed home. It was barely 7am and the Tube trains were already full of office workers.

For Kelvin, April 7, 2015, had begun like any other working day. The nation had enjoyed the hottest Easter for four years and the temperature that morning was above average and rising. He did not know it yet, but it was going to get a lot hotter for Kelvin that day. The papers were full of coverage of the forthcoming general election, which they said was too close to call. In the international news pages, *The Times* reported that Kenyan warplanes had bombed two camps belonging to Islamic extremists in neighbouring Somalia in response to a horrific attack on a university.

The chaos and destruction of the world seemed a long way from Hatton Garden that morning. As normal, a street cleaner swept the pavement and jewellers were beginning to open up their shops. George, a muscular security guard with huge hands, was at his usual spot in a shop doorway eyeing the people coming and going. Everything appeared just as it always did when Kelvin arrived for work just after 8am. He let himself in through the black wooden main door of the HGSD building. It housed around 60 business tenants, most of them jewellers, over seven floors. In the basement was the vault. Built in 1948, it held 999 locked safety-deposit boxes that were entombed in a layer of steel, 20-inches of reinforced concrete and protected by a two-foot-thick Chubb door that weighed 10 tonnes. The custom-made portal had two combination locks and a key. Just to reach the vault door you had to pass through five locked doors and two sliding iron gates. Not to mention the state-of-the art CCTV system and digital alarm linked to a central headquarters that was programmed to activate within 60 seconds of a break-in. There was good reason why the vault had never been penetrated in all of its 67 years.

Kelvin shut the front door behind him before punching in the four-digit code to the glass sliding doors that led to the unstaffed lobby. Waiting for him was his colleague, fellow security guard Ronald Kamara, who did not bother with formalities. "I think we've been burgled," he blurted out. It was no longer just another Tuesday morning for Kelvin.

He dashed across the grey marble floor and opened a door beside the lift, which led to a descending flight of stairs into the basement. At the bottom, to the left, was another wooden door, with a mortice deadlock. Kelvin immediately noticed the top lock was missing. He peered through the hole where it should have been and saw the vault had been ransacked. The lights were on and the bars of a second security door had been cut and forced up, apparently to let someone in. Kelvin turned and ran along the corridor to a fire exit that led to a yard outside the basement. He slid back the two bolts on the door and pulled out his phone to check if he had a signal as he dashed into the open air. At exactly 8.10am he dialled 999 and told the operator on the emergency police line that there had been a burglary at the Hatton Garden Safe Deposit Ltd.

Jamie Day was the first detective on the scene. The quietly spoken 43-year-old was measured and watchful. But Detective Constable Day's relaxed demeanour masked an implacable determination that had helped him to get a job in Scotland Yard's elite Flying Squad. The team had a distinguished history and Day wore the navy-blue tie bearing the squad's logo of a descending eagle with pride. The raptor was a fitting symbol of the way the Flying Squad worked, quietly watching their criminal quarry, unseen and from above, before striking without warning.

Day arrived to find Kelvin waiting outside on the pavement along with a local uniformed officer who had evacuated the building. The anxious security guard explained what he had found and Day cautiously descended to the basement vault area and peered through the broken lock. The corridor was covered in dust and debris and the floor was strewn with papers, crowbars and power tools, including an angle grinder and a huge diamond-tipped drill. The metal lift shutter had been forced open wide enough to let someone squeeze through. Next to the huge, locked vault door, between a grey office chair and a black coat stand, was a neatly drilled hole that had given the raiders access to the vault. Inside the strongroom, empty safe deposit boxes had been stacked almost to the ceiling in one corner by the thieves. Ransacked paper jewellery packets, envelopes, letters and plastic shopping bags lay scattered around the floor. Also left behind were a collection of war medals. Whoever did this was not callous enough to steal those treasured items. Some of the boxes appeared to have had the locks smashed off, while others had been jemmied open, apparently at random. A brass plaque on the wall warned customers: "NOT RESPONSIBLE FOR PERSONAL PROPERTY".

Day set up a cordon around the crime scene to protect it from contamination. Within the hour the vault was crawling with forensic scientists clad in blue body suits. They would remain in the building carrying out painstaking tests for the next week in the hope of gathering evidence that might nail whoever was behind the burglary.

News of the raid spread up and down Hatton Garden like a bushfire and, in an age of social media, soon broke to a country that was slowly returning to work after a four-day break. The street outside the vault was filling up fast with angry jewellers desperate for news on whether their boxes were among those that had been emptied. It was rumoured that between 300 and 600 could have been smashed open. Many had their life savings stored in the vault and were not insured.

Day and his colleagues were under intense pressure to find the burglars and retrieve the stolen goods. Britain's top police officer, Met Commissioner Sir Bernard Hogan-Howe, had been informed of the raid and he wanted results. The Prime Minister David Cameron and Home Secretary Theresa May would want to know what his detectives were doing to catch the burglars and recover the loot.

In total 73 boxes had been emptied and it was estimated that between £10million and £20million worth of cash and jewels had been snatched. It was beginning to look like one of the biggest burglaries in British history.

Day and his team had certainly never seen a crime like it and could not think of any comparison in recent history. That was because there was none. This had been planned and executed with ruthless precision and the master thieves had not left a single clue in the building. They had spent many hours in the vault and had probably eaten in there, not to mention performing other essential bodily functions. Yet there was no DNA or fingerprints. The place had been cleaned by the raiders to remove every last trace of forensic evidence.

Then there was the hole in the wall. They had used a diamond-tipped industrial drill that had to be cooled with many litres of water that they had brought with them. The monster bit of kit could only be operated by someone who had been trained. And the disabling of the high-tech alarm system needed an expert engineer. The cover had been calmly removed without activating the tamper switch and the wires cut. This had to have been planned over many months, if not years. The gang had intimate knowledge of the building's layout and security systems. It would have involved at least five people lugging heavy tools but there were no witnesses. The noise of the drilling would have been deafening but nobody heard a thing. There was not one image on the building's internal CCTV because the intruders had taken the hard drive with them.

The mastermind who had executed such an audacious crime must rank among the leading felonious talents in the world. Intelligent, methodical, a stickler for detail and a strategist of the highest order. Who could have been responsible for such an impressive piece of work?

Five Weeks Later

The capital was abuzz with rumours about the heist of the decade, quite possibly the heist of the century.

Weeks earlier a gang of masterful burglars had broken into a seemingly impregnable vault in the heart of the capital's jewellery quarter. It was a ludicrously ambitious feat believed to have involved lock-picking, abseiling, drilling and, most brilliant of all, getting away with it. The gang were the most wanted criminals in the UK, maybe Europe, and among the most admired. These guys were experts, the crème de la crème. A German gang had been fingered, or the rival Pink Panthers from Eastern Europe. They must have been extraordinarily fit, a contortionist was reputed to have been amongst their number. The hole left by the drillers in the concrete-sided vault − like an unfinished Audi logo − had become an instant icon. But this was not about your Vorsprung durch Technik, you know. This was old school. You don't pick up how to do this stuff overnight.

Helping to clog up London's polluted streets on this May day was a 14-year-old blue Citroën Saxo, nicknamed Beeney by its overweight retired owner. Beeney got a lot of use. Sixty-seven-year-old grandfather Terry Perkins did not walk anywhere if he could avoid it. Sitting in the passenger seat was Danny Jones. Seven years younger than Perkins and in much better shape.

They discussed the previous month's burglary.

"No, they can't work that out," said Perkins. "That is the biggest robbery that could have ever ever been."

"Yeah," nodded Jones.

"That will never ever happen again," said Perkins.

"No," agreed Jones.

"The biggest robbery in the fucking world, Dan, we was on," went on Perkins, warming to his theme, "and that cunt…"

"Yeah."

"The whole fucking 12 years I've been with him… three, four bits of work… fucked every one of them," said Perkins bitterly.

That "cunt" was Brian Reader. Now 76 years old and suffering from prostate cancer, Reader was at home in Kent making the most of his long-overdue retirement. It had only started six weeks ago. For the previous sixty years he had barely stopped working, carving out a career that was unique in British criminal history – he was the country's most prolific burglar. A genuine master in this dying craft. The real, quietly spoken deal in a world full of wannabes and show-offs. He had been intimately involved in pieces of work that had graced the front pages of the national press no less than four times over more than 40 years. That is surely a record. These jobs were worth, in today's money, more than £150 million – another record that looks unlikely to be bettered. Yet, virtually no one knew Reader's name. That was about to change.

His final job, his 9th Symphony, his Sistine Chapel, his Battle of Trafalgar, was decades in the planning. The assault on the Hatton Garden vault, breathtaking in its ambition, was to be his swansong. And, if it came off right, nobody would ever know he'd done it.

But it didn't come off right.

"The biggest cash robbery in history at the time and now the biggest in the history of the fucking world, that's what they are saying," said Jones in Perkins' Saxo. "And if you listen to the Master, you walk away."

"And what are the odds, what fucking odds?" pondered Perkins.

"What a book you could write, fucking hell?" mused Jones.

This is our attempt at writing that book. The history of Brian Reader is, more or less, the history of spectacular, acquisitive British crime over the last 70 years. We asked Reader to help us tell his story. As is quite right and proper, he refused. A true criminal of Reader's calibre never brags, never rats. Not publicly anyway. We are fortunate to have had help from some of his friends and relations. As we write, Reader is not in the best of health. In speaking to us, they felt that Reader's extraordinary life deserved a telling, an honest and open appraisal. There may never be another like him.

When researching the life and times of such a cunning and resourceful criminal as Reader, it is inevitable that we will be left with gaps. We have decided not to fill those gaps with conjecture. Some of the quotes you will read are anonymised and for good reason. But every word spoken in this book came from the mouth of a real person, whether in hushed tones in a London pub, over a mug of tea in a suburban kitchen or over a trusted phone line from a Spanish bolt-hole. Where we don't know what really happened, neither will you. You really couldn't make it up. There's simply no need.

CHAPTER 1

Eton for Criminals

Brian Henry Reader was born into the harsh poverty of London's docklands on the southern shores of the River Thames on February 28, 1939. Reader was the first child of Doris, 19, and Henry Reader, 24, who had married five months earlier after discovering Doris was pregnant. They had grown up living next door to each other in the Victorian terraced houses of Prior Street in Greenwich. It was not unusual at the time for several families to squeeze into a two-up-two-down. The communal kitchen and outside toilet was often shared between six adults and 10 children and there was no running water or electricity.

Reader's arrival came on the eve of what Winston Churchill would describe as "Britain's Darkest Hour". Within two years the skies above south east London were filled with the hum of Hitler's bombers. Reader was too young to join the children being evacuated, so when the bombing began, Doris would take him down to their Anderson shelter at the bottom of the garden at 64 Cressingham Road, Lewisham.

On the first night of the Blitz, nearly 1,000 German and Italian fighters and bombers attacked the capital. Like a huge swarm of metal locusts, the fleet extended for miles across the skyline and the ground shook with the noise of their roaring engines. Their main targets were the densely populated docklands area where Reader's family lived and 600 tons of high explosives were unloaded. The effect was catastrophic as large swathes of the city were reduced to rubble. Plumes of black smoke glowed red and orange as fires raged in bombed-out factories and homes. The dust-laden atmosphere pervaded every corner of the capital, leaving the streets covered in a layer of soot. That first attack, on September 7, 1940, saw Reader's home coming close to destruction when the house next door was bombed. Official records show an incendiary device fell on number 63 Cressingham Road at 6.40pm. Earlier that day the Woolworth's store a mile away in New Cross Road was hit, killing over a hundred people. Three years later, German planes attacked the local Sandhurst School in Catford one lunchtime and sliced a little girl down with a round of machine-gun fire as she skipped in the playground. They then dropped a 1,100lb bomb from the Focke-Wulf FW 190A-4 directly onto the school building, killing 32 children and six staff.

Reader would later tell friends his first lessons in crime came from his father, known as Harry, who would buy and sell goods arriving and then stolen at the docks. Harry made the most of the rich pickings from the cargoes unloaded. The son of haulage contractor Thomas Reader, Harry's day job driving lorries gave him ample opportunity to get his hands on items in demand. The Second World War and its aftermath provided a chance for men like him, who described themselves as "general traders", to make money from their ability to provide what was wanted, often at short notice. Harry lived on his wits and his streetwise savvy. Reader was to inherit all of this, along with an ability to find a trusted and secret marketplace for items of questionable provenance. One family member said of Harry: "He was a dodgy geezer, a good talker who knew lots of people and was always doing deals. But he never went to prison and was a hard worker."

Barrel-chested Harry had the tough exterior needed to survive on the streets of one of the poorest parts of London and was prepared to use his fists to settle an argument or protect his street business. Just 5ft 3ins tall, he joined the armed forces soon after war was declared when Reader was just six months old. A family member said: "He was at Dunkirk and, though he wasn't the biggest of men, he was muscular and knew how to look after himself. Once he got into an argument with a bloke; I think the man must have poked Harry because the next thing I knew he'd punched the chap square on the chin and he was lying flat out on the road. Harry always spoke like a cockney and he said: 'Get in the bloody motor quick.' We drove off and left the bloke lying there."

Reader's first winter was the coldest on record for 45

years and resulted in an eight-mile stretch of the Thames freezing over. Left alone with her first child, Doris got by on Harry's army pay of 14 shillings per week, worth £100 in today's money. Reader remained very close to his mother for the rest of his life. At the time of writing, she is 98 years old and living in a care home. Described by family friends as a "diamond" and a traditional south London matriarch, Doris instilled in Reader her Calvinistic work ethic along with a steely determination and unwavering commitment to putting family first.

Harry returned from the war in 1940 and the couple had three more children. A daughter was born in Bermondsey in 1941, followed by a son in Greenwich in 1948 and another girl five years later in Deptford. Food was rationed throughout Reader's childhood and there was no such thing as social security. It wasn't unusual for families in the working-class neighbourhood to own no furniture or bedclothes. An army coat on a mattress on the floor would be where they all slept.

Battling to keep her children fed and clothed during the tough post-war years, Doris was forced to move around south east London regularly and Reader was sent to a succession of schools. A friend said: "He always said that every time he went to a new one he would have to fight to prove himself. The docker children would always dig out the new kid and it made him even more independent. Brian knew that if you didn't fight back then you would always be bullied so he stood up to them. He was a tough kid. He wasn't big but he was strong and always had stamina, even from a young age."

It was during this period while at St Peter's School in Greenwich and then South East London Technical College that Reader became friends with a group of boys who would stay loyal pals to this day. One old friend said: "He's still got a lot of his old mates from school all those years ago. Every time I go to a funeral they would be there. Brian's a loyal person and he never forgot his old school friends even when he made his money. They're a staunch mob." The group have done well for themselves but Reader's generosity is reflected in the fact he has lent them money to put down deposits for houses over the years. "That's what he's like. Brian is a loyal friend and he stands by his mates and they have helped him over the years as well," the source said.

His first brush with the law came early in life. Reader was aged 11 and stood just four-and-a-half feet tall when he set out on his career path. Like all villains he started on a small scale. Reader got a conditional discharge at the East London Juvenile Court for 12 months on November 24, 1950, for four offences of "stealing tinned fruit by means of store-breaking". The charge was for burglary of a "non-dwelling". This type of crime would go on to become something of a speciality for Reader.

Reader had learned to help his mother by stealing on the side, while also working as a butcher's boy at the weekends and after school. An easy way for small children to make a few pennies was to pilfer the petrol coupons from public libraries and then sell them. That would be combined with legitimate earners like selling worms to fishing tackle shops and delivering papers and milk. Reader's friend said: "In those days every kid in your class would have at least one job on the go and many would bunk off to work full time or steal. If you wanted something you couldn't ask your parents to get it for you. You had to get it yourself, whether through stealing or earning the money. If you wanted a bike you had to think of a way of making it happen because no one else was going to get it for you."

Electoral records show that by 1947, when Reader was aged nine, he was living with the family at 1 Stanton House in Greenwich. The modern red-brick, ground floor council flat was on the shores of the Thames and only a few yards from Saint Alfege Church where Doris and Harry had married. It was a luxury for the family to have the whole flat to themselves, along with running water, electricity and an indoor toilet. But in 1953 they moved again, this time to 9 Liardet Grove in Deptford into a house that had been built for railway workers and which was demolished a few years later.

Harry abandoned Doris when Reader was a teenager, leaving the boy as the family's main breadwinner. It was a bitter blow that was to stay with Reader for the rest of his life and may have provided some of the motivation for him to go on and become one of the most successful thieves of his generation. A lifelong friend said: "It wasn't easy for him not having his dad around, and maybe that was part of the reason he worked so hard to be the best in the game. Brian was never given anything in his life, ever since he was a kid he had to earn it or take it using his own initiative. Brian had to be the head of the family from a young age and it made him grow up even faster."

Harry had met a woman 20 years his junior called Joyce Emms in the Mitre pub in Northampton in 1959, during a period of work tarmacking the Watford section of the new M1 motorway. He had got into the building and demolition trade in the post-war years as money was pumped into replacing homes destroyed in the bombing and improving the nation's infrastructure. Joyce was a beautiful blonde mother of four. Originally from Dagenham on the eastern fringes of London, she had moved to Northampton with her husband Patrick, who died a few months before she met Harry. Her daughter, Susan, said: "My mother had the most striking natural blonde hair and one night she was out with my grandmother, Mabel, when this man just sat down and started talking to her. In those days there was a photographer who would take pictures of people in the pub and he got one of my mum and Harry that night. Just as it was being taken Harry grabbed her hand and you can see the look of surprise on her face." Susan still has the black and white picture of the pair with Mabel.

Harry soon moved in with Joyce and the kids. His

business, "Reader's Demolitions", was booming and he employed a group of men who knocked down many of the old buildings in Northampton after the war. At various times he also owned a timber yard, a children's clothes shop, a fruit and veg shop and a general store. But Susan says that domestic life had become horrendous for her mother and siblings. She said: "Before mum passed away she told me that it was after he moved in that he punched her in the face for the first time. She said, 'I never knew why.' My mother was a beautiful woman and he was very jealous. By the end he wouldn't even let her go to buy the Sunday dinner because he thought the butcher fancied her. He kept hitting her and she would often have the bruises to show for it. He could be very frightening and would stand in front of the TV staring at us and blocking our view." The claim Harry beat Joyce is backed by a second source who described him as a "Jekyll and Hyde" character who could turn on the charm with outsiders while being a bully behind closed doors. The source said: "He worked hard and earned well but never had much money as it went on the horses or in the pub. He never talked about his other family, it was a taboo subject." But Susan says that Harry would always send money back to Doris for Reader and the other children. She said: "You could see Brian loved his dad."

Susan remembers Harry taking her down to London when she was a child. She said: "He would sometimes go and see Brian and his other children. We would all wait in the car. One day he came running back and jumped in saying Brian's mother was after him and we never went back again." Susan remembers Reader taking his own children to see their grandfather when they were very small. She said: "His mother was never allowed to know about it. I was young at the time but I remember thinking Brian was very handsome and a lovely man, not arrogant and nothing like his dad."

Despite the alleged violence, Harry and Joyce went on to have their own son, Reader's half-brother, in September 1967. Harry's business hit the skids in the 1970s and he was forced to sell their spacious detached home and move into a two-up-two-down. The lifelong *Daily Mirror* reader loved betting on the horses and would squander large amounts of money gambling. Harry had smoked Players No6 cigarettes all his life and in the late 70s he was diagnosed with lung cancer. Susan said: "The last time I saw Brian was just before Harry died on November 28, 1981, when he came in a big car with his wife Lyn and his brother and sisters. I remember he was shocked to see Harry had lost so much weight and was living in a small house because he had lost all his money. Before Brian came, Harry combed his hair and said: 'Joyce, will you get me my two-bob coat? It's got my teeth in the pocket.' Brian and his siblings all stood at the bottom of the bed. I remember wanting them to go forward so Harry could see them. You could see they all loved him." Harry died within the next few days. Reader did not attend the funeral.

Reader left school in July 1955, aged 16, soon after Harry moved out. He started working full time as a butcher's boy in Lewisham as he helped Doris feed and clothe his younger siblings, who were aged 14, seven and two. But helping housewives with their meagre meat rations did not live up to young Reader's lofty plans for himself and he soon left to become a fireman with British Rail. That job could have set Reader on the straight and narrow for life but it only lasted for seven months. In June 1957, now aged 18, the law caught up with him again when he was convicted at Brighton Magistrates' Court of stealing four pounds, 15 shillings and sixpence – now worth more than a hundred pounds, from a tea hut. Reader escaped with a conditional discharge of 12 months and was made to pay 10 shillings in costs.

The die was cast. The pattern was set. Only the targets would become bigger. Five months later he was to appear at the Old Bailey for the first time, marking a serious escalation in his offending. Perhaps because of his young age and difficult family circumstances, the judge dealt with him leniently and Reader escaped with only two years' probation for the very serious crimes of causing grievous bodily harm with intent and burglary. Now that Reader had dodged jail by the skin of his teeth, Doris decided it was time her oldest son should do his national service. This was compulsory for all young men until

1960. It had already been deferred so he could help his mother look after his siblings. Reader was posted to the Royal Engineers which were based in barracks close to Wormwood Scrubs Prison in West London. This meant he was able to return home at the end of the day to help care for his brother and two sisters. Official records reveal that: "On discharge his character assessment was shown as 'good'."

Different areas of London had traditionally been known to harbour villains who specialised in different types of crime, often a reflection of the transport links to those particular places. In the tenement buildings around the terminuses of King's Cross, Euston and St Pancras, were railway-raiding gangs, while on the north side of the London docks, lorry hijackers took advantage of the goods being driven from the eastern coastal ports of Tilbury and Harwich.

Greenwich, Deptford and neighbouring Bermondsey also had the docks and over generations the families that lived there developed an ingrained culture of disregard for the law. It was a place where outsiders were treated with suspicion, including people who had lived in the area all their lives. To be a proper local you have to be from a Greenwich or Bermondsey family. A contemporary of Reader's who grew up in Greenwich said: "It was a real community and there were a lot of scallywags but everyone was tight-lipped and followed the code never to rat. We stood shoulder-to-shoulder and though we were poor it was a great place to live." One of Reader's old friends said that in the post-war years everyone on the docks had a scam on the go. He said: "I knew a guy who worked down there who had a secret box fitted under the engine of his car and he would fill it up with stuff stolen off the docks when he drove in and out of work. If you came out of a working-class area like Deptford in those days, like Brian did, you had to have a little bit of enterprise to improve your situation. Crime becomes a way of life because it's the only way to get out."

Professor Dick Hobbs, who specialises in studying organised crime and has spent much of his academic life speaking to criminals, described the area as a "den of thieves". He said: "It was the blagger docks. All the dockland areas produced the top villains in London, particularly on the south side. Along with Reader, you had the Richardsons, Freddie Foreman, Frankie Fraser, the Brindle family… it goes on and on. For someone like Brian Reader, it was like going to Eton. It all started with the docks – the thieving from the docks, doing a deal with this person. In East London, the river front was the biggest in the world. It went on for 26 miles. But on the south side it was far more compact. Bermondsey was just one of those places that produced villains. The most famous armed robbers during the golden age of armed robbery from the 1960s to the 1980s were the Bermondsey Blaggers. On the opposite side of the river you had the Canning Town Blaggers. On the south side you could live right up close to the river and the docks. On the north side you had a massive wall to keep the thieves out, but in Bermondsey the wharves and the houses were side by side."

The leading criminal family in the Greenwich area were the Hayward brothers, Billy and "Flash Harry". They had a pub in Deptford where you could buy stolen goods, firearms and drugs. Billy Hayward was jailed for eight years in 1966 after a gang fight at Mr Smith's Club in nearby Catford with the notorious Richardson family and "Mad Frankie" Fraser, which left one man dead. One former armed robber, now living in Spain, said: "There were certain parts of London where you found like-minded Herberts when you were 14 or 15. Tufnell Park and Bruce Grove in the north and Bermondsey in the south. You had robbers like Micky McAvoy, Tony White, Harry Wright – Harry the Rat – coming out of there. They were the cream of the crop. Bermondsey and Peckham were probably the areas where the most daring and the biggest robbers came from."

Upon leaving the army, Reader gave his official job title as "haulage contractor", but in fact it was at this time that the young man made the conscious decision to pursue a life of crime full time. A friend said: "He bought a tipper truck when he left the army but legitimate, above-board work never appealed to Brian." He met Bill Barrett, a seasoned criminal who was 11 years his senior and may have helped to fill the hole left in his life by his father's departure. One of a new breed of up-and-coming criminals rising out of the mean streets of Bermondsey, Barrett would become his early mentor in crime. Barrett's generation of successful, working-class thieves and armed robbers were seen by young men like Reader as clever, independent of spirit and audacious. Unlike the brutal and bullying violence of the extortionists like the Krays in East London and the Richardsons in the South, who made their money by bleeding people dry, these men used their wits to pull off huge burglaries and robberies where the victims were often faceless banks or big businesses.

Though Barrett had no particular specialism, one old thief who knew him said he was a good all-rounder who could be relied on to do a job. The source said: "There are people like that who don't seem to be able to do anything but end up on some of the biggest jobs. Billy Barrett took Brian under his wing and I know they had a touch out of the docks early on that gave them a few bob." The pair had got their hands on a consignment of mercury, which they sold on the black market for a healthy profit. But Barrett was jailed and would later relish telling friends how he had conned his former employers at the *Daily Mirror* during his three years inside. The source said: "He worked in their distribution department bundling up the papers when they came off the printers when he went down. But he managed to keep it quiet and got his mates to sign him in so he got paid throughout his time in the nick."

Reader began to develop his burglary skills and after he was released Barrett realised he was a quick learner who was willing to work all hours to achieve success. But Reader was back before the courts on April 22 1960 when he escaped with a fine for possession of an offensive weapon – a broken bottle. Another ageing criminal who first met Reader in the early 1960s said: "By that time, he had already had one touch with Bill on a job and Brian had some burglary skills. He wanted to get on our firm because we were quite a successful gang. We had already been on bank jobs and were using a thermic lance which was new in Britain. Brian wanted to come on board because he was ambitious and like anyone in any line of work, he was looking to work with the best."

It was while his criminal career was beginning to take off that Reader met the woman who would become the love of his life. Lyn Kidd was an attractive 20-year-old from Camberwell who was working as a bookmaker's assistant when Reader, then 24, asked her out on a date. He was one of her regular customers and Reader's good looks and quiet confidence had caught Lyn's attention. Soon they were going steady and, during this period of post-war austerity, she was impressed by the fact Reader was always well turned out in a different smart suit and was never short of a few bob to take her out with. It would take her a little while to discover that his earnings did not come from the car dealership he claimed to run. This fact would be shielded from her family for many decades. Handsome and charming, Reader was always popular with the opposite sex. But despite the opportunities, his friends are convinced he stayed faithful to Lyn for the rest of their 50 years together. A lifelong friend said: "He's never been one for chasing women. Brian would go home every night to Lyn and unlike most successful criminals he never had mistresses. He wasn't one for nightclubs and the fast life. Brian's a quiet family man and he did everything for Lyn." For her part, Lyn played the role of the master criminal's wife to perfection – always loyal and discreet. Reader told her only what she needed to know and nothing more.

The couple married in 1963 and their son, Paul, was born the following year. A daughter, Joanne, arrived a year after that and the Reader family was complete. Reader was a doting father and gave his children all the things Harry had failed to provide for him. A retired detective who would later arrest Reader said: "He never did a day's legitimate work in his life so he had lots of time with his kids and wife. He was a family man. He loved his holidays and would take the kids to the French Alps, the whole family were good skiers. They would also spend a lot of time in Spain. He gave his children all they needed in life." Holidays were very important to the family and in the early years Reader would take them all to a caravan park at Coghurst Hall near Hastings every summer along with Bill Barrett's family and other friends from south east

London. Reader bought caravan number 92 on the site in 1967 and kept it up until the early 1980s.

CHAPTER 2

Working in the Garden

As the 60s wore on, Brian Reader developed a network of contacts centred on Hatton Garden, which would remain the epicentre of his criminal activity for the rest of his life. "The Garden", as it is affectionately known to those who work and deal there, had a long history as a centre for villainy. Sitting on the edge of the City of London, the Garden has also been at the heart of the nation's jewellery trade for generations.

It has its name thanks to Sir Christopher Hatton, a personal favourite of Queen Elizabeth I, "who danced with grace and had a very fine form and a very fine face". So fine was he, that her majesty gave him a manor house where Hatton Garden now stands. In those days, the house stood in countryside outside the city walls. The River Fleet, which later gave its name to nearby Fleet Street, ran alongside it.

The street that would be recognisable today as Hatton Garden began to take shape in the 1600s when a fine row of townhouses was built on the site of former monasteries. But the well-off new occupants found themselves surrounded by some of the worst slums in London for the following two centuries. Notorious highwayman Dick Turpin was a regular at the nearby Red Lion Inn, an infamous haunt of low-lifes and criminals. During the following century, Charles Dickens lived for a couple of years in nearby Doughty Street and he set his novel Oliver Twist in the area. The fictional hideout of Fagin and his gang of young pickpockets was a couple of streets from Hatton Garden in Field Lane.

At the same time, skilled craftsmen were beginning to make the area their home, transforming it into a bustling centre for business. Immigrant Italian, French Huguenot and Jewish craftsmen settled in the area called Clerkenwell. As it was positioned just outside the city walls, they were able to carry on with their trade without belonging to one of the city's guilds. These medieval guilds were a kind of early trade union, formed to keep standards high and chancers out. But, in time, they turned into a closed shop. In order to join, you had to serve long apprenticeships – or you could buy your way in through family connections. So skilled foreign craftsmen instead set up workshops in Clerkenwell and began selling their wares directly to the public. Slum clearances during the mid 19th century radically changed the area again, with thousands of the poorest residents moving to other notorious slum areas in the East End.

The birth of Hatton Garden as a repository for unbelievable riches was beginning. The way was paved at

the start of the century with the establishment of Johnson
and Co in the street, later renamed Johnson Matthey
– still a globally famous brand in precious metals today.
Percival Norton Johnson pioneered ways of refining
platinum from gold. He also invented new methods of
measuring the purity of gold and other bullion. After
George Matthey joined the firm and added his name,
Johnson Matthey were appointed Official Assayers and
Refiners to the Bank of England. Johnson Matthey was
soon handling vast quantities of gold and silver for refining
from mines in South Africa and South America. Hatton
Garden was coming up in the world.

This helped the burgeoning local jewellery industry.
Johnson Matthey supplied the raw materials for the
craftsmen and also provided local tradesmen with a
smelting service, turning the dust and scraps from their
workshops back into metal, which was then credited to
their accounts. The next gamechanger for Hatton Garden
was the creation of De Beers, by three Englishmen, to
form the world's biggest diamond mining firm. By the end
of the 19th century, this cemented London's position as the
diamond trading capital of the world with Hatton Garden
at its core. More than 100 diamond traders were based
there by the turn of the 20th century.

Hatton Garden had gold and it had diamonds. But
pre-war Hatton Garden still looked very different from the
glitzy retail experience of today. It was a warren of
workshops, grubby and industrious, with no shopfronts.

One veteran said: "Hatton Garden before the war was a Dickensian-looking place with a patchwork of run-down houses. There would be a setter in one room, a polisher in another, an engraver in another, and if you opened a door sometimes a rat would run out." The devastation of the Second World War hardly helped. The area was badly bombed and jewellery was now sold on the black market. But many of the master craftsmen had gone and the quality of the work deteriorated. Jewish refugees from Antwerp, fleeing the Nazi invasion of Belgium, brought with them their skills in cutting rough diamonds and kept Hatton Garden alive.

By the time Reader began to frequent Hatton Garden, the main draw for the non-criminally minded was Gamages department store, which had opened in 1878. Until it closed its doors in 1972, it was one of the most popular stores in London – and was reputed to have the best toy department in the country.

But the future of Hatton Garden didn't lie in toys. The first major jewellery shop to open on the street was City Jewellers in 1968 and it is now home to the largest cluster of jewellery shops in the UK. There are 60 retail shops and over 300 separate companies linked to the jewellery trade. For much of the 20th century, virtually every stone that ended up in a British bride's engagement ring passed at some point through Hatton Garden.

It has provided the most tempting targets for the likes of Reader and his ambitious young associates. Number 87 was at one time home of the London Diamond Club, which was set up for traders in rough diamonds. The nearby London Diamond Bourse was for dealers in cut diamonds and other precious stones. The Bourse, founded after the Second World War, was originally based at Mrs Cohen's Kosher Cafe on the corner of Greville Street and Leather Lane. Visitors described a chaotic place filled with smoke and Yiddish, but where large diamonds were traded over tables piled with chess sets and coffee. Security was minimal. Hatton Garden veteran Dave Harris told Rachel Lichtenstein, for her book Diamond Street: the Hidden World of Hatton Garden, "They had on the door there a very tough, old, retired Jewish policeman from the 1900s. He was a rough old thing. You could only go into the place if you were known. Occasionally, robberies did happen. One dealer, who had his pocket picked in the place, had a parcel of fine diamonds worth over £10,000."

Hatton Garden also attracted a more enterprising type of thief. The local *Westminster Budget* newspaper reported in September 1854 that an "elegant young man of 30 with Bond Street references" rented an office at 70 Hatton Garden under the name T.C. Morris. He was described as having a foreign accent, a dark moustache and wearing "lavender kid gloves and other well-fitting appurtenances of civilisation". He became accepted within the community. So much so, that a leading diamond dealer visited Morris's office and showed him some stones he had recently brought back from Amsterdam. The dealer woke up some time later to the smell of chloroform and a nasty blow to the head. The stones had disappeared – and so had T. C. Morris.

But for much of the 20th century, elderly dealers would think nothing of walking up and down the Garden with thousands of pounds' worth of diamonds hidden in secret pockets. One former apprentice who started learning his trade in the 1930s, described taking precious items from his workshop to the nearest safe-deposit vault in Chancery Lane. Other traders just carried their diamonds and gems back home with them. Dealers used to openly buy and sell diamonds in the street. The whole place ran on trust.

Lichtenstein wrote about deals sealed with a handshake after much haggling: "This is the way the flow of business has taken place in Hatton Garden for over a century. It is a secret, private, hidden world that operates according to a strict set of unspoken internal laws: never screw the partner; and once the deal is done it must be adhered to." One dealer told her: "Everyone knew and trusted each other in the 50s; there was a different atmosphere, the businesses were long established. Now it is a bit more fly-by-night. Businesses come and go, they open up a shop, they go bankrupt, then disappear. But then you knew if you were established you could be trusted and there was nothing to worry about."

Newspaper cuttings from the 1950s reveal the concentrated wealth in Hatton Garden made it a magnet for crime. In 1955, the *Daily Mirror* splashed a story on its front page with the headline "Jewel raid sensation – the runaway 'Woman in Red' found dead in hotel room". Thelma Madeleine Johnston-Noad, wife of a millionaire fraudster "Count" John Edward Johnston-Noad had taken her own life. She was wanted for an £8,000 Hatton Garden gem raid in which a jewellery dealer had been drugged before being robbed. The reporter wrote: "She lay in bed in the Pack Horse Hotel, Staines, as her accomplice in the raid was being sentenced at the Old Bailey. A man whom the police also wished to interview in connection with the raid, was dead beside her. They were clasped in each other's arms in an oyster satin coverlet."

Hatton Garden became a particular target for burglars and safe-blowers – in a three-month period during 1987 Hatton Garden suffered six robberies and 10 burglaries. Not only was Hatton Garden a target for London's most accomplished criminals, it was also where they turned to offload the loot. Until his death in 1991, middleman Moshe Riyb was known as "The king of Hatton Garden". Peter Finch, a customs officer, told journalist-turned-academic Dr Paul Lashmar: "Moshe would arrive on the street corner at 10.30 in the morning and wander round the Garden. He had cash on him to buy anything – legal or illegal. If you needed short-term funds he could provide it; the complete Mr Fixit. People beat a path to his door. He bought anything – proceeds of robberies, smuggled gold, old lady's heirlooms… When we raided him, we found nearly £2million of stock in all forms of gold –

including fine gold bars in his tiny office in Diamond House. Even the doorstop was a big lump of silver."

By the early 1960s Reader was a regular at the Chop House restaurant in Clerkenwell, where London's thieves and gangsters would congregate, including the Kray twins and the Great Train Robbers. Gordon Goody, who along with Bruce Reynolds, plotted the iconic 1963 robbery, shared a flat in Clerkenwell with a man who was to become one of Reader's closest friends and fellow master burglars.

Many of the Great Train robbers had come from Reader's old stomping ground in south east London and the huge publicity around the heist helped fuel an increase in the number of young men turning to crime. The robbers achieved the status of heroes in the eyes of many working-class people and this was especially the case in those areas of London they had grown up in. One gang insider said: "Armed robberies started to become the big thing after the train robbery in '63. Every lump in Bermondsey was going across the pavement with a gun, but Brian knew there were cleverer ways to make your fortune. You could get very big sentences for armed robbery but with burglary there was, and still is, much less jail time."

Court records reveal that, by 1962, Reader was operating in and around Hatton Garden, handling stolen gold and jewels. He was convicted on March 3 that year at Clerkenwell Magistrates' Court of "receiving" and fined

£50, worth more than £1,000 today. If he was unable to pay, the court threatened to send him to prison for three months.

Clerkenwell had become known as London's "Little Italy" following an influx of economic migrants from the country after the First World War. The feared crime families in the area included the Cortesis, Fuscos, Monte-Colombos, Falcos and the Sabinis. Clerkenwell-born Darby Sabini, known as "the king of the racehorse gangs", dominated the London underworld during the interwar period. Sabini, who was immortalised as the gangster Colleoni in Graham Greene's Brighton Rock, is regarded as the first of the gangland bosses in the UK. By the time Reader was frequenting the area, that title had been passed on to Jack Spot and Billy Hill. But the Krays were beginning to rise up the criminal pecking order.

One of Reader's former gang members revealed how they were going about doing the same: "At that time Clerkenwell was the place where all the thieves and gangsters would congregate from around London. Everyone knew everyone and it was a place where deals would be done and jobs planned. Me and Brian would meet every day around 10am in Clerkenwell. There were always bits and pieces that needed doing, scoping and getting the latest technology. At one time Brian would say, 'But we never have a day off!' We had so much work we didn't have enough hours in the day to get it all done. It's changed now but in those days everyone knew what everyone was doing. We never wrote anything down, it was always in our heads. If you enjoy what you're doing then you become successful and money comes and that was what it was like for us. It was a full-time job for us and we enjoyed the work. It's a challenge to pull off the job. We did a bit of work together and it was a success and we worked together from then on. We never got involved with armed robbers. Because of our reputation we used to have people coming to us with work – often armed robbers – but we would always turn them away. It wasn't our cup of tea. These guys would do a robbery and then go out bragging about it and then wonder why they got nicked two weeks later."

CHAPTER 3

Forming the Firm

Brian Reader was now a key member of what would become his gang in the decades to come. They would not always go on the same jobs. It depended on who found the work and who was available. And who was not in jail. Paul Lashmar has spent decades investigating the group and has met Reader. He said: "These were guys all born around the time of the war. They grew up mostly in London and deprived inner city areas. They fell naturally into criminality for one reason or another. Reader, like the others, started with fairly minor crimes and then worked his way into burglary and a bit of GBH. He also gets into receiving and handling stolen goods. The die is cast. That's what he does. He just upgrades it all the time. The size of the proceeds gets bigger and bigger."

When Reader started off with the small-scale stuff in the 1950s and early 60s there wasn't a lot of choice. Britain was still in full post-war austerity. Lashmar said: "There wasn't that much of anything around, particularly valuables. But as the country got wealthier in the 1960s, the jewellery sector started to fly. There were shops and warehouses full of fur coats and all sorts of expensive consumer items. For Reader and his gang there were a lot more juicy targets and the guys were adapting to that. They gradually skilled-up. They were learning how to do new things and their targets got bigger."

One of the most respected members of Reader's network was south Londoner Tony Hollands. Known as "Dirty Tony", he was widely regarded as the best safe cutter in the country at that time. Tony was a member of a loose affiliation of burglars dubbed the "Boffin Mob" by the press because of their ability to deploy cutting-edge science and technology to get into vaults. A source has revealed how Hollands was "top of the division" among safe cutters in London and behind a huge raid on Carrington & Company, the prestigious jewellers on Regent Street, over a November weekend in 1965. The underworld source said a south east London criminal was suspected of murdering Hollands, while trying to extort money out of him. The alleged killer's favourite tactic was to tie his victim's hands together and make him stand on a stool with a noose around his neck while he rocked it with increasing ferocity until the terrified subject gave up his money. Hollands was found hanged in the 1980s and, though he was officially ruled to have killed himself, the source suspects the villain, who cannot be named for legal reasons. He said: "He did the same thing to another thief but did not kill him. He put a noose around his neck and made him stand on a pair of steps and then rocked the steps until he told him where his whack was."

Another member of Reader's network, an "alarm man" called John Woodley – known as "Ginger John" – had overcome the security system at Carrington. The raid appeared on the front page of the *Daily Mirror* under the headline: "Yard Big Hunt for £300,000 Jewel Gang". Described as "one of the biggest jewel thefts ever carried out in Britain", the *Mirror* said it was the latest raid by the Boffin Mob, whose haul for that year was estimated at £2million.

Police had attended the shop while the gang were inside after a "mysterious call to Scotland Yard's information room" from a man who refused to give his name. He told the operator he had seen people acting suspiciously near the one-time jewellers to Queen Victoria and George V. Legendary *Mirror* crime reporter Tom Tullett and his colleague Barry Stanley wrote: "A police car raced to the shop but there was no sign of a break-in. The police returned to West End Central police station and it was another one-and-a-half hours before the robbery was discovered." Whether the officers were paid off or were simply unable to see any sign of the six raiders we will never know.

Dirty Tony and Ginger John had used skeleton keys to enter the store as shoppers passed by on the Saturday lunch time. They made for the basement where they cut through the armour-plated doors of the strong room using acetylene burners. Another of the raiders at Carrington, according to the source, was Reg Dudley, a criminal who would later be jailed for life for the murder of two London gangland figures, Billy Moseley and Micky Cornwall. Moseley's slowly thawing head was found in a public toilet in Islington six weeks after Dudley was jailed in 1977 and 25 years later he had his conviction quashed. Dudley, who was said to be feared in north London where he ran a gang called Legal & General, was freed after evidence was uncovered showing police had set him up.

Along with Dirty Tony and Ginger John, another leading member of the team who Reader met in the early 1960s was John "The Face" Goodwin. The wiry little criminal, originally from Beckenham, south east London, got his nickname from his remarkable looks. Goodwin, also known as "Little John" and "Scarface", had a boxer's broken nose gained during his childhood in the ring. His cheeks and forehead were covered in scars and pock marks after he was the victim of a horrific acid attack as a young man. A former member of Reader's gang said Goodwin had been disfigured when he was in his early 20s by a criminal who lived around the Richardsons' heartland of the Walworth Road in south east London. Goodwin moved there in the 1950s. The former gang member said: "When John was about 22 or 23 he had acid thrown in his face by a criminal who was known as a nasty bastard. From that day on he was called The Face because the acid destroyed his face. He looked scary but he wasn't hard at all."

Goodwin's appearance would have been even worse if he had not been treated by a team of doctors formed under pioneering surgeon Sir Archibald McIndoe, who had developed early plastic surgery techniques on Battle of Britain fighter pilots. Sir Archibald was one of the most influential exponents of reconstructive surgery, treating injuries mostly caused when aircraft fuel tanks ignited and pilots were caught up in the inferno before they could parachute to safety. Goodwin was treated at McIndoe's plastic surgery unit at the Queen Victoria hospital in East Grinstead, Sussex.

The former gang member said: "He was always very grateful for the work they did for him. John was a good talker but he wasn't a burglar. I remember on one job I gave him a long jemmy and told him to open a door and when I came back 10 minutes later he was just standing there and the door was still locked. He didn't have a clue how to use the thing. John's skill was finding people with the right skills, insiders with the information or keys we needed to get into places."

Lashmar said Goodwin, like Reader, was a dedicated family man. He said: "He married into the Tibbs – a very heavy London crime family. Goodwin was a cautious man. He invested his money. There were holidays and all of that sort of thing but he was not being flashy. Goodwin was really shrewd, he was a thinker. He was always thinking: 'How do we avoid getting caught? Where is there a weak spot?'" Goodwin would go on to make more money out of legitimate business than crime and owned a successful pawn shop in Islington, north London. The gang insider said: "He would always say: 'How many villains do you see driving Rolls-Royces compared to straight people?' His point was that criminals hardly ever looked after their money well, whereas he always did."

One remarkable character who joined the group in the early 1960s was a man called Joe, an illegitimate scion of a well-known wealthy family. Always on the lookout for ways of making money, Joe was a reporter covering Marylebone Magistrates' Court in his early life and would take money from defendants in exchange for binning stories about them. A former gang member said: "Joe was a good all-round thief. He was very thorough and wouldn't tell lies. His weakness was gambling. I remember we had to do a job at short notice because he had lost money and needed to pay a debt. Luckily, it worked out but by the end of the night he had gone and gambled it all away." Joe, who married an actress, was also a ladies' man. The source said: "He was very handsome and women would stop and stare at him when he walked past them in the street."

Another leading player and close associate of Reader's who he met at this time was a criminal known as "Little Legs", a popular nickname for short men at the time. Little Legs, originally from Tottenham, north London, was widely regarded by his peers as one of the best lock pickers and burglars in the country. Little Legs' skill and intelligence are reflected in the fact he escaped a major jail sentence, only doing short stints for minor offences as a young man before spending much time abroad, on the run. Little Legs, who is a year younger than Reader, cannot be named for legal reasons. He was to be by Reader's side in some of the biggest heists of the 1970s and 80s.

Little Legs is believed to have been responsible for bringing Tony Gavin in to the "mob". Eight years older than Reader, Gavin was a forceful personality and had a propensity to be physically threatening. An underworld source said: "Tony could have a right row if he wanted to. If it came down to it and trouble started, he would be involved in the thick of it. Once we were waiting for him in Clerkenwell. It was unusual he was late, because normally he was a stickler for time, and would arrive early and be sitting there reading the paper. All of a sudden he turned up all dirty and red faced. He said: 'Go and get my car, I've left it up on the Holloway Road.' He was a very good driver and he said he had been cut up by three blokes. When they stopped at the lights he got out and climbed onto the roof of their car and jumped up and down on it."

Five-feet-eight-inches tall, Gavin had been a PT instructor in the British army. He was a barrel-chested, tough north Londoner. He had a sideline driving second-hand furniture from London to Glasgow once a week, leaving on Saturday morning and returning on the

Tuesday.

It was Gavin who brought on board the final member of the group. Mickey "Skinny" Gervaise was an electrical engineer and alarm expert who would become one of the most prolific burglars and armed robbers in British history. Tall and slim, as his nickname suggests, people who knew him say he looked like the Monty Python star John Cleese. "Alarm men", or "Bell men", were greatly prized because of their scarcity and the fact that a reliable one could allow a gang access to the best vaults in the country while minimising the chances of getting caught. They were highly skilled and had to keep abreast of the latest developments in technology. When he was first tipped off about Gervaise, Gavin knew nothing about him apart from the fact he was a trained alarm technician and where he parked his car. In those days you could find out who owned a number plate if you paid a small fee at the local town hall and that's what the gang did to get his name and address. Gavin approached Gervaise, who agreed to come on board.

Lashmar said: "Gervaise was an alarm man, but he was adaptable. He worked for an alarm company but he got turned. And, boy, when he came over, he came over big time. I once calculated that Gervaise was personally involved in burglaries and robberies worth £40million at the time, which is an absolutely enormous amount of money. Gervaise didn't take home £40million, he took home his slice. He lived the life of the big-time criminal.

Gervaise was married but had the reputation as a ladies' man. He was making big money and spending it on expensive cars and big houses."

The gang had no leader or obvious hierarchy, making it highly adaptable and fluid, with members going off to work with other criminals outside of the circle. It did not matter if some members were caught because the others could go off and recruit more, allowing them to continue developing their skills, contacts and technology. Lashmar said: "This was the best group of burglars in the country. This was the London team. The Old Bill knew about them but they were pretty careful. This was also the era of police corruption. There were deals to be done all the time. They were able to keep going. There was a hardcore of 10 or so. Some people did get done, some people did go down. They needed to be replaced. Reader had a reputation for being able to get into anything but they brought people in with other skills. This was a group whose abilities varied and who had a range of skills. If you had information about a jeweller's near Hatton Garden that you wanted to hit, you saw who was around, who had the skills you needed. This group was largely non-violent. They were prepared to carry out some violence occasionally but most of them were against it. They were versatile. They were up on a roof, they were in through the windows. They were working full time at this. They were at it in various combinations. They were not interested in houses. They were interested in warehouses and specialist jewellery places."

One member of the gang said they would spend much of their time talking to alarm and lock experts and researching the latest developments in security technology. Every year Reader would travel up to Birmingham to attend the Master Locksmith Association's annual conference. He said: "We would make it our business to get to know people with specialist knowledge: safe engineers, locksmiths, specialist drillers and alarm experts. Someone might say, 'My father-in-law works for Chubb,' and you'd try to get to meet them and go from there. Everyone's looking for the big buck." The source said they treated their work like a full-time profession and put in long hours. He said: "If you enjoy what you're doing then you become successful and money comes and that was what it was like for us. We enjoyed the work. It's a challenge to pull off the job."

Hatton Garden was the perfect place for Reader and his team to work. Half the people were trying to do an honest business, while the other half were crooks. Lashmar said: "The gang knew about the movement of people and valuable items. They knew if someone had got a load of diamonds in. If they had a target then John Goodwin, Brian Reader and Mickey Gervaise would go down there and get inside. They put on a brown coat. They would walk up and they would put a blank lock in the door. It's called voiding the lock. After that, any key would open it. They would do it just before it closed up for the day.

Gervaise would go inside and look at the alarms. He would do something in the day that would neutralise the alarm. He would do something to the wire that would stop it working that night."

Though we do not know about all of the crimes Reader was involved in during the 1960s, a general flavour of the kinds of capers his gang were up to can be found in the list of offences Gervaise would later admit to. They start in December 1963 with the attempted burglary of the sub-Post Office in Highbury Corner in north London. Metropolitan Police documents state: "With others, forced entry to Post Office, with intent to steal from safe, attempted to negate alarm but activated same and decamped empty handed." This would appear to be Gervaise's first offence and his inexperience is reflected in his failure to disable the alarm. But the gang had more success in September the following year when they got away with more than £18,000 in cash and stamps – worth £350,000 today – after returning to the same Post Office and blowing up the safe with gelignite.

Gervaise said he and others did exactly the same thing a month earlier at the Post Office in Bruce Grove, north London, making off with more than £18,000 in cash. The gang made a failed attempt on another Post Office a few miles south in Camden Town later the same year. Another crime the thief admitted to committing that decade was the attempted burglary of an unnamed cleaning company in York Way, north London, on an unspecified date in either 1964 or '65.

A gang insider said Reader was on at least one of the raids on Gervaise's list during this period. On the evening of December 7, 1969, Reader and his team broke into the Post Office on Albemarle Street in Mayfair and made off with more than half-a-million pounds' worth of cash and stamps. One man got into the premises and smashed the alarm off the wall with a hammer before cutting the wires and using an acetylene torch to burn a hole in the safe. The insider said that at the time they had a network of buyers for postage stamps and benefit stamp cards which were issued by the Post Office until 1975. He said: "The Post Office was a vast organisation in those days. It took a few months to get rid of the stamps but they could be sold for 40 per cent of their value so it was worth it. Among those our regular buyers would sell them on to were people working in Post Offices who would pass them back to customers at the full cost and pocket the cash themselves." Reader was near the top of a huge underground black market network of small businessmen and women, operating on the fringes of criminality.

After his conviction for receiving stolen goods in 1962, Reader managed to stay out of trouble until March 1970, when he was fined £30 at Woolwich Magistrates' Court for handling a stolen camera. By this time his team had reached their zenith in terms of skills, contacts, knowledge and equipment. But in May 1971 Reader would come close to death after being interrupted while scoping out a bank in Reading. He was in a telephone exchange with another gang member trying to find the "line" for the bank's alarm. At that time security systems were linked to local police stations via the British Telecom network. If you could identify the line then it could be cut, disabling the alarm.

The gang insider said: "They were in the exchange when they heard someone coming in. The other chap escaped out the first floor window and got down but Brian's foot slipped as he followed and he done himself, landing straight on his head." He was out cold and when Reader woke up he was lying in hospital with a policeman at the foot of his bed. He had suffered minor brain damage and it was weeks before Reader was able to leave hospital. He was moved to a rehabilitation unit in Hertfordshire where he had to learn how to walk again.

The insider said: "It affected him for the rest of his life. He was in a very bad state and never fully recovered. Even to this day, if he carries two cups of tea Brian struggles because it messed up his balance." To add insult to injury, police records show he was convicted of burglary with intent at Reading Magistrates' Court on May 14, 1971, and fined £35. But serious injury was not going to stop him. Four months later Reader would be participating in, what remains to this day, one of the biggest burglaries in British history.

CHAPTER 4

The Bank Job

By the time Reader and his gang came to plan what would be their biggest job yet, he was 31 years old and – but for his head injury – should have been in the prime of his life. Now a father of two young children, he was determined to give Paul, then aged six, and Joanne, five, all of the things his own father had failed to provide for him, such as stability, a comfortable home and family holidays they would always remember. If the audacious raid on the basement vault at Lloyds Bank in Baker Street was a success, then he could guarantee their security for the rest of their lives. It marked a serious escalation in the scale of Reader's ambition, both in the size of the prize and sheer amount of effort required.

The burglary would take place over two weekends in the late summer of 1971, just five months after Reader's fall in Reading. He had only been out of hospital for a few weeks when the final decision was made to go for it. Though Reader was still weak and unsteady on his feet, there was no way he was going to miss what would prove to be the biggest payday of his life. He would be an adviser, co-ordinator and most importantly, safe deposit box opener if the gang managed to get into the vault.

Planning had begun in 1970 when Gavin, then aged 38 and one of the main brains behind the job, realised the bank on the southern edge of Regent's Park held a huge amount of cash and valuables. Gavin brought in car dealer Reg Tucker, from Stoke Newington in north east London, to recce the vault. Tucker, who was not known to the police, opened a bank account at the Baker Street branch on December 7, 1970, with a deposit of £500 using the fake name G Edwards. The 37-year-old ran a car dealership in Forest Road, Walthamstow, East London, but gave the bank a false home address. Two months later, he applied to rent a safe deposit box in the same building at a cost of £2.50. This gave him regular and easy access to the room the gang hoped to breach.

To access his box, Tucker needed to sign a card using his false name and was then taken into the vault by two members of staff. Each box had two locks – Tucker would open one with his key and then a member of Lloyds bank staff would open the other. It was then standard practice for the staff to leave the box holder alone in the vault, giving Tucker plenty of time to do what he needed to do in peace. Bank records show that he went back to the vault 13 times. But he kept next to nothing in it.

Reader's gang had given him the vital job of memorising the inside of the vault and to later draw a plan of it for them to base their whole operation on. Portraying himself to bank staff as a respectable businessman, Tucker always carried an umbrella with him during these visits. Once alone, he used it to measure the height of the vault and the floor. He also used his arm to measure the walls, as he knew the length from his shoulder to his fingertip. The regular nine-inch floor tiles helped Tucker check his measurements. A gang insider said: "Tucker wasn't a professional burglar and didn't have any particular skills. He was brought in by Tony to do odd jobs."

The vault was thought to be impregnable. It was built of thick reinforced concrete. There were two doors to the vault behind a locked sliding grill. The main door was alarmed and on a time lock which meant that no one, not even the bank's security staff, could open it while the bank was not open for business. But Reader's gang had another plan.

Two doors up the street from the Lloyds bank at 189 Baker Street was Le Sac, a struggling leather goods shop that had never made a profit for its owners and, in May 1971, they decided to sell up. It wasn't widely advertised but word got to the gang after one visited the place by chance and saw the basement with his own eyes. They hatched an audacious plan to dig a tunnel. The gang asked a recently bankrupted businessman they knew, Bennie Wolfe, to make enquiries. The 64-year-old Australian Jew and "scallywag" had previously run a jeweller's shop in Kilburn, north west London, until it went bust.

Wolfe was trading from home in jewellery, antiques, anything he could get his hands on to turn a profit. He contacted Le Sac's owners together with his former shop assistant Molly Adams. After the Kilburn shop had shut, Molly had started a new job for "fancy goods" dealers A.S. Brown Ltd. But they had talked about going into business together. Wolfe mentioned this shop he was interested in on Baker Street. As an undischarged bankrupt, he told her he wouldn't be able to run the business in his own name and she agreed to put it in hers. When they visited 189 Baker Street, "Sale" and "15% off" posters filled the windows. He was told he needed to speak to the leaseholder and director of Le Sac (London) Ltd, Morris Levy. Through solicitors, they negotiated a price of £7,500 for the business and £2,000 for the stock. This was agreed on August 21. Wolfe closed the shop and put a sign up in the window stating it would re-open on September 1. This never happened.

Tucker's visits to the Lloyds Bank vault had become more frequent. He visited once in February, twice in March and once in April. After just two visits in the following three months, he went into the vault five times in August alone. Le Sac had a basement that was level with the bank vault next door but one. Only 40 feet and a fast-food outlet called Chicken Inn separated the two buildings. Another car dealer, Thomas Stephens, also unknown to police, was asked to acquire the tools the gang needed for the next stage of their plan.

A gang insider has now revealed that Reader requested his old friend Bobby Mills be brought on the job as a favour to him. The pair had known each other since they were teenagers, growing up together in south east London. Though "Millsy" was regarded by some of the others as a liability who brought nothing to the party, he was allowed on board. The six-strong line-up for the raid had now been finalised. Along with Reader, Gavin, Tucker and Mills were two other mystery men, one now a legitimate businessman who lives in Mayfair and the other a long-time member of the gang and explosives expert.

The gang insider said: "On the first night they turned up at the agreed meeting point in Marylebone at 5pm all ready with their sandwiches and gloves. The tools were already waiting for them in the shop. All of a sudden Mills turns up 10 minutes late and says, 'I've been very ill and the doctor said I mustn't go into any buildings or confined spaces'. Everyone looked at each other and rolled their eyes because it was obvious his arsehole had gone. It was embarrassing for Brian because Mills was his man and he'd shown him up." It was therefore decided that Mills would be the lookout or "outside man" and he was taken to the top of a building overlooking the bank with the help of one of the gang who had worked out a route by picking locks.

The men began work later that Friday night, the first day of the August bank holiday weekend. Gavin, Tucker and a third gang member drilled a hole into the basement floor of Le Sac. The six inches of concrete was chiselled out until the London clay was exposed beneath and the gang began to dig. Reader was still recovering from his fall and took no part in the digging. He was saving his energy for what lay ahead. If they were successful, the gang were relying on his skill at opening the deposit boxes. This vital job would determine how much loot could be taken and he was highly skilled at jemmying them open quickly.

After digging below the shop, the gang hit their first obstacle - the foundation wall of the building was sunk below the level of the floor of the basement and was blocking the progress towards the bank. Tucker was ordered out the way as Gavin and the second gang member dug further down under the wall and then up the other side until they hit the concrete basement of the Chicken Inn. The insider said: "The bottom of the restaurant was used as the ceiling for the tunnel and once they got past the sunken foundations it was reasonably steady work digging the soil, which became pretty sandy. A tray was filled with the soil and passed back into the shop and soon the basement was full of earth."

Gavin led the work in the tunnel. He had a very muscular physique and used to run around the track at Parliament Hill in North London to stay in shape. But this digging was arduous, backbreaking work. Gavin lost one-and-a-half stone in weight during the job. The gang had decided to only dig at the weekend to try to avoid raising suspicion. Baker Street was a bustling area of shops and offices from Monday to Friday. But like much of central London, it was largely deserted at weekends. The few local residents lived in flats above shops and offices, comfortably distant from the work that was now taking place below ground.

By Monday morning, they had tunnelled the 40 feet beneath Baker Street and made it to the bottom of the bank. They had excavated a space seven-feet wide and five-feet high directly under the vault. Above them lay a fortune, separated by 18 inches of double reinforced concrete. A jack was brought down the tunnel and placed onto some railway sleepers. It was used to push against the vault floor above them. But the only thing that moved was the sleepers, which began sinking further into the ground. In desperation they kept hammering the jack but the sleepers only sunk further and further. The raiders had underestimated the thickness of the concrete floor of the vault. The insider said: "They had thought it would be the same as the floor of the shop, six inches, but it was three times that. Though they got to the bank on the first weekend it was impossible to get through so they had to down tools and stay cool hoping nothing would be noticed until the next weekend." So the gang walked out and went back home to their families.

That week, Tucker cooly continued to remove the dwindling cash from his Lloyds Bank account. He took out £55, leaving a balance of just £1.36. On the Monday, Wolfe went back to the shop. The sign in the window was removed and replaced with one that said they would re-open on September 14. Tucker visited the vault twice that week on the orders of the gang, on the pretence of inspecting his safe deposit box, number 317. If they were ever to get into the vault, it had been decided, they needed to take risks. A gang member bought a small amount of gelignite from a reliable contact. Explosives were still relatively easy to obtain, if you knew where. The IRA's bombing campaign on mainland Britain was yet to take hold and, once it did, explosives would be much more closely guarded. But it was not an easy decision, to set off a small bomb in a confined tunnel in central London. Nervous about the noise it would make, Gavin instructed Stephens to hire walkie talkies so those inside Le Sac could stay in touch with outside-man Mills in case they attracted attention.

At 5.30pm on the Friday, September 10, 1971, the Lloyds bank guards closed for the weekend as normal. As one guard later told police, "I went to the vault where the security boxes are stored. We put the trolleys inside the vault, turned off the power, put the cable inside the vault, shut and locked the grill door, took the footplate up and locked the main door to the vault. Everything was intact and secure when I did this. The sliding door was then shut and this sets off the time lock on the vault door."

At the same time the gang entered Le Sac and Mills

was positioned back on top of 94 Baker Street, a five-storey Georgian town house that had an uninterrupted view of the bank. Three years previously, the building had been a huge draw to the area, briefly the home of the Beatles' Apple boutique. The shop was opened, according to Paul McCartney, to create "a beautiful place where beautiful people can buy beautiful things". It was a financial disaster, plagued by shoplifters and thieving staff, and closed its doors within eight months.

Back in the tunnel, the gang's explosives expert drilled into the concrete of the vault above the tunnel and packed the holes with gelignite. The railway sleepers which had been used as a base for the jack were turned on their ends and used to push some folded sheets of roofing felt against the concrete to hold the explosives in place. A series of 10ft-long yellow cables were connected together and run along the length of the tunnel back in the basement of Le Sac. An electric detonator was wired to the end of the cable.

The insider said: "The opening to the tunnel was closed to minimise the noise and they got in touch with the outside man to co-ordinate the explosion with the movement of the traffic. A battery was used to detonate it at around 12.30 in the morning when the traffic lights were green and cars were moving. Luckily it worked with one explosion as you can only ever get away with one. If people hear a second bang they call the police."

The muffled thud could be heard at the end of the

tunnel. There was an anxious wait while the dust and smoke cleared. Mills confirmed from the roof of number 94 that all was quiet on the street outside. Gavin and the explosives expert crawled back along the tunnel to the bank. Looking up they found a hole measuring about six inches in diameter right under a bank trolley, which had been left out on the vault floor. "You always need some luck and they had it there because the trolley muffled the noise of the explosion," the insider said. It wasn't big enough to slip through but the hole was gradually widened using hammers and chisels until it was big enough for the smallest member to squeeze through.

He poked his head into the middle of the vault. Tucker's measurements and the gang's calculations had been spot on. The room was still thick with smoke and dust from the explosion. The blast had left scorch marks on the ceiling above. The insider said: "It was a great feeling for them to get in but the job wasn't finished. The first man in was handed a hammer to smash the hole from above so it was big enough for Gavin, Reader and Tucker to get in."

The next day, Saturday, September 11, the unwitting gang was to come within a hair's breadth of being caught in the act. A keen amateur radio enthusiast was about to stumble upon the crime of the decade. Robert Rowlands owned an American Forces radio receiver – "a very good set", as he put it – and was in the habit of switching it on when he got into bed or if he woke up in the night.

"About 11pm on the 11th September, 1971, I got into bed and turned the radio set on," he later explained. "I suddenly heard a voice, which was clearly being transmitted locally because of the clarity of the signal. I heard a man's voice. It appeared to be the tail end of a message and the man said something to the effect, 'Do you understand, over?' There was a silence for at least five minutes. I then heard a man's voice but I'm not sure if it was the one I first heard and he said words to the effect, 'We now have two-hundred-gee and everything's going fine'. Another man then answered, who was later referred to in the conversation as 'Bob' and he said words to the effect, 'You'll have to cut down on the noise as the traffic is dying down.' I had the impression that the man Bob was outdoors. Another man then answered and said words to the effect, 'We will call you when we are coming out.' It was at this stage that I decided to call the Marylebone Lane Police Station and, as a result of speaking to them, I took a tape recording of all further transmissions."

Thanks to Rowlands, the next stage of the Baker Street raid was captured in the burglar's own words. Various gang members, including Reader and Gavin, took it in turns to speak from Le Sac to Mills, keeping lookout across the road. The gang, exhausted after spending the day opening safety deposit boxes and choking from the fumes, were planning to stop work and continue after a rest the following morning.

"Right, listen carefully." Gavin ordered Mills: "We

want you to mind for one hour from now until approximately one o'clock and then go off the air, get some sleep, and come on the air with both radios at six o'clock in the morning. Over."

"That's a bit ridiculous, mate," replied Bob. "I'll never wake up like that. Over."

"Well, what time do you think you'll wake up, over?" asked Gavin.

"Well, I might just as well come out and come back in tomorrow, mightn't I, if I'm going to do that?"

"Yes, but how are you going to get back up there tomorrow?" asked Gavin. "It'll be daylight, won't it? Over."

Mills said: "I suggest that we carry on working tonight, mate, and get it done with. Over."

"Look, the place is filled with fumes where we was cutting," explained Gavin. "If the security come in and smell the fumes, we are all going to take stoppo and none of us have got nothing. Whereas this way, we've all got three-hundred-grand to cut up and when we come back in tomorrow... at least we've got something. Over." There was a pause. "You read me? Over."

Mills offered to slope off and come up the back stairs the following day: "I should think I've got half a chance."

There was a heated discussion in the vault. Some choice words were exchanged. Minutes later, Gavin was back on the radio to Mills. "They all say that you should stay there. Over."

"My eyes are like organ stops, mate," complained Mills. "I'm not going to be any good this morning."

"You can have eight hours' sleep. Over," said Gavin.

"Where am I going to sleep, mate," asked Bob. "Who's going to wake me up?"

"Listen, if you don't wake up after eight hours you're not a normal person then, are you? Listen, it's not a bad rate of pay, is it? It's 30 and probably another 30 to come or more, so, like, er… what about that, then?"

Mills complained: "Mate, honestly, it's no use. Money is not my god. Everyone's entitled to their opinion… I'm telling you that if I go to sleep here tonight, first of all, I won't wake up and, secondly, I won't be able to sleep anyway, cos it's freezing cold and everything up here. Over."

"You know what you've got to do, Bob," answered Gavin. "Please your fucking self… the only reason we're not staying in is the fumes. I know you're tired. We're all tired. If it was possible for us to work on, we'd all be working on. I've been working non-stop all day. We just can't work on because of the noise. The fumes is secondary, the noise is the main fucking reason. We've done 90 per cent of the easy ones and we are now back to the hard ones… anyway, so your problem is getting back up. If you're worried about not waking up in the morning, put the earplug in your ear and go asleep somewhere comfortable in there, which I'm sure you can find. We will call you up from eight o'clock onwards… we will fucking wake you up and it will be like an alarm call, won't it? Over."

"All right, I won't go to sleep, right?" said Mills. "Can you try and get in a little bit earlier, that's all? I'll sit up and wait here. Over."

Finally losing his cool, Gavin said: "Fucking... we're all just like you are. None of us have had any more sleep than what you've had. That's fucking obvious. We've none of us had to do what you've had to do but we're in a bit of a rough state ourselves. If there was any way we could get you out, we would. But there isn't a fucking sensible way of doing it... we will get in as early as we can get in. When we go, will you mind it for an hour at least because that's the dangerous time?"

"Roger, I will do that," replied Mills. "Now, listen, if by any chance I doze off, right, someone will have to come into the window, don't come up the ladder, cos that's the dangerous part, come into the window and call me. Over."

The complaining from Mills, who was only there as a favour, added to Reader's embarrassment after he brought him onto the gang. Not only had Mills refused to go into the bank after losing his bottle, he was now refusing to do his job. The insider said: "He was a disaster and an example of Reader being a poor judge of character."

In another snippet, one gang member said: "The hard ones are very hard. I want to leave but the other three... everything's going very well. I'm getting over the shock!"

The following morning the gang were back. Mills had survived his night on the roof. "How's everything? OK?" asked Gavin.

"Everything's fine," replied Mills. "No intruders whatsoever. Over."

"Right, now you've done a good job, Bob. Listen, we're not going to work too late. We're going to finish the rest of the easy ones off. We're going to have a go at some of the other ones. We're going to clean up in here. We should be coming out this afternoon. You'll have to bluff your way straight down off the roof, OK? Over."

"Roger, will do. Over." said Mills.

"Before we come out, we'll arrange a meeting place for you, so that we can go where we're going to, OK? They're in there now, so pay absolute attention to that front door. Over."

"Roger."

"I don't suppose you'd see the lights if they came on, would you?"

"No – no."

"So you just have to pay a particular attention to that, eh, Bob?"

"Roger," said Mills, remembering that they had agreed to use false names. "Is that you, Steve, by the way? Over."

"Yeah."

"Sorry about last night, mate. I was a bit knackered."

"We was all the same, tell the truth. Over."

The police had all of this. So what were they doing

about it? From Sunday morning, police patrols started searching the area, looking in particular for a man keeping watch from a high building. But they didn't know where to start. The security departments of all banks with branches in the area had been contacted by midday. Commander Bob Huntley was informed of the suspicious broadcasts. Huntley was in the final few years of a distinguished police career. He was commander of CID Area 1, which covered central London, including Baker Street. During his service, he received 26 commissioner's commendations and one high commendation. In 1971, as the IRA bombing campaign began to spread out of Northern Ireland, he was also put in charge of the newly formed anti-terror division known as the bomb squad.

After he was told of the broadcasts picked up by Rowlands, Huntley left home and headed into Marylebone Police Station. If the suspicions were right, they had a unique opportunity to catch a gang of burglars red-handed. Detective Chief Inspector William Barnett was already in charge of the response. Huntley said: "There was no indication from the messages which had been picked up of the method of attack, though from the scraps of information which were available it did appear that a bank or some such stronghold was involved."

Police needed technical help and fast. They asked the BBC and the Post Office for assistance in tracking down the broadcasts in the hope of catching the burglars in the act. Barnett added: "We did receive considerable assistance, but the equipment they had was of a type which was not much help. We were told by one of the radio-detection experts that we should search an area within a seven-mile radius of Mr Rowlands' flat and this involved a huge number of banks and similar premises." That advice left police with an area of 154 square miles of central London to search. It contained hundreds of banks and officers began the process of contacting the head offices of all of them. The most likely targets were selected for officers to visit in pairs. Some banks refused to open up for the police, they were so confident of their security systems. Others arranged for managers or security staff to travel into the city to meet the police outside and carry out checks.

It was 3.55pm before Sergeant Tony Lundy and his partner got to the Lloyds branch in Baker Street and, once inside, they found there was a time lock on the door to the vault. Barnett said: "The guards were able to go only to the vault door and no further." One security guard said: "The outer door of the strong room was secure. The windows of the bank were locked and there were no signs of anything having been disturbed. I heard no noises and smelled nothing. Outside the premises, I looked about but saw no suspicious person or vehicle." It was not often that Lundy, then a young up-and-coming police officer, missed his man. As we shall see, this was the first but by no means the last time that he crossed paths with Reader.

The hours passed with no breakthrough. Perhaps it was

a false alarm. Both Barnett and Huntley stayed at work late that night, not leaving until gone midnight. They went home to their beds anxious, but confident they had done all they could.

The gang was of course oblivious to the chaos they had caused around the capital. They were delirious with joy at what they now possessed. It was the payday they had all been dreaming of and working towards. They had a van in an underground car park behind the shop and they began filling it with sack after sack full of cash, gold and jewels. Their luck was in that day and they lugged the gear unseen out of the back of the shop, before driving to Tucker's home in Chingford, Essex, for the "cut-up". They had left a scene of destruction behind them that would reverberate around the country.

CHAPTER 5

Lid on a Scandal

The same guard who locked the vault up on Friday night re-opened it at 9am on Monday morning. "I opened the sliding door and the main door of the vault and immediately saw that the vault was in complete disorder," he said. Police were called and returned to the place their colleagues had left just 17 hours earlier.

Detective Chief Inspector Jack Candlish was told about the break-in when he arrived at work. He immediately contacted Commander Bob Huntley and the pair headed straight to the scene of the crime. "There was a hole in the floor of the vault and the deposit boxes were lying everywhere with the property strewn all over the place," Candlish later said. He suggested sending a police officer down the tunnel to see where it led but Huntley was worried in case there was a gas leak. "First of all we thought that the tunnel might have come from the underground but then we looked at the neighbouring shops," wrote Candlish. They tried to unlock the front door to Le Sac with help from the owners but the keys didn't work. "I then went to the back entrance with

Commander Huntley," Candlish went on, "and forced open the back door, which was secured with a bolt on the inside. We found all the earth and the hole with property lying around in the tunnel and at the entrance."

In the years after Baker Street, a number of myths have grown up around the job. One of the earliest misconceptions surrounded an alleged police cover-up in the aftermath. It has been claimed that a D-Notice was issued asking the press not to publish any detail of the raid on grounds of national security. This has led to decades of salacious speculation about the raid. One wild theory, which inspired the 2008 film *Bank Job* starring Jason Statham, was that the burglary was carried out on the orders of Michael X, an infamous black rights activist.

Michael X (not to be confused with US black rights campaigner Malcolm X) was born Michael de Freitas in Trinidad in 1933. After emigrating to the UK in his youth, de Freitas became an enforcer for the notorious slum landlord Peter Rachman. He went on to become a leading figure in the growing black power movement in the 1960s. The rumour was that Michael X had got hold of compromising photographs of the Queen's sister, Princess Margaret, on holiday on the Caribbean island of Mustique with her lover, Roddy Llewellyn. This version of events has it that Michael X kept them a box in the vault at Baker Street and MI5 organised the break-in to spare the Royal Family's blushes. Under police investigation, Michael X fled to his native Trinidad in early 1971. He was arrested the following year for murdering two members of his Black House commune on the island and executed by hanging in 1975. It made for a highly entertaining crime caper in the *Bank Job*, but we are sorry to say that very little in that film rings true.

Another myth about the raid is that the gang spray painted "Let's see how Sherlock Holmes solves this one" inside the vault before they left for the final time. It's a lovely idea, adding to the mystery of the masterminds who were never caught but, again, sadly untrue. The real scandal remained a secret until we started speaking to gang members in 2015. Among its great riches, the vaults also offered up disturbing pictures that could spark a national scandal. But the scandal was never to happen.

In one of the safety-deposit boxes, Reader found a hidden stash of child pornography. Equally shocking, he told those closest to him that the pictures belonged to a prominent Conservative politician and cabinet minister. The disgusted gang members made sure to leave the pictures strewn around the floor of the vault where police were bound to find them. The fact that these horrific snaps stayed secret was taken by them as proof that the police were bent. It was one rule for them, quite another for a senior member of the establishment. They weren't hurting anybody. He was abusing kids and clearly revelling in it. In fact, the truth of the tale is more complex.

Many of the official files from the case are in the

National Archives but remain closed for 100 years. This has fuelled suspicions of an establishment cover-up. But one recently released document reveals that police did attempt to silence the media. They didn't want the gang to know they had been recorded without their knowledge. Detective Chief Superintendent Robert Chalk later wrote in a police memo that their work was "made all the more difficult by the fact that the news media refused to take any notice of a confidential memorandum issued to them and which it is now known had the effect of causing the gang to scatter".

There was huge interest in the case from the off. "Why?" asked the *Daily Mirror* on its front page on Tuesday morning. "Police probe into bank raid that should never have happened." Reporters had got hold of details of Rowlands' recordings and they were printed over two further pages of coverage inside. The gang were dubbed the "Moles of Baker Street". "Just like an Ealing comedy," the paper went on, "with cops in a flap over crooks they could hear, but couldn't catch."

Not for the last time, Reader and his cronies were causing the Met acute embarrassment. Chalk was paranoid about leaks. "After warning them of the dire consequences of any leakage to the press," he said, "I took a calculated risk and decided to keep all members of the team fully acquainted of what was going on, as it was going on. This was done through regular conferences behind locked doors. The pressures exerted by the press, and the temptation to talk, were immense, but everyone stood firm and kept their mouths firmly shut."

The real cover-up, other new documents reveal, appears to have been carried out by Lloyds Bank. These show there was a "heated argument" between detectives and senior bank officials inside the ransacked vault. Detective Sergeant Barrie Newman later wrote in a statement: "When the burglary at the bank was discovered, the vault was in complete disarray with property, including jewellery etc, being scattered about the floor. Any property dropped by the thieves was, in fact, retained by the bank on their insistence that it was on their premises and their responsibility. Police are not in a position to say exactly what was left behind and what the bank did with this property. Police have not even been given a list of this property."

His senior officers agreed with this version of events. Candlish wrote: "Whilst the bank provided us with every facility which we required during our investigations they were extremely uncooperative when it came to dealing with the stolen property itself." He described how bank staff asked police to leave the vault and set up tables in the entrance hall outside at the foot of stairs leading up to ground level and "they then piled the property which was on the floor of the vault onto these tables".

Huntley got involved in an attempt to break the deadlock. He later wrote: "I recall that there were various inspectors of the bank at the premises and I spoke to the chief inspector and the manager who told me that they had decided not to hand over the property. This was probably on the basis that they felt there was a duty of secrecy to their clients. I told the bank representatives that I thought that this property was stolen property and ought to be handed to the police but after considerable discussion I was unable to convince them and accordingly the bank retained the property." He added: "The bank collected all the property together including even a bag of stamps which was found on the stairs of the empty handbag shop. When I went back during the following few days, all of the property was laid out on tables with people looking at it apparently attempting to identify their own property. It was quite clear that there was no particular system for this distribution of the property. The bank's delay in giving us the names of box holders hindered us considerably."

The management of Lloyds Bank were only prepared to name the box holders with their permission. Any box holders implicated in the raid, like Tucker, were hardly likely to agree to this and so would remain anonymous. The investigation was losing valuable time. In another attempt to solve the problem, one of the Met's Assistant Commissioners wrote three days after the break-in was discovered to the head of security at Lloyds Bank asking for his help. "Although it cannot be positively confirmed at the moment there is indication that the losses are extensive. Further, that the method employed in effecting the entry to the strongroom strongly suggests that extensive planning and knowledge of the room was known by the persons responsible. You will probably agree that this source of information could have originated from a deposit box holder and it is for this reason that it is vital for police to be supplied with all possible information as to the identities of these persons and all visits made by them to the bank storeroom."

The bank inspector replied five days after: "May I say that the substance of the third paragraph of your letter is fully understood and appreciated by me and the general management of this bank, but it has been a fundamental concept of British banking to preserve secrecy over the affairs of those who utilised its services. Your letter is being very seriously considered but at the moment our decision only to supply the names of those depositors who have given permission remains good."

According to two of our sources, Lloyds staff may have been covering up evidence linking one of the most powerful men in the country with child sexual abuse. The files show that Lloyds stuck to its guns and refused to reveal what was left in the vault or who owned it. Chalk later wrote: "There was a considerable quantity of property left in the vault and tunnel but after a heated argument with bank officials they took possession of it. This property was never handled by police and to this day it is not known what that property consisted of or its value." Eventually, a list of 210 box holders was handed over to police but internal Scotland Yard documents show it "was not believed to be a full list".

First reports suggested that around £500,000 was stolen. Two weeks after the burglary, the *Daily Mirror* was reporting the true figure was closer to £4 million. "This makes the raid the biggest ever in Britain," the paper reported, "well above the 1963 Great Train Robbery haul of £2.6 million." Police estimates varied from £1.25million to £2million. In real terms, it remains one of the biggest burglaries in British criminal history. But despite the initial stonewalling from Lloyds Bank, the investigation began to make some headway.

Detectives were split into four teams, one dealing with "outside enquiries", another examining what was left at the scene, a third contacting the victims and the last taking care of the office work. The first team, dealing with outside enquiries, was led by Detective Inspector Alec Eist. Eist was ideally suited to the role, boasting a network of underworld informants that was almost unrivalled in the Met in the early 1970s. Documents found in the National Archives reveal how Eist got the first leads in the case. "It very soon became apparent that there would be no evidential help from fingerprints or forensic experts," recalled Chalk, "and that great reliance would have to be placed on the intelligent use of informants and the gathering of intelligence on the men believed to have taken part. Quite early on in the inquiry, it was learned from an informant that two of the men engaged in the break-in were a 'Tony' and a 'Reg'. Almost at the same time, from another informant, it was learned that one of the men in the gang had acquired a pub on the northern outskirts of London and had done considerable rebuilding and redecoration, costing in the region of £10,000."

The Flying Squad asked police stations along the northern border of the Metropolitan Police district whether they knew of any properties that fitted the bill. But these inquiries drew a blank. Chalk took matters into his own hands. "I then used a helicopter and discovered a place which fitted the description, at the top of Tring Hill, on the Hertfordshire/Buckinghamshire border. Aerial photographs were taken – these were to prove invaluable at a later stage when the roadhouse had to be searched - and the information obtained was checked with a discreet visit to the premises."

Chalk's officers contacted local police and obtained all the paperwork relating to the property. It was called The Crow's Nest, a large and busy pub on the A41 out of London towards Aylesbury. One of the directors of the company that owned The Crow's Nest was Gavin. The previous manager was traced to Wellingborough, Northants. Officers were sent to meet him and grill him about Gavin and his circle of friends and family.

An underworld source has revealed new details about how Gavin and Tucker came to the notice of the police after they fiddled Reader and the other gang members out of £150,000 in cash taken from the bank. The money had been left in the van they used to transport their loot back to Tucker's home in Chingford for the cut-up.

The source said: "Using explosives gives you a headache, so after the job the explosives man had a raging pain and was lying on the settee in Tucker's house with his eyes shut. They had done the cut-up and Tucker said, 'I'm going to put the van away.' Brian went with him and the explosives man said, 'Keep your eye on that cunt.' Brian didn't and Tucker took the bag of money. It was a cricket holdall with around £150,000 in it.

"When Brian and the explosives man left, Tucker brought Gavin into it and they split the money. But Tucker was no good and was connected to a man called John, who was a toerag from Hoxton and also a police informant. Tucker wasn't well-liked either and within a few days of the robbery he was driving around Hoxton with a brand new Mercedes. What an idiot! Anyway, someone told the police he had been involved with Baker Street. It was karma and they deserved to get nicked."

Thanks to this information, police decided that Gavin along with two of his associates – Thomas Stephens and Reg Tucker – were possible suspects. And all had recently left their homes. "None of these men were known to police in the accepted sense," said Chalk. "They did not frequent clubs or gamble and very little of them was known in the underworld." Through a contact on the south coast, Hampshire Police found that Gavin had a yacht called Captain Beppe. The boatbuilder in Southampton was traced, who revealed that Gavin had changed the vessel's name to Articus. Police were given access to the files of the shipyard, which revealed further business links between Gavin and Tucker.

It turned out that Gavin and Tucker had already sold Articus for £7,000 and asked about buying a larger 38-foot vessel capable of being sailed in the open ocean. Gavin had specifically asked about buying a Nicholson yacht, an attractive and sought-after vessel made by master boatbuilders based in Gosport, Hampshire. They had set a budget of £15,000 and had told the shipyard that they wanted to make certain modifications as they planned to sail it to the West Indies.

Hampshire police spoke to a broker who specialised in Nicholsons and he found out that Gavin and Tucker had already bought a yacht called the *Osprey of Doone* from a boat sellers in Glasgow for £8,000. The pair had set sail from Scotland just two days previously and it was believed they were heading to Kemps Shipyard in Northam, near Southampton, for some planned modifications. Police in Dublin, Belfast and Liverpool, all possible alternative destinations, were contacted and the boat was next spotted by HM Customs and Excise in Liverpool Bay, heading for the open sea.

With the help of HM Coastguard, the *Osprey of Doone* was tracked heading south through St George's Channel, between Pembrokeshire, South Wales, and County Wexford, in the Republic of Ireland. But a storm blew up and the yacht was lost to sight. Police along the south Wales, north Devon and north Cornwall coasts were alerted and it was discovered that the Osprey of Doone had been towed into Bideford harbour by the local lifeboat with engine failure. The two men on board, who were believed to be Gavin and Tucker, had left on a train for London. "At least it was known that two of the suspects were back in the country," said Chalk.

Meanwhile in London, officers were hard at work trying to find out as much as possible about the four suspects, their wives, cars, children, children's schools and family. Ten addresses were identified and teams of officers, driving their own cars and staying in radio contact with the operations centre in St John's Wood Police Station, made continuous circular loops, passing each address four times every 24 hours. Every car visiting each address was logged and the owners and sellers traced.

Another informant told the Flying Squad that Tucker's father was dangerously ill in hospital in the East End of London. Tucker was an occasional visitor. Gavin, meanwhile, was believed to be visiting a close relative near Biggin Hill, Kent, according to the same informant. "It was decided to play a waiting game until such time that as many of the suspects as possible, particularly Gavin and Tucker, could be arrested on the street," explained Chalk. "To arrest anyone at his or a relative's address would have caused the rest of the gang to scatter again. Eventually, patience was rewarded."

The informants told officers that Tucker was to meet two men at the Cumberland Hotel at the end of Oxford Street, near Marble Arch. Later that evening he was due to visit his father in hospital. Gavin was expected to visit his relative in Biggin Hill that night, while Stephens was due to go home. It was decided that it was time to spring the trap.

Undercover officers were placed at the hotel and they watched as Tucker handed a bag over to two Pakistani men. At 10.20am on Friday, October 29, 1971, Eist and Sergeant Roy Davies stopped the Pakistanis driving a Ford car on The Mall. One said, "I don't know anything. I'm only going to see a doctor. I don't know anything." The pair were taken to Paddington Police Station where they were charged with dishonestly handling £32,000. The other said, "I understand everything but there was £35,000 in there, not £32,000."

Chalk began questioning the Pakistani suspects later that night. Both were reluctant to talk. "I don't know anything," said the first. "I didn't get out of the car. I don't want to say any more."

"I believe you were going to take the money out of the country for the men you collected it from," Chalk told him.

"No, never, sir," he replied.

"What were you going to do with the money then?" Chalk pushed.

"Not another word passes my lips, sir," he answered.

Chalk got no further with the second man in custody. "I cannot talk, sir. I would get my throat cut," he claimed.

Shortly after leaving his father's bedside at Whipps Cross Hospital in Walthamstow, Tucker was arrested driving his Mercedes west down Lea Bridge Road that same evening. Tucker was questioned the following day by Candlish and Chalk. He admitted: "Yes, it's the bank's money. But I didn't take part in the burglary." That morning, October 30, Gavin and Stephens were arrested. Gavin was tailed from Biggin Hill driving into south east London and stopped in Bromley. Stephens was arrested as he left his work.

Later that afternoon, under questioning, Stephens too confessed. "I got the tools and the jack. I knew it was dodgy but I didn't know what job it was until I read the paper on Monday morning," he said.

"Who did you get the stuff for?" asked Candlish.

"I am not giving a name," replied Stephens. "I suppose you think I am the 'Steve' when they were talking over the radios?"

"I don't know," said Candlish, "but you will be charged with being concerned in the burglary."

Later that night, it was Gavin's turn to be questioned. "I suppose you do voice comparisons?" he said. Chalk didn't reply. "All this talk about £3million – I don't know how they do it. My business was to dig the tunnel. Every time I saw a cartoon in the papers about your lot, I thought, 'There goes another nail into my coffin! They will never give up until they catch us.' I felt like writing to the papers telling them to turn it in. I will tell you everything you want to know – except names. I just want to do my bird and return to normal life. I was a fool to allow myself to become involved."

Chalk said: "The tunnel is described as being the work of an expert. How long did it take you to construct it?"

Gavin replied: "We were in there for two weekends. I lost over one-and-a-half stone in weight."

Gavin told the detectives about a locker he had at Euston Underground station. The following morning, Candlish and Chalk opened left luggage locker No50 and found a bag containing jewellery and coins. They took it back to the station and showed it to Gavin, who confirmed: "That was my share. I have handed it in because I genuinely want to make amends." Gavin was asked where the £1,627 he had on him when he was arrested had come from. "Where do you think?" was his reply.

The next morning, on November 1, 1971, he made the following written statement: "Because I am very fit I was approached by an individual whom I knew some years ago. He said he needed someone who could withstand many hours of arduous work and asked me would I be interested. This I agreed. He later told me it was the Lloyds Bank at the corner of Baker Street NW1. Because I had some experience in the building trade, I confined my activities to constructing and building the tunnel. All my share in the proceeds you have now recovered as I arranged for you to do."

Bennie Wolfe, the bankrupted businessman who had rented Le Sac to the gang, continued to deny being involved. But he couldn't explain why he was able to let himself in with the new set of keys on the second weekend of the tunnelling. "As I have already told you, Mr Candlish," he said, "how do you prove that you cannot drive a car?" He claimed he couldn't remember the name of the man who first told him that the shop was for sale: "I have a dreadful memory." Wolfe was told he was going to be charged in connection with the burglary but made no reply.

The following morning, Tucker asked to see Candlish and confessed that his share of the loot was at the left luggage office at Waterloo Station. Candlish collected a holdall that had been deposited under ticket 1083. He later showed the bag of jewellery to Tucker at Marylebone Magistrates' Court, who insisted: "That is all I had out of the raid." Additional manpower had been made available and over the next few days 120 officers searched 40 addresses linked to the men and their families.

"Many relatives and friends were brought to the station but were allowed to leave after questioning," said Chalk. "When eventually the three men were questioned, the value of all the background information obtained was brought home. There can be no doubt that the many hours of hard and patient work… led the prisoner to think we knew much more than in fact we did." Yet more loot was recovered nearly one month after the arrests. Police received a phone call from an informant at the end of November 1971. They were told to go to left luggage locker 733 at Victoria Station, where they found three parcels of jewellery.

Police recovered 609 separate items of jewellery and coins. They sorted the stolen gear into envelopes and waited for it to be claimed. By now, more than 200 victims had come forward. Victims were shown envelopes containing stolen items that matched the descriptions given to police. If anyone claimed anything, they were asked to provide proof of ownership. Chalk said three years later: "Several items were claimed by various people and these are still in the possession of the police." He added: "The losers often tried to exaggerate their losses, obviously with the intention of defrauding the insurance claims. Others, for reasons best known to themselves, refused to divulge the contents of the deposit boxes."

All received something but they were still hugely out of pocket. Items worth £750,000 were recovered – less than half what was known to have been stolen. Apart from Gavin's admission, there was no evidence that any of the other arrested men had taken part in the burglary itself. Wolfe had an alibi. He was in Rotherham on that weekend.

At their trial, Gavin, Tucker and Stephens were each

sentenced to 12 years in jail, while Wolfe got eight years. Gavin, Tucker and Stephens appealed against their sentence in May 1974, but only Stephens was successful in cutting his down from 12 to eight years. Wolfe appealed against the conviction and sentence but was unsuccessful in both.

After their conviction, Gavin and Tucker angrily confronted police, demanding to know what the officers who had investigated them had done about the child pornography Reader had left in the vault. But they were confused about the identity of the child abuser and believed, from the type of images they had seen, that he was a schoolmaster.

Meanwhile, Reader and the other masterminds of the crime had got away scot-free. Reader was snapped with his young family on a beach in Spain months after the raid, waiting for the heat to die down. It was later claimed that two senior officers on the case had pocketed £1million in diamonds from Baker Street in exchange for letting them off the hook. These sensational allegations were made by notorious porn baron Jimmy Humphreys from his cell in Gartree Prison, Leicestershire.

Humphreys cut a colourful figure in 1960s Soho but his downfall in the following decade was even more spectacular, ending the careers of dozens of corrupt police officers. When vice squad officers raided rival porn shops, they would ring up Humphreys and offer him the magazines they had confiscated. He would turn up in his

Rolls-Royce and fill it up with smut. It was part of a lucrative arrangement that saw Humphreys pay £3,000 a week in protection money to a roster of bent officers. His business, run with his second wife, June Packard, was flourishing. They owned a luxury flat in Soho along with a 28-room farmhouse in Kent. They had the lease on seven porn shops and two strip clubs, where June regularly appeared under her stage name Rusty Gaynor.

But all this came tumbling down after the *Sunday People* published a picture in 1972 of the head of the Flying Squad, Detective Chief Superintendent Kenneth Drury, on holiday in Cyprus with Humphreys. The paper made devastating allegations about payments to senior officers in exchange for Humphreys being allowed to ply his illegal trade without interference from the law. Drury was eventually jailed for eight years after he and 10 other officers appeared at the Old Bailey in what was dubbed "The Dirty Squad" trials.

The Yard also mounted a full investigation into Humphreys' empire, raiding his premises and searching his flat. June was arrested at Heathrow Airport carrying a gun and was jailed for four months.

After serving one month in prison, June was released but Humphreys found out she was having an affair with a small-time crook, Peter Garfath. Garfath was attacked and badly cut up. A court later heard that Humphreys had ordered his henchmen to cut off Garfath's hands. Humphreys always maintained that he was framed and, when he found himself in prison serving an eight-year sentence, decided to open his diaries, which detailed his dealings with corrupt officers.

He invited campaigning Labour MP Robin Corbett to visit him in prison and told him that a detective superintendent and another officer had helped themselves to £1million worth of gems from the Baker Street raid and sold them on the black market. Humphreys claimed that a detective chief inspector had visited him and June at their flat soon after the raid. He had been sent by another corrupt officer, it was alleged, and showed Humphreys some of the jewels that were wrapped in tissue paper in his pocket. He asked Humphreys if he wanted to buy some for June and help him dispose of the rest. June spoke to a reporter from the *Sunday People* and backed up her husband's story. "Jimmy wasn't interested," she said. "He knew nothing about jewels."

By the time Humphreys had finished spilling the beans on the vast network of police corruption, 74 officers had been arrested, 12 had resigned, 28 retired and 13 were jailed. It was the biggest police scandal in a century. Just two years into his sentence, Humphreys was rewarded with a royal pardon.

Of the officers on the Baker Street case, it was Eist who was by reputation the most corrupt. One former colleague told former solicitor turned author James Morton for his 1993 book *Bent Coppers*: "He was the best informed police officer in London. What he took off one criminal he gave back to another. If he got £200 from a villain for giving him bail, Eist would give £195 to cultivate an informant." Neil Darbyshire and Brian Hilliard wrote in their history of the Flying Squad: "Detective Sergeant Alec Eist established two reputations. One was as a specialist in the arrest of lorry hijackers, the other as one of the most corrupt officers of his era."

Alexander Antony Eist was born in Cardiff on 26 March, 1929. He served as an Able Seaman in the Merchant Navy from 1945 until 1948, when he joined the Met. In 1967, he was awarded the British Empire Medal for Gallantry. Along with two colleagues, Eist was investigating a series of house burglaries when they visited a suspect's house. While one officer spoke to a woman at the front door, the suspect tried to escape out the back door carrying a rifle. Eist recognised him as someone who escaped from prison. The suspect threatened to shoot the officers and raised his gun at them. But Eist and his colleagues threw flower pots at him and managed to overpower him. Along with his British Empire Medal and War Medal, Eist received a Police Exemplary Service Medal and letters of congratulations from both Buckingham Palace and the then Home Secretary Roy Jenkins.

He was a star detective. Yet another commendation came for his role in securing four convictions over the Baker Street heist. This was one of 13 commendations in his career, the last coming in January 1975 "for outstanding diligence and detective ability leading to the arrest and conviction of an active and violent gang of robbers". He was also commended at the Central Criminal Court and by the Director of Public Prosecutions.

But his downfall came in 1975, when he was arrested by anti-corruption officers. He was acquitted in his subsequent trial and returned to uniformed duty in November that year, but Eist resigned on grounds of ill-health three months later. Reg Dudley was one of Eist's underworld contacts. As outlined in Chapter 3, he had loose links to Reader's gang and was a self-confessed "fence" – a buyer and seller of stolen property. He later said: "I also had a close relationship with a bent detective, Alec Eist. My friends knew that if they were in trouble, for a few grand channelled through me, Alec would do what he could to make evidence 'disappear'." After Eist was arrested, Dudley was convicted of a double murder but always insisted on his innocence. It was 25 years before he cleared his name and he wonders if Eist's downfall made him a target.

It is not known if Reader, Mills and the other two unnamed raiders who all escaped charges, ever paid corrupt police officers to keep them out of trouble. A gang insider said: "It was a normal thing in those days to pay off the police. After a burglary they would come to the house at five am and it was understood they would get their share, normally through a middleman. All the CID were at it in those days and if you weren't they would put you on traffic duties."

We understand that at least one other raider — the explosives man — was named to police by Gavin. Benny Wolfe later showed him Gavin's witness statement proving it. Police interviewed him but, for whatever reason, he was never charged.

Bobby Mills moved to Brixton, south London, where he became a cannabis smuggler using the cover of a beach bar in Devon to import consignments of the drug. The insider said: "He had two boats that he would use to do the handovers out at sea." But the steel-lined warehouse he used to store the drugs in Penge, south London, was raided by customs officers and he was jailed in the late 70s for seven years. Mills went on the run to Spain where he died around 10 years ago and is buried under a false name. The insider said: "No one went to his funeral because they didn't hear about his death until long afterwards."

Of the two other Baker Street raiders, one is believed to have gone straight soon after the burglary and is now living in luxury in Mayfair. The other is understood to have given up crime and is living somewhere in the UK.

CHAPTER 6

The Betrayal

A tall, authoritative-looking man dressed in a police sergeant's uniform stepped into the dual carriageway. He raised his right hand deliberately and signalled at a lorry travelling towards him to stop. The officer's set jaw and determined stare immediately convinced the driver to hit his brakes and the vehicle came shuddering to a halt in a layby. Flanked by what appeared to be two Ministry of Transport officials, dressed in white smock coats and dark glasses, the man in uniform made his way towards the lorry. As the baffled driver started to wind down his window, a blue van loomed up from nowhere in his rear view mirror. Five masked men carrying shotguns and a pistol jumped out screaming at him to get out. Within a minute, the driver and his colleague were tied up and their lorry was being driven away with one of the hijackers behind the wheel. Watching it disappear into the distance with its cargo of 321 silver bars worth £3.5million, the lanky, balding figure in the police uniform smiled to himself. Mickey "Skinny" Gervaise knew he had pulled off what was, on that grey March morning in 1980, one of the biggest robberies in British history. But Gervaise had no inkling of the huge repercussions the heist would have.

A life of crime seemed an unlikely future for policeman's son Michael Anthony Gervaise when he was born in Aberdeen in 1943. His parents, Walter and Dorothy, moved to King's Cross in north London shortly afterwards and young Mickey grew up with no hint of a Scottish accent. The only child was a gregarious and bright youngster and did well at school, paving the way for him to train as an electrical engineer. His first job was designing new wireless portable radios for a British firm called Perdio, and the comfortable life of a middle-class professional beckoned. When the company relocated from London to Sunderland in 1963, Gervaise had no problem getting a new job as a burglar-alarm technician. But a knock at his door later that year would change the course of his life forever. Gervaise was approached by Reader's gang and went on to become one of the most prolific thieves in British history.

But by the end of the 1970s he had become greedy and careless. Gervaise was now living the life of the big-time criminal, splashing out on expensive cars and large houses. Though he was married with two children, he had gained a reputation as a ladies' man and enjoyed showing off the trappings of his success. The need to fund this expensive lifestyle meant he soon became unwilling to stick exclusively with Reader's gang, who abided by strict rules in order to reduce to a minimum the chances of getting caught. A job would only get the green light if they had examined all the angles and were confident of avoiding arrest. That meant rejecting a lot of potentially lucrative work. Gervaise wasn't willing to be constricted by these rules and he began running with armed criminals like Lennie Gibson and Mickey Sewell, men who he would later do the Silver Bullion job with. The gang insider said: "Gervaise started working for everybody. He even got in with shoplifter Roy "The Bear" Green, a big lump who would go thieving from jewellery exhibitions in Brussels and Amsterdam. By the end even Tony Gavin, who had been like Gervaise's PR man on the firm, had had enough of him. Tony was very jealous and had the idea Gervaise was getting more than his fair share."

Gervaise committed at least 41 high-value burglaries between 1963 and 1980, including 14 in the Hatton Garden area. The biggest was the £8million raid on the Mayfair branch of Bank of America in October 1974, at that time said to be the largest bank burglary in the world. The insider said that Reader was given the option of taking part but turned it down because of concerns over the other raiders. His hunch proved correct when most of the gang were jailed for a total of 100 years as a result of evidence from Stuart Buckley, the inside man who turned police informant. Buckley, who had worked at the bank as an electrician, obtained the safe's combination by hiding in the roof space above the vault door and peering through a hole in the ceiling as officials opened it.

In 1973, Gervaise plotted to raid four Barclays banks in central London, including branches on Park Lane and the Brompton Road. Two years later he stole watches worth a quarter-of-a-million pounds from Roamer Watches, close to Hatton Garden. In 1978, he was involved in at least eight big burglaries on commercial premises and a year later that number rose to 10. Sources say that by 1980 it was obvious Gervaise's avarice would lead to his downfall. By then he had become involved in the far riskier crime of armed robbery. It was this group of villains who were being pulled in by Scotland Yard in their droves by detectives using the flawed supergrass system. The feeling of elation Gervaise had experienced following the success of the Silver Bullion raid did not stay with him for long. A few weeks later he was arrested in connection with a string of burglaries after being "ratted on" by a fellow gang member. North London safe cutter Chrissie Wren had been persuaded to turn supergrass and, in addition to Gervaise, he had named a second member of Reader's gang, John Goodwin.

The police investigation that grew out of Wren's evidence was codenamed Operation Jenny and would eventually see 17 men convicted for 83 robberies and 105 burglaries. Spearheading it was Tony Lundy, who as a young sergeant had unwittingly come within a hair's breadth of foiling the Baker Street burglary. He was now Detective Chief Inspector Lundy, Scotland Yard's most prolific and controversial thief-taker. Lundy was an ambitious, straight-talking Lancastrian who had been a leading exponent of the supergrass system during the 1970s. The practice of persuading criminals to turn "Queen's Evidence" came to prominence in 1974 when a small balding man with a walrus moustache gave evidence in the oak-panelled surroundings of Court Two at the Old Bailey. After Derek "Bertie" Smalls left the witness box, the seven defendants sitting in the dock suddenly burst into song, belting out the 1940 vocal harmony number "Whispering Grass" by the Inkspots, which included the line: "Why tell them all your secrets?" More ominously for Smalls, the armed robbers then made gun gestures while singing: "We'll Meet Again." The meaning of this unusual musical performance was clear to all of those watching. Armed robber Smalls had given evidence against his old friends and former brothers in crime, breaking the unwritten law of omerta among criminals: never betray your fellow villain. A 38-year-old with a comb-over, Smalls had been "turned" after he was arrested in connection with a £237,000 bank raid in Wembley in August 1972. During a succession of trials at the Old Bailey over six months, his evidence jailed 28 villains who received a total of 414 years. Smalls had admitted to his part in 20 robberies but was handed total immunity from prosecution in return for betraying his former gang, known as the "Wembley Mob". Chief Superintendent Jack Slipper, who solved the Bank of

America robbery, said after the robber was jailed: "Smalls is the greatest weapon the police have ever had against the underworld. He will have to spend the rest of his life with a £1million price on his head because so many people want to get even with him."

Smalls was the last informant who admitted taking part in armed robberies to be granted full immunity. In future all supergrasses would be sentenced with the judge taking into account the help they had provided the police and prosecution. The first to be dealt with in this way was Maurice O'Mahoney in 1974 when he admitted robbery, burglary and attempted robbery at the Old Bailey, with a further 92 offences taken into consideration. He was given just five years in jail for offences that would normally attract a 20-year tariff and two more of his gang joined him in giving prosecution evidence. O'Mahoney helped to jail 20 robbers, and throughout the 1970s and early 1980s supergrasses often comprised a large part of the prosecution case in armed robberies.

The rise of the supergrass system coincided with one of the darkest chapters in Scotland Yard's history. Though there had been an acceptance among senior officers in the post-war period that corruption was widespread, the problem was largely ignored. In 1955, the *Daily Mail* reported that a superintendent had written to the then commissioner revealing how officers at West End Central police station were receiving up to £60 a week from pimps and gaming-house owners. The report was mothballed and the commissioner personally visited the station to give the officers his full backing. It was only thanks to some brave and brilliant investigative reporting by journalists at *The Times*, then the establishment's newspaper of choice, that the problem was finally forced on to the political agenda. The front page exclusive story by Garry Lloyd and Julian Mounter was headlined "London policemen in bribe allegations. Tapes reveal planted evidence". Three detectives had allegedly taken cash in exchange for dropping charges and allowing criminals to "work unhindered". Using the latest technology, Lloyd and Mounter had recorded conversations between the officers and a south London villain who had approached them to blow the whistle on the corruption. One of the detectives was taped saying: "We've got more villains in our game than you've got in yours, you know." The same officer bragged: "I'm a firm in a firm. Don't matter where, anywhere in London, I can get on the phone to someone I trust, that talks the same as me." The three detectives were later jailed despite the fact that Bill Moody, the officer put in charge of the investigation, turned out later to be one of the most corrupt in the force.

Reader and his team would exploit the corruption, usually working through a middleman to pay off a superintendent who might pass a percentage down to his junior officers. A number of Reader's gang would go to jail over the years but the man himself and a few other key players managed to avoid doing time until the early 1980s.

By then deals had become harder to come by following a clampdown on corruption and the ending of unrecorded conversations between detectives and villains in cells with no solicitors present. A former gang member said: "The whole of the CID was corrupt in the old days. It's all changed now, but in those days the governor of the police station would turn up after a robbery, have a look and then go to the pub with his sergeant to think about how they were going to get some money out of it. I've had to pay police officers quite a few times over the years. After a job they would come to the house at five in the morning. Everyone knew who was doing which jobs, so if we knew another mob were planning a big one we would leave the country so we wouldn't get lifted. The police would beat us up sometimes as well. That was always a good sign because it meant they didn't have anything. You would get a beating now and again that was part-and-parcel of the way things worked."

By 1972 the situation had become so bad that when Sir Robert Mark became Commissioner of the Metropolitan Police he said in his inaugural address: "A good police force is one that catches more criminals than it employs." It was the Criminal Investigation Department and its most elite unit, the Flying Squad, responsible for targeting armed robbers, top burglars and high-profile gangsters, that was the target of Sir Robert's comments. At the time, some Flying Squad detectives had become known for their close relationships with their criminal targets. Among them was Detective Chief Inspector Tony Lundy.

So by the time Chrissie Wren was arrested for armed robbery in May 1980, just two months after the Silver Bullion raid, Lundy's methods were already in the spotlight. His approach to supergrasses, honed over many years, involved confronting a suspect with the bombshell news that a friend had spilled the beans on them and given an account of their crimes so detailed that they felt it would be impossible to wriggle off the hook. Lundy would regale his shocked prisoner with the specific ins-and-outs of all the offences, convincing them he had more than enough to send them to jail for 20 years. At this point he would plant a seed in their mind. There was a way out, he would say. If the suspect held his hands up and came clean they would only get five years. This often had a domino effect, with the next villain naming others who Lundy would then pick up as quickly as possible and repeat the process. The trick was to hit them hard and fast, before the criminal networks had time to confer or consider the consequences.

This worked with Wren, who started singing like his namesake. Despite having no previous convictions, he was a serious criminal whose father was also a leading villain. Wren had links to some of the top robbers and burglars in London, including one or two in Reader's gang. Up until this point supergrasses had been used mainly to jail armed robbers. Lundy realised Wren and Gervaise would give him a once-in-a-lifetime opportunity to smash Britain's gang of master thieves, a group that had been successfully operating in London for two decades, with the ringleaders beyond the reach of Scotland Yard.

Lundy told author Martin Short in his excellent biography of the officer: "For two weeks we were charging people by the dozen, in and out of court, working day and night. We recovered firearms and even police uniforms. The pressure on me and my officers was immense." The total value of the crimes committed by Wren and his gang was £3million. Lundy said: "One big breakthrough came when we hit some lock-up garages Wren had told us about. They were an Aladdin's cave full of the best gear any burglar could want: thermic lances, petro-chemical lances, radios tuned to police wavelengths, stuff that villains dream of. Wren claimed that Tony Fiori had stockpiled the lot for many years [the garages were very near Fiori's home] so he too rolled over and became a supergrass. Now we could really crack the organised burglary side of London crime."

Fiori was another leading burglar with loose links to Reader's network. Confronted with the evidence from Wren, both Fiori and Gervaise agreed to turn supergrass. But slippery Gervaise was a calculating character and Lundy believed he was holding back. A suspect could only qualify for supergrass status if he told the "whole truth" and it was clear to Lundy that Gervaise had not.

Lundy told Short many years later: "I didn't agree with Gervaise being a supergrass. He wanted to help and started to talk but I said, 'No way! He's an out-and-out liar.' He was admitting loads of burglaries, but he was denying three or four robberies we knew he had committed.

"Cunning bastard that he was, he'd taken part in a £400,000 jewel raid in Hatton Garden in May 1978 [Patel] and another worth £800,000 in April 1980 [Gemco] but he kept them both back until my deputy, Pat Fleming, and I dragged them out of him! We were getting him down from Whetstone back to Finchley and strapping him about crimes he would not admit – until we got to the Nth degree. Then he'd have to admit them and also admit he's lied.

"I said, 'You can't use a man like that. What kind of a supergrass is he? He'll be the destruction of the entire system!' But I was overruled. I was told to keep my place and told Gervaise would be used."

He had started off by admitting 31 burglaries starting in 1963 but was denying involvement in any robberies. Among those he held his hands up to was a raid on Gemco diamond merchants in Hatton Garden on April 15, 1980, just a month after he had pulled off the Silver Bullion heist. According to a source, Gervaise had been tipped off about the vulnerabilities of the shop by a younger alarm man called Roy who had previously managed to get into the building. The underworld source said: "Roy told him he could go through a side-door and do the wires of the alarm, and that's exactly what he did.

Gervaise went in with two south London armed robbers and waited for the Jewish manager to come back. When he did they gave the poor man a hiding and did some real damage to him when he first refused to open the safe." When the manager relented, the trio escaped with nearly £1million in diamonds.

Gervaise had nowhere to hide his "whack" so he put it in a briefcase and left it with a friend called Alfie, who stuck it in his shed at the bottom of his garden in Potters Bar. Protected only by a flimsy padlock, the diamonds were squashed in with rusty old tools next to a second briefcase belonging to Gervaise containing around 200 broken luxury watches. He had bought them from Reader, who had stolen them during a raid on luxury watch makers Piaget in Birmingham. When Gervaise admitted the Gemco heist, Lundy insisted he return the diamonds and gave him permission to speak to his wife, who went to Alfie's house to get them. The source said: "She picked up the wrong suitcase and Lundy went spare when he found out he had a load of broken watches instead of the diamonds." In the meantime, Tony Gavin had heard about the whereabouts of the diamonds and took them from Alfie before going on holiday. After missing Gavin's return from Heathrow Airport, Lundy's team eventually caught up with him and got the diamonds back.

While this was happening Lundy was tipped off by his number-one informer, Roy Garner, about Gervaise's involvement in the crime every detective wanted to solve.

Garner contacted Lundy one Saturday to tell him that his prisoner had been on the Silver Bullion job. The detective rushed to Gervaise's cell with his boss, Superintendent Reg Dixon, where he had to attempt to get him to confess without letting on he had been told about his involvement. If Gervaise knew he had been grassed up, it would put Garner in danger. Lundy told Short: "When he looked at me, his bottle dropped out and he knew. I never told him, I didn't have to. Here were we, coming in on a Saturday afternoon, out of the blue, when he knew we were all supposed to be having a weekend off, and he was locked up in peace at Enfield. He knew it had to be something special when all of a sudden we're there: the superintendent and the chief inspector."

But sly Gervaise was not going to admit to anything before working out exactly where he stood. He was worried about Lundy's relationship with armed robber Lennie Gibson, one of the Silver Bullion gang. Lundy knew Gibson through the Finchley Amateur Boxing Club where the criminal's son had been one of a hundred north London boys learning to box. The officer had become heavily involved in the club and would drink with Gibson in the Torrington Arms nearby. Gervaise told Lundy, with Dixon out of the room, that the crime "involves Lennie", adding: "You don't realise how serious it is." Lundy responded: "Get one thing straight: Lennie is a likeable type but I have no allegiances to him or anybody else. If they are involved in villainy, they will be nicked and dealt with like anyone else."

According to Lundy's account, this led to Gervaise breaking and saying: "Well, perhaps you will understand why I have been worried – I was on the Silver Bullion job with Lennie Gibson." At this point Lundy told Dixon to return to the cell and Gervaise gave them the names of three more of the gang: including Mickey Sewell and Dudolpho "Dolph" Aguda. Gervaise said: "I was the policeman but the uniforms and guns were provided by the others." He denied having any idea where the stolen bullion had been hidden. Lundy went on to arrest the gang and they eventually revealed they had hidden the silver in a lock-up garage in Belgrave Close in Southgate, north London. Lundy's informer Roy Garner was paid £180,000 as a reward for providing the information that led to the discovery of the silver. A smaller amount of money was given to Wren for setting the ball rolling by naming Gervaise.

The investigation had been a huge success for Lundy, but that would turn sour a year later. In February 1981 an anonymous letter landed on the desk of Scotland Yard's commissioner accusing Lundy of plotting to ensure the Silver Bullion reward would go to an informant who was not entitled to it. The note appeared to have been written by a senior Scotland Yard officer. That, coupled with allegations from supergrass Billy Young, would spark a corruption investigation into Lundy led by Deputy Assistant Commissioner Ron Steventon. Steventon eventually sent a file to the Crown Prosecution Service, who decided he should not face criminal charges. Lundy told the world he had been cleared and in 1985 was put onto the ongoing Brink's-Mat police investigation. What was not made public at that time was Steventon's finding in the unpublished report. He wrote: "I feel bound to express a personal opinion and regrettably there is a dearth of evidence to support it, but it is my belief that Lundy is a corrupt officer who has long exploited his association with Garner." Lundy resigned from the force citing poor health in 1988 while facing another corruption probe.

The Silver Bullion investigation had grabbed all the headlines but in the background it had led to Reader and Goodwin being charged with three burglaries totalling more than £1,250,000. On Friday May 30, 1980, Reader was arrested during a 7am raid at his four-bedroom house on Goddington Lane, Orpington, south east London. He was locked up before being questioned by Detective Inspector Albert Patrick and Scottish-born detective John Davidson, known to his colleagues as "Obnoxious Jock". Davidson would go on to be accused of having a corrupt relationship with criminal Clifford Norris – the father of one of the racist killers of black teenager Stephen Lawrence.

Patrick, now retired, said of Reader: "I had respect for him, he never gave me a hard time and never made any stupid allegations. He was a good, old-style villain. I don't think he had an ounce of violence in him. He wasn't a 'yes sir, no sir' type either. He respected me and I respected him. He had a job to do and he knew I did too." Patrick questioned Reader at West Hendon police station before charging him with burglary and remanding him in custody. He said: "Reader was a total gentleman throughout the whole process and ended up confessing to one of the burglaries. He made a statement, called a 992, because of the pressure he was under knowing that Gervaise had named him. But he didn't admit the other crimes. I think there was one in Hatton Garden and another on the Clerkenwell Road. After he put his hands up to the one he was remanded in custody."

But five months later the detective, who lived in Blackfen, got a surprise when he bumped into Reader close to his brother's car showroom, which was also in Blackfen. Patrick said: "By that time he wasn't my responsibility and he had been bailed after someone put up a surety. Even so, he did try it on with me. It was obvious from his demeanour. He used words to the effect of: 'Can you help me out?' I said 'forget it' and reported it and that was the end of the matter." As time went on, it was becoming increasingly apparent that Reader might not need any help to get him off the hook. The star prosecution witness in his case, Mickey Gervaise, had turned hostile. Gervaise had given a poor performance in the witness box during the trial of Bob Deanus, a jeweller he had fingered over the Silver Bullion robbery. In his summing up to the Deanus jury, Judge Peter Slot said of Gervaise's testimony: "You would not honestly hang a dog on his evidence, would you? You would not dream of finding a man guilty on the basis of his evidence alone, would you? Well I would not." Sure enough, Deanus was acquitted in January 1982.

Three months later, the slippery supergrass told Reader and Goodwin's trial he had made it "abundantly clear to everyone" that he didn't want to give evidence. He told the court: "I even wrote to the prosecution saying I didn't want to get involved." Gervaise withdrew his evidence, claiming detectives had told him to falsely accuse the defendants of burglaries they had nothing to do with. He told their trial: "I went along with what was required. Goodwin's name was suggested – he should be involved as an extra. I was expected to involve him. I was doing a deal and I just went along with it… The police officer said Goodwin and Reader were to be implicated – they had to go, to use police terminology – to be put away. It was left to me to involve them in whatever role." He also sensationally claimed that a retired robbery squad inspector had committed a number of burglaries with him in the 1970s and was ordered to keep quiet about his dealings with bent cops when he turned supergrass. But instead of being cleared, Reader and Goodwin's trial was abandoned after the judge was told of claims they had been trying to "nobble" the jury.

At the burglary retrial, the 12 jurors - who this time

had 24-hour police protection – found them not guilty after two days of deliberations. There was cheering from the public gallery.

Discharging Goodwin, Judge Slot said: "Before we part, I don't think it likely that we will meet again. I would like to thank you personally for the restraint, self-control, propriety and dignity, if you will allow me to use that word without appearing to be patronising, with which you have conducted yourself throughout these trials. No one can fail to recognise the tremendous strains and pressures you have been under."

Goodwin would be back at the Old Bailey, however, when he was convicted of interfering with the jury in the earlier trial and jailed for seven years in March 1983. The allegations related to the abandoned trial of him and Reader the year before. Eight other people, including a juror, were sentenced for their parts in what prosecutor Kenneth Richardson described as a "determined attempt to poison the fountain of British justice". Mr Richardson said that four jurors, and possibly four more, had been offered bribes of £1,000 each to bring in not guilty verdicts against Reader and Goodwin. It was believed that others not identified had accepted the bribes. But the plot failed because one member of the jury panel, Grace Ellicott, a 36-year-old waitress from south east London, reported to the court that an approach had been made to her. Mr Richardson said that all the defendants were engaged in "a wholesale conspiracy to pervert the course of justice", playing different roles. Many of the jurors in the burglary trial came from Reader's home turf in south east London and were known to use the Jolly Marshman pub, where some bribery approaches were made.

Two of the men jailed with Goodwin included Reader's former mentor Bill Barrett and another old friend Geoff Donovan, who were both handed four-year sentences. Barrett and Donovan had spent summer holidays with the Readers at Coghurst Hall caravan park near Hastings. The court heard that Reader and Goodwin had been spotted while on bail during the burglary trial by two police officers meeting Barrett and Donovan in a Wimpy restaurant at Exmouth Market in Clerkenwell. It was the day before Ms Ellicott was offered cash to find them not guilty. The officers said they heard the men saying: "We'll see the women tomorrow." Chief Superintendent Ronald Hay told Goodwin's trial: "The four men were leaning across the table – huddled together conspiratorially."

Goodwin appealed against the conviction claiming the judge had been wrong to describe him as "the leader of a gang of jury nobblers". Instead he passed the blame over to his friend, stating: "Reader was plainly the leader and the instigator of the said attempt." The Houdini-like villain was freed and his sentence quashed when he was cleared at the Court of Appeal in May 1984. Goodwin, dubbed "Mr Fix-it" following his conviction, was released because of concerns over the evidence from two witnesses. One Appeal Court judge said: "However suspicious we are, we have to look at the quality of the evidence and quality was lacking."

It was the latest in a string of close escapes for Goodwin who, after two re-trials, was eventually acquitted of burgling a bank in Whitechapel, east London, in 1978. The jury were unable to reach a verdict in the first trial and the second had to be dropped when Goodwin hoodwinked the court by pretending to have a heart attack. The crafty thief, who went on to become the chairman of non-league Bishop's Stortford Football Club, was sensationally cleared in the third trial after he produced a recording of a detective appearing to take a bribe from him. He had stashed a recorder in a friend's Christmas tree shortly before the officers had called for a festive tipple and the evidence saved him from jail. Three detectives later faced trial accused of taking £8,500 from Goodwin to help him escape the bank burglary charges. Two were cleared and the third had his conviction overturned at the Court of Appeal.

In April 1983, while Goodwin was still in jail, his wife Shirley was kidnapped at gunpoint from her home by the evil villain Charlie Pitts. Among his siblings were Shirley Pitts - AKA "Queen of the Shoplifters" - and Henry "Adgie" Pitts, a bank robber who died in a car crash at the age of 29. When Shirley Pitts passed away in 1992, the Kray twins sent their condolences and Buster Edwards, the Great Train Robber, turned up in person to pay his last respects. Charlie Pitts was one of four masked men who forced their way into Goodwin's house to grab terrified Shirley Goodwin in her dressing gown and slippers as her children looked on.

A handwritten ransom note sent to Goodwin's sons Bradley and Spencer stated: "JOHN PUT MUM IN THIS POSITION SO JOHNS MONEY CAN GET MUM OUT OF IT. I CAN BE A NICE GUY OR A WICKED BASTARD. ITS YOUR CHOICE OKAY.... ALLS FAIR IN LOVE AND WAR. AT THE MOMENT MUMS BEING TREATED WITH KID GLOVES. BUT IF YOU GO TO THE LAW THEN MUM WILL THINK SHES IN BELSEN THAT A PROMISE. SON IM TRYING TO GET IT OVER TO YOU JUST OUR NASTY IT COULD GET. SO SON GET BUSY GET ALOT OF MONEY PUT TOGETHER AND WAIT FOR OUR CALL."

Detective Sergeant Dick West was tasked with helping to find Shirley despite having spent the previous few months investigating her husband over the jury nobbling claims. The retired officer said: "About a week after Goodwin was jailed Commander John Blann came to me and said, 'You've been dealing with Goodwin and his wife and you know what she looks like. She's been kidnapped so go and find her.' This was a woman who had been spitting fire and brimstone at us for months and now we had to rescue her."

Goodwin was visited by detectives in Wandsworth prison and he revealed his longstanding feud with Pitts.

Working with Scotland Yard, the family pretended to agree to pay £10,000 and the kidnappers were put under surveillance. Pitts, his son-in-law Sean McDonald and a third man were arrested simultaneously. West then interviewed McDonald in an attempt to persuade him to reveal the whereabouts of Shirley. The suspect had been stripped of his clothes and was wrapped in a blanket while sweating heavily, his head buried in his hands.

The following exchange was recorded in the officer's notebook. West warned: "She may already be dead and if she isn't she's certainly in grave danger. If you have any conscience at all you'll tell us where she is."

McDonald replied: "I can't tell you or they will kill me."

West continued: "Have you considered the implications for you if she were to be found dead? What you are involved in is bad enough but you should realise that you could be party to murder if she is killed." He added: "This is England. You don't walk into some mum's front room and drag her out in her slippers at gunpoint. You don't lock her away for a week, threaten her life and demand money for her return without people getting a bit upset about it."

McDonald replied: "She'll be all right, honest, they won't kill her."

Trying to convey the seriousness of the situation, the officer asked: "Do you know what panic is? Do you have any idea how people react in a situation they can't control, when things go horribly wrong and they can see no way out? People do some terrible things just to save their own skins."

McDonald cracked and admitted to being at the kidnapping but claimed he did not go into the house and had no idea what had been planned. West asked: "We believe you but where is Shirley? Her life may be in your hands." McDonald then revealed that she was being held in chalet 56 at the Warden Bay holiday camp on the Isle of Sheppey in Kent. He admitted booking the holiday home three weeks earlier after Pitts told him to reply to an ad in *Dalton's Weekly*. He said the gang had made audio tapes of Shirley describing her husband's villainy, naming others involved and their crimes. He even claimed the tapes, which he said had been buried, included details of the involvement of corrupt police. It is not known if they have ever been recovered. Pitts was jailed for 18 years at the Old Bailey after being found guilty of robbery, blackmail, kidnapping and false imprisonment. McDonald was handed an eight-year term.

By the time of the kidnapping Reader had "gone on his toes" to avoid being jailed over Gervaise's burglary allegations. He took Lyn and the kids with him to Europe after dropping off his surety of £40,000 at the Old Bailey and telling the clerk of the court: "I'm off to park my car." Instead, a friend waiting outside the court drove him to Dover, where they caught a ferry to Calais. A gang insider said: "They stayed with a friend in Paris before Brian met up with his family." They moved on to Spain, which had become popular for British criminals on the run after the collapse of a 100-year-old extradition treaty in 1978. A new agreement was made in 1985, which closed the loophole.

This was to mark one of the happiest periods in Reader's life as he took Lyn and the children, who had by then left school, on a tour of France and Spain. They spent that winter with a friend in the exclusive Alpine resort of Meribel, where Reader hired a chalet and became a decent skier, despite his poor balance caused by the accident in Reading ten years earlier. In the summer, they stayed in a villa owned by another friend in the quiet resort of Javea on Spain's Costa Blanca. It was a life far removed from Reader's war-ravaged childhood. He got his yachting licence after doing night-classes and would take the family out on to the crystal blue Mediterranean waters every day.

Lyn would later tell *Guardian* crime reporter Duncan Campbell that it was not such a happy time for her. "We went to France, then to Spain. I hated it. I thought, you can't go home when you want to. People think it sounds glamorous but it was awful changing homes all the time. I used to get plants and flowers whenever we went to a new place to try and make it look like home. Then I got a message that my mother was ill, so we had to come home. But we still had to keep hiding because of what Gervaise had said and have different identities." It was during this period that Reader and Lyn began calling themselves Mr and Mrs McCarthy, an identity Reader would continue to deploy decades later.

Lyn said she would later see the film *Buster*, starring Phil Collins, with her daughter Joanne, known to the family as Joey. The romantic comedy tells the story of Great Train Robber Buster Edwards and his long-suffering wife, June, played by Julie Walters. The couple go on the run to Acapulco, Mexico, but June becomes unhappy and returns to the UK. Lyn said: "Half-way through she [Joanne] said, 'Oh, this is the worst thing I could have done,' because it's all about being on the run and wanting to have English things to eat when you're abroad. And I said: 'Well, at least I didn't ask for steak and chips, did I?'"

A source has revealed that in 1983, while still a fugitive and with no passport, Reader allegedly pulled off one of his most audacious burglaries yet when he sneaked back into the UK via Jersey. Under the noses of Scotland Yard, he executed a £3million raid – worth £9.5million in 2016 – on the Lloyds Bank in Holborn Circus, just a stone's throw from his Hatton Garden stomping ground. He entered the country by hitching a ride on a private yacht from France, after being told a contact had obtained a key for the bank. The source said they broke in one weekend, bypassed the sophisticated alarm and entered the vaults where many Hatton Garden jewellers kept their possessions. Reader ransacked the safety deposit boxes and then slipped back out of the country.

A judge would later criticise police for failing to act on a tip-off from a former detective who had been approached by one gang member before the crime had been committed. Sentencing six of Reader's accomplices, Judge John Hazan said ex-officer Alan Tolmie was working for security firm Chubb when he was offered a £10,000 bribe in return for details of the alarm system. Mr Tolmie reported the approach to the Flying Squad, who ignored it. Judge Hazan told the Old Bailey: "One can only wonder whether, if the proper action had been taken by somebody before this criminal activity, a £3million burglary could have been avoided." It was only after detectives followed up Mr Tolmie's tip in the wake of the raid that gang members were jailed for 55 years in February 1984. Once again Reader and at least one other leading member of his gang had escaped prosecution. But his lucky streak was about to come to an end.

CHAPTER 7

Fool's Gold

The neighbours thought the McCarthys at number 40 were just a normal family like everyone else on the street. The middle-aged husband always smiled and said hello as he left for work as a car dealer, driving his green, second-hand Vauxhall Cavalier. His attractive wife would stop for a fag and a gossip with the other mums to talk about the weather or the recent birth of Princess Diana's second son, Harry. They were new to this particular part of London but both had local accents and they impressed everyone with their knowledge of the area. Their pebble-dashed, four-bedroom house on Winn Road, in suburban Grove Park, south east London, looked like all the others on the leafy street. A very keen-eyed observer might have wondered why it was the only one with white, Spanish-style shutters on the windows. Had they spent some time living abroad? It would have taken a dedicated curtain twitcher to have noticed Mr McCarthy coming and going at odd times with so many different briefcases. Though the net curtains on the street did do more than their fair share of twitching, none of the busybodies behind them could have guessed at the truth. Not in their wildest dreams.

Because the McCarthys were not the McCarthys at all. Neither were they a normal family like everyone else on the street. They were in fact the Readers, and Mr Reader was one of Scotland Yard's most wanted fugitives. The different suitcases he had been carrying were stuffed with huge bundles of £50 notes that he was exchanging for consignments of gold bullion, stolen in the Brink's-Mat robbery, the biggest ever in Britain.

Brian Reader had perfected the art of living an outwardly respectable and unremarkable middle-class life because it came naturally to him. Unlike many, less successful criminals, he had no desire to be a "face" on the nightclub circuit that was packed with plastic gangsters. In the 1960s, while the Kray twins became celebrities on the Swinging London scene, Reader was keeping his head down, working hard and spending his evenings with his family. The idea of being photographed by David Bailey or socialising with Lords, MPs or actors like George Raft, Judy Garland, Diana Dors and Barbara Windsor was an anathema to him. Recognition would mean failure in his line of work and Reader was happy with his life as an inconspicuous success.

Now aged 47, he had helped to mastermind some of the biggest burglaries in British history. The total haul from his work so far was already in the tens of millions. He had not spent a day in prison and only a handful of Scotland

Yard detectives and members of the London underworld had ever heard of him. It goes without saying that the most successful professional criminals are the ones the general public do not know because they have not been caught. But the horrendous events of the coming months would ensure his anonymity would be lost forever.

As we have seen, he and Lyn had slipped back into the UK in the summer of 1984 because she had not enjoyed life abroad and wanted to return home to be with her sick mother. We know they were living under the false name McCarthy because of a letter we have uncovered written by Reader's daughter, Joanne, from the French ski resort of Meribel, dated January 23, 1985. It is stored in the National Archives and the green envelope with a French postmark is addressed to "Mr and Mrs McCarthy, 40 Winn Road, Grove Park". Joanne tells her parents about the weather in the French Alps and adds: "Last night I cooked veal cordon bleu (or cordon blue as Jay used to say) and to my astonishment it turned out really well. So I promise when you come out I'll do lots of cooking and Dad you can finally see that your money wasn't wasted!" Reader appears to have paid for his daughter to complete a ski chalet cooking course. Though she has used false names, in all other respects the letter is typical of any 19-year-old writing to her parents and is signed, "Lots and lots of love and kisses".

The house on Winn Road was owned by a member of Reader's "staunch mob" of former schoolmates who would stick by him through thick and thin. The friend, a publican, did not need to think twice when Reader called him from Spain to say he was coming back to the UK and needed somewhere to live. Though he had a good payday with the Holborn Circus job a year earlier, Reader never liked to be off work. It wasn't long before he was offered something by millionaire gangster Kenneth Noye. Friends say Reader had been introduced to Noye by his brother, a "flash" property investor who had a showroom selling second-hand Rolls-Royces in Blackfen, south east London. Noye, 10 years younger than Reader, would later claim that it was the older man who approached him first at his wife's squash club to suggest they go into business together. Whatever the truth of the matter, the men were undoubtedly working together by the end of 1984 in a plot that would see them both becoming front-page news for the first time in their lives.

The conspiracy was founded on a robbery that had taken place a year earlier, on a cold November morning in 1983. Armed masked men forced their way into the Brink's-Mat warehouse, Unit 7 of the Heathrow International Trading Estate near the airport on the western outskirts of London. Described as "the crime of the century", in less than two hours the armed gang escaped with three tonnes of gold bullion worth £26million, approximately £82million in today's money. They had doused the terrified guards in petrol and threatened to torch them if they did not give up the

combination of the vault. Led by Brian Robinson, the
brother-in-law of security guard and inside-man Anthony
Black and trilby-wearing Micky "The Bully" McAvoy, the
violent thugs managed to get rid of most of the gold before
they were arrested. Robinson and McAvoy were later
sentenced to 25 years in prison while Black got six years
after turning supergrass. But most of the stolen gold bars
had not been recovered and the search for them would
continue for years and stretch across the globe.

As every thief involved in high-profile, large-scale
robbery or theft will testify, stealing the gear is normally
the relatively easy part, compared to the bigger challenge
of monetising it. The pure gold bars had to be melted
down to get rid of their traceable serial numbers and then
smelted with other metals to reduce their purity so as not
to attract suspicion on the open market, where such a
high-quality product would immediately raise eyebrows.

That was where Reader and Noye came into the
equation. They would become the middlemen, with Noye
the man connected to the original robbery gang and
passing the gold to Reader, who would exchange it with
his trusted Hatton Garden contacts in exchange for large
amounts of cash. Though he had a low profile for a
criminal who had spent most of his life breaking the law,
by the early 80s Reader had been known for some time
among certain detectives at Scotland Yard as one of the
most accomplished and ambitious burglars in London.

Also developing a reputation with detectives in Kent

and London, Noye had managed to stay out of jail by cultivating friends in the police. Powerfully built and with a broken nose that added to his menacing appearance, Noye had grown up in post-war suburban Bexleyheath, south east London. His father was an inspector for BT and mother a manager at a greyhound racing track, then one of the favourite haunts of the criminal world. A bright kid and always a hard worker, he had left school at 15 with a number of O-levels before going to college. After doing a milk round and selling newspapers on the Strand, Noye gained an apprenticeship as a Fleet Street printer.

The business-minded young man saved enough to set up his own haulage company. After a string of property deals, he had accumulated enough money by the late 1970s to buy 20 acres of land outside the village of West Kingsdown in Kent, 15 miles down the A20 out of London from Reader. A bungalow that had been on the site burnt down in mysterious circumstances and it was here that Noye built a mock-Tudor, six-bedroom mansion complete with indoor swimming pool, which he named Hollywood Cottage.

The contrast between Noye's nouveau riche and ostentatious country pile and Reader's suburban semi could be seen as a fair reflection of the differences in the two men's characters. While Reader was happy to go about his business quietly, with no fuss or need to show off his wealth and success, Noye wanted to be known as a country squire who had made millions. One retired detective who later investigated both men described the pair as being "like chalk and cheese". He said: "It was a business relationship. Reader is the last of the gentleman thieves. He was a likeable bloke, not arrogant or aggressive like Noye and many other villains. Reader didn't have the swagger or the bravado. He was a humble man and he listened to you and gave you respect when you spoke to him.

"You have violent criminals like the Krays who relish hurting people and then you have another sort of villain, people like Reader use it to try to improve the lives of their families. They use the money to put their kids through school. He gave his children all they needed. He never did a straight day's work in his life so he had lots of time with his kids and wife. He was a family man."

A longtime friend of Reader's said his pal was not always a good judge of character and had been too easily impressed by Noye's confidence and bravado. The friend said: "Brian used to think the sun shone out of Noye's arse and would often say he was a clever bloke. For a while it was often 'Ken thinks this' and 'Ken said that'. Brian told me a story about Noye once that says a lot about him. One day he handed his car over to be cleaned knowing that in the back was half a million in cash and a blade that would be found by the kids cleaning it. He wanted everyone to know about his money and enjoyment of violence. I told Brian then he was a complete cunt and he would stitch up anyone and that's what happened. If Reader hadn't got involved with Noye he never would have gone to jail."

Not long after meeting Noye, Reader had witnessed first hand his volatility and propensity to violence. The friend said: "They were out at a nice restaurant one Saturday night along with Reader's brother, a fourth man called Roy and all their wives. When Roy started singing, Noye joined in. Roy got on the table, making quite a noise. One of the diners stood up and said: 'Excuse me there are other people eating'. Then it all went off and Noye lunged at the man shouting: 'You cunt.' But it was obvious this bloke could handle himself so Noye pulled out a blade and stabbed him. Luckily, the bloke wasn't badly hurt and Brian and the rest of them got out of there by a miracle. Nothing ever came of it but can you imagine, doing that in a busy restaurant on a night out with the wives? I bumped into another of Brian's friends later and he asked me: 'How did he ever get involved with that Noye?'"

The close shave should have been all Reader needed by way of a warning for what was to come but he continued the partnership. It was not long afterwards that the pair came on to the radar of the police. In December 1984 a detective inspector in Scotland Yard's Criminal Intelligence Unit, then known as C-11, with extensive contacts in the south east London underworld, picked up intelligence that Noye was moving large amounts of gold. The officer had also learned he was working with a new associate by the name of Brian Reader. Unbeknown to the

Yard, at the same time Customs and Excise were picking up information about large gold transactions in the UK which had to involve the proceeds of Brink's-Mat. They had begun watching a group of gold dealers in the West Country who would soon be linked to Reader and Noye.

The man heading the police investigation into the whereabouts of the stolen gold was Acting Detective Chief Superintendent Brian Boyce. Boyce was a former soldier who had been on the team who served under the legendary Scotland Yard thief taker Leonard "Nipper" Read when they nailed the Kray twins. Boyce was respected by his men because he wanted to stick with hands-on police work and had no desire to climb the greasy pole at Scotland Yard.

By January 1985 the officer decided intelligence reports on Reader and Noye warranted putting them both under surveillance using only Flying Squad officers, known then as C8, to begin with. But Boyce was immediately faced with a difficulty. Not only was Noye a registered informant for controversial Yard detective Ray Adams, but he was also friendly with Kent Police's local Regional Crime Squad. Noye was suspected of being part of a gang of lorry hijackers who would hand over half their stolen loot to bent cops as a way of keeping out of trouble. For this reason Met officers had not told Kent police when they arrested Noye in 1977 for receiving stolen goods. Boyce was worried about letting the neighbouring force know about the highly sensitive operation but procedural rules meant he had to. In the end he informed only the most senior Kent officers about the plans.

The action started almost as soon as the police surveillance teams moved into position on the morning of January 8, 1985. Reader was seen leaving Noye's home in his green F-reg Vauxhall Cavalier at 9.10am and then made the half-hour drive back to his own place. Twenty minutes later he left his home at 40 Winn Road and was shadowed by four unmarked Flying Squad cars as he drove to Cowcross Street, near Hatton Garden. He parked outside Farringdon Station, where he made a phone call in the ticket hall. An eagle-eyed officer who had managed to slip into a booth next to him observed that Reader had dialled the number of a nearby jewellery shop at 9 Greville Street in Hatton Garden called "Pussy Galore". Reader waited a few seconds before walking out on the street, looking up and down. He then returned to the booth and dialled the same number. He repeated this process one more time before going into a cafe over the road, where he was followed by two more undercover officers.

He was sitting at a table with two men, one of whom would later be identified as Tommy Adams, a 24-year-old up-and-coming north London gangster and member of the infamous Adams family. The other was Chrissie Weyman, a gold dealer and fence who ran a shop called Lustretone, also on Greville Street. Weyman, who died in the early 2000s at his home in Brighton, was a well-known "scallywag" who grew up a stone's throw from Hatton Garden in Little Italy. One of Reader's extensive network of criminal associates, he was the son of Nell Falco, a member of the Italian family with mafia connections. His uncle, Tommy Falco, had been slashed by self-styled "King of the Underworld" Jack Spot in 1956 during a battle for supremacy with fellow crime boss Billy Hill. Falco had also been shot at in the Central Club in Clerkenwell by the psychotic Ronnie Kray.

Undercover detectives watching the men were aware of their criminal pedigree and they knew that one false step could destroy the operation and endanger lives. Aware that he could be under close surveillance, Reader stayed completely silent. He scribbled on a piece of paper, which he showed to Adams and Weyman. They all then got up, walked out of the cafe and got into Reader's Cavalier, where Adams produced a heavy parcel about a foot long. He got out of the car and put the parcel in the boot of a white Mercedes sports car parked close by and drove off.

Another team of detectives staking out Hollywood Cottage had that morning seen a Ford Granada driven by a man aged about 20. The car left soon afterwards and was later seen outside Noye's old home in Hever Avenue, in the town of West Kingsdown, near Brands Hatch, which was now the home of another notorious south east London criminal, John "Little Legs" Lloyd. He is not to be confused with the "Little Legs" who was a member of Reader's gang.

In 1981 Lloyd had been charged, along with feared south London gangster Mehmet Arif, with the £1million Bluebell Hill robbery, in which a gang hijacked a lorry after shutting off a road in Maidstone, Kent. But the case was dropped without explanation and none of the stolen money was ever found. Scotland Yard later learned that a senior Kent detective, who was an officer on the Bluebell Hill robbery, was also a regular dinner guest with Noye at the Forge restaurant close to Noye's home. They were also passed claims from a police informant that Lloyd had escaped prosecution over the 1981 robbery by paying off a corrupt Kent police officer. DCS Boyce was unaware of this at the time. His team ran a check on the Hever Avenue house and found Lloyd had bought it from Noye a few years earlier. Just a few hours into the operation and detectives were already uncovering a network of known criminals who appeared to be engaged in some kind of plot.

Later in the afternoon Noye and another man left Hollywood Cottage in his blue Range Rover and drove towards London on the A20. They turned off on the south eastern outskirts of the capital in Sidcup and stopped in the car park of the Beaverwood Club, which was hidden from prying eyes by a screen of trees. Police were to follow Reader and Noye repeatedly to the Spanish hacienda-style nightclub as it became apparent it was their secret meeting place, situated conveniently between their homes on the A20.

Though the Flying Squad had not obtained enough evidence to warrant arrests, their first day's work had found links between Noye and Lloyd as well as Reader and Hatton Garden gold dealers. Boyce was sure his team were watching the middle men of Brink's-Mat robbery at work, but he needed the finest surveillance officers in the country if they were going to get the evidence they required.

The next day, January 9, he rang Scotland Yard's elite team of undercover watchers. Known then as the Specialist Surveillance Unit or C11, the handpicked group of just eight included experts from the Special Air Service (SAS) and had to pass the toughest training tests of any police officer at the Yard. Among the gruelling tasks they had to complete to make the grade was hiding in a hole in open countryside for more than two days and lying beneath floorboards for over 60 hours.

The C11 team joined forces with the Flying Squad, who briefed them on the finer points of the operation. The idea was to try to get the surveillance officers as close as possible to Noye's home, which was in the middle of 20 acres of grounds and surrounded by a large wall on a secluded country lane. A command centre was set up in a ground-floor room of the Stacklands Retreat House, a home for elderly and sick members of the church, which was opposite Hollywood Cottage on School Lane. At the gate of the house the C11 team carefully constructed a hide under an oak tree, which allowed them to keep watch on Noye's gate 24 hours a day. A video camera was placed in a bird box up a tree to give another view of Noye's gate. Meanwhile, outside Reader's house detectives hid in a number of vans to keep an eye on his movements.

The following day, the police teams followed Noye and Reader to a slip road off the A2 in Kent where Noye handed over a black briefcase. A C11 detective named Myrna Yates, then aged 36, had managed to get out of her car and remain unseen by the men while they did the hand-over.

Day three of the surveillance operation, January 10, was to provide a major breakthrough. The destination of the heavy briefcases, which police believed contained the Brink's-Mat gold, was revealed to be Scadlynn Ltd, a bullion dealers in North Street, Bedminster, Bristol. The West Country link was uncovered thanks to some more brilliant work by detective Yates.

In the morning Reader again met Noye at the Beaverwood Club before being tailed to the Royal National Hotel, off Russell Square in Bloomsbury, central London. To check if they were being tailed, Noye followed his partner for a short distance into London before disappearing. But Yates was too good to allow the operation to be compromised and she managed to keep tabs on Reader without being spotted by either man. The officer followed her target into the hotel lobby, where she saw him talking to Weyman and Adams, the men he had been seen with in Hatton Garden on day one of the operation. All three left and Weyman and Adams were seen driving off.

Their Mercedes was tailed to Paddington Station in west London after taking a route via the north of the capital, known to be Adams' home turf. Adams was by now carrying a heavy brown briefcase and police believed both men appeared agitated. They made a couple of phone calls and bought first-class tickets to Swindon, before boarding the train along with a number of undercover Flying Squad officers. They made more calls at their destination before shaking hands and appearing to part company, making a show of waving each other goodbye. But instead of splitting up, they were practising an anti-surveillance technique, with one man walking away before being followed by the other in a move designed to flush out any police officers who might be following them. Again the detectives were too experienced and expert in their work to fall for the trick.

Believing they were in the clear, the pair met up at a fish-and-chip shop and waited until a black Jaguar XJS pulled up, driven by a 42-year-old gold-bullion dealer called Garth Chappell. He was the managing director of the Bristol company Scadlynn Ltd. With Chappell was a demolition expert and scrap-metal dealer from the city called Terence Patch. The two London men put the briefcase in the boot and got in the car.

Boyce and his team had now made the vital West Country connection to the plot to smelt and sell on the

Brink's-Mat gold bullion. Chappell was a partner with another man who at the time was unknown by the general public but would later gain infamy. John Palmer had left school at 15 to sell paraffin door-to-door in his hometown of Solihull in the West Midlands. He had moved down to the West Country after branching out into estate agency and selling second-hand furniture and flooring.

In 1980, he formed Scadlynn Ltd with Chappell, which initially struggled to keep afloat. But accounts for 1984 showed a huge spike in business, with the firm handling £9million worth of bullion. Investigators were also very interested to see the lifestyles the two men were leading.

Palmer, then 34, lived in the converted coach house of a country mansion called Battlefields on the edge of the village of Lansdown near Bath along with his wife, Marnie, two daughters and two Rottweiler guard dogs. Chappell had a mansion with a swimming pool called Stonewalls in the Somerset village of Litton.

After meeting the West Country side of the gold-bullion plot, Adams and Weyman appeared back in London the same day. They were tailed to Russell Square where they handed a briefcase to Reader. It appeared Reader was handing over the gold and collecting cash in return.

For the next fortnight, the surveillance teams watched Reader shuttling from his home to Noye's and back into London, exchanging packages with Adams and Weyman.

After 18 days of the surveillance operation, Boyce decided it was time to move in on the targets.

On the afternoon of Friday, January 25, he briefed a tight group of around 20 officers at a south London police station about his plans to move in on the suspects. Magistrates had granted warrants to raid 36 addresses in London, Kent and the Bristol area. Boyce had a huge job on his hands coordinating the movements of scores of teams as they attempted to arrest the main protagonists before they became aware they were under suspicion and destroyed evidence or left the country. It was clear Reader was a conduit between Noye and the Bristol arm of the plot, but Boyce was far from certain where the gold was being stored and he needed to recover as much as possible to build a watertight case. How and when the teams moved in would depend on the movements of the suspects in the coming hours and days.

Five Flying Squad units were put on stand-by for the operation, which was given a maximum time limit of 72 hours. One was outside Hollywood Cottage, the second around Reader's house and a third in Hatton Garden. A fourth was deployed in the Bristol area, while a fifth was mobile, ready to provide back-up. Boyce would watch the middle men at work and decide when to strike depending on the movements of the two prime suspects – Reader and Noye.

Though all of the officers could have been armed, Boyce made the decision not to issue them with firearms.

He was aware that Noye kept a collection of shotguns at his home but decided they were only for show and, along with his Barbour jacket and Range Rover, were part of his attempts to promote himself as a legitimate businessman and country gentleman. At that time Noye had no record of using violence and Boyce was concerned that if he issued his men with guns then Kent officers would have to join the job. That meant Noye was more likely to be tipped off. The actual hands-on coordination of the operation was put in the hands of Boyce's deputy, Detective Chief Inspector Ken John.

The events that would unfold in the grounds of Hollywood Cottage in the coming hours began a dark new chapter in Reader's career.

CHAPTER 8

Death of a Detective

"Dogs – hostile." The staccato message that came crackling over the police radio could mean only two things: the Brink's-Mat police operation was on the verge of being compromised and the lives of police officers were in grave danger. The warning had come from Detective Constable Neil Murphy, a member of Scotland Yard's elite Specialist Surveillance Unit or C11, who had been deployed along with his colleague Detective Constable John Fordham 10 minutes earlier to enter the grounds of Noye's home.

Snow had fallen on the afternoon of January 26, 1985, and as darkness approached, the idyllic Kent countryside was white and silent. It was bitterly cold and few ventured out of their homes. Behind the imposing wrought-iron gates, a warm glow could be seen coming from the windows of Hollywood Cottage. The apparent serenity of this chocolate-box scene gave no hint of the bloody violence that was about to erupt.

At 6.15pm the outlines of Fordham and Murphy could just be made out as they emerged from the black, dense undergrowth in the garden opposite the house. The pair crouched as they crept across the road. The crisp crunching of the snow under their feet was the only sound of their approach. Before them was a long open driveway, illuminated by lamps, which glistened on the lawn that swept away to the right-hand side. Thick shrubbery lined the left of the grounds and it was this area the men had decided to aim for.

Fordham and Murphy were good friends and had worked together for five years. They were among the most experienced close surveillance officers in the country. Fordham was the senior partner, having served on the unit for nine years. The soft-spoken father of three and former soldier from Romford, Essex, was known as "Gentleman John" by his colleagues because of his thoughtful and polite manner. He had won four commendations for bravery and had served with Murphy, also a former soldier, in Northern Ireland.

Though the junior partner, Murphy was accomplished in his work and had the high fitness levels and keen observational skills needed for the job. Fordham had been Murphy's tutor in C11 and the pair had often worked together after the pupil made the grade.

Earlier that day, their C11 colleagues Russell Sinton and Stephen Matthews had been on duty since first light and had watched Noye's wife, Brenda, getting ready to take her children to visit her mother. But the Ford Granada failed to start and Noye came out to try to fix what he thought was a faulty battery. The criminal was to later claim in court that it was while he was cleaning the battery terminals of the car that he got a knife from the kitchen and having finished with it, casually threw it into the footwell of the passenger side.

Back at Winn Road there was no movement until Brian Reader was seen driving off in his green Cavalier at 1.10pm in the direction of Noye's home, tailed by two Flying Squad officers. Following a well-worn pattern, he turned off the A20 and into the car park of the Beaverbrook club, only to drive away when Noye was nowhere to be found.

Reader then drove up and down the A20 as he waited for his partner who was never to arrive. It later emerged that the men had agreed to meet at 1pm and Noye had been on time only to leave 20 minutes later when Reader failed to show. After losing patience, Noye had gone to meet an unnamed woman. Unaware of this, Reader was seen by officers arriving at Hollywood Cottage at 2.25pm, only to find the gates locked.

The cue that police were waiting for came at 6.12pm when Reader returned and was let into the house. Detective Inspector Bob Suckling, the officer in control of the Hollywood Cottage team, said later: "I felt a search was needed then and there, as this might be a rare opportunity to strike at Hollywood Cottage when an exchange was taking place." Suckling ordered the C11 team to enter the grounds at 6.15pm.

Fordham and Murphy were using a two-way radio to communicate with their command post but once in position they were fully responsible for their own actions. Dogs were an occupational hazard for the pair and they knew it would probably be a factor after spotting the canines earlier in the day during a scout of the grounds. Noye had already shown himself to be highly aware of police surveillance techniques. He would also naturally have concerns about being targeted by other criminals after a slice of his wealth. Fordham and Murphy carried a bottle of yeast pills, to feed to the dogs and make them drowsy. The men also each had night-vision binoculars, rubber body suits, a balaclava, gloves and camouflage caps.

After receiving the order to move in, the men left the observation post under the oak tree in the front garden of the Stacklands Retreat House, where they had set up base opposite Hollywood Cottage. They wanted to get as close to the house as possible to pass on the details of anything they could see. Silently listening for any movement in the house, the men painstakingly edged forwards in the winter darkness towards the house.

Minutes later the operation began to go wrong. Suddenly, two snarling Rottweiler dogs emerged from the darkness, their white teeth exposed as they circled around the officer. Fordham's position was badly exposed. He was down on one knee, deep into the garden but still around 60 yards from the house. Murphy later said the sight of the animals was shocking, admitting: "I was terrified of them."

He threw some of the yeast tablets to the dogs but they ignored them and instead kept up their loud barking. It was then that Murphy radioed: "Dogs – hostile" and began to retreat after silently gesturing to his colleague that they must get out of the garden. He later told the Old Bailey that the first thing a C11 officer is taught is "blow out rather than show out". He said: "It was obvious to me that because of the noise the dogs were making the occupants of the house would come out, so I moved away." At 6.26pm he radioed: "Neil out towards fence." A minute later Fordham's voice came across the airwaves: "Somebody out, half-way down drive, calling dogs."

Murphy moved to a wooden fence separating Hollywood Cottage from Noye's neighbour and perched on top to get a better view of the person approaching. He could see a man where the dogs had been, searching in the undergrowth with a torch. Murphy tried to create a diversion by pretending to be an angry neighbour and he kicked the fence, shouting: "Keep those dogs quiet." He later told the Old Bailey that the figure with the torch started moving towards him so he jumped into the neighbour's garden. The officer said he then heard someone say: "Show us your ID. I will blow your head off."

The man with the torch was Kenneth Noye and he later told a jury that he stabbed Fordham 10 times. He would claim that he was terrified for his own life after discovering a man in a balaclava hiding in the pitch dark in his garden. He said he had been in his study scolding Reader for failing to make the planned meet earlier that day, when he was alerted to the dogs Sam and Cleo by his wife. He shouted to her, telling her call them in, but she replied: "I'm not going down there, it's too dark."

Noye put on his leather jacket and went to his Granada, where there was a torch conveniently lying next to the knife he had dropped in the footwell earlier that day. Claiming he had found the blade by chance on his way out would help Noye later when he tried to convince his murder jury that he had not intended to cause anyone harm when he went into the garden. When he got to the dogs he began scanning the undergrowth by swinging the torch around. "I was looking mainly on the floor," he would later say. "I thought there may be an animal that might be trapped. It's happened before, so I was looking in front on me."

He said a noise made him shine the beam to his left where it illuminated a masked figure just a few steps away. "I just froze with horror. All I saw when I flashed my torch on this masked man was just the two eyeholes and the mask. I thought that was my lot. I thought I was going to be a dead man. As far as I was concerned, that was it."

Noye then claimed the man hit him in the face without warning with what he thought at the time was a weapon. He said the blow, "woke me up. Made me so I could move again. Immediately the blow came across my face I put my hand up. I dropped the torch, obviously, and put my left hand up to his face and grabbed his face or head. I shouted out 'Brenda, help,' and started striking with all my strength, as fast as I could, into the masked man. I didn't have to think about using all my might. I thought I was a dead man.

"When he came straight at me I struck into the front of him, all five times. As far as I was concerned, I was fighting for my life. I had struck the man in front, but it didn't seem to have any effect. He was overwhelmingly on top of me. He just looked grotesque, big.

"I am totally amazed at the amount of wounds the man had – I just didn't think it was having any effect. He was just totally overwhelming me... I suspect in a way I was bringing him towards me because I had hold of him. He looked like a giant. I didn't really relate to the masked man as a human being – I stabbed him in a panic."

He said they fell to the ground together. "I don't think I fell under his weight... it might have been his weight or me losing my footholding. Over we went. He came down on top of me and, as he came down on top of me, I struck him again. This was my only chance to get away because I was having no effect on the person. I got up and started running up the drive, looking over my shoulder to make sure he wasn't coming after me. When I looked, I saw the man running towards the front of the wall. My dogs were with him." Blood was pouring out of a wound on the left-hand side of Fordham's heart and he fell before reaching the gates of the cottage.

Hearing her husband's shouting, Brenda Noye said she went and got a shotgun from his bedroom cupboard and began loading it as she ran. Wearing her dressing gown and slippers she sprinted into the garden followed by Reader. They came across a blood-smeared Noye, who shouted: "There's a masked man down there." He grabbed the gun from Reader, who was by now holding it, and returned to Fordham. The officer was bleeding to death from two wounds that had penetrated his heart.

"Who are you?" Noye repeatedly shouted before adding: "Take that mask off." Noye claimed Fordham said he was SAS, and took off his mask, adding: "On manoeuvres." Noye could see now that his victim was very pale and must have guessed he was dying. Noye told his wife to call an ambulance and get a camera so he could get photographic evidence of his injuries. Fordham's jacket then fell open exposing the blood pouring from his body.

Noye would tell the jury trying him for murder: "I knelt down to him because I could see the man was in a very bad way. I said, 'What on earth are you doing here?' but he didn't answer. He didn't say anything. His head was down and I put my arm under him to put it in a better position. Then a car drove in." Explaining his actions, Noye said: "I didn't want him to get away in case he came back another time, when I wasn't there, to sort Brenda and the children out."

As soon as the two-word warning about the dogs had been issued the C11 back-up police team had taken action with Detective Constables Sinton and Matthews returning to the edge of the house to see if they could attract the dogs. At 6.37pm Murphy warned on the radio: "Man compromising John. Stick/shotgun." Suckling immediately ordered all units to raid Hollywood Cottage.

Murphy then moved back to wait by the front gate, where he said he saw two men and a woman. All three were shouting. Controversially, it was not until three months after the incident that Murphy made a statement saying he saw the man not holding the shotgun make a kicking motion but was unable to tell if it made contact. "It was obvious to me at the time that he kicked John," Murphy said. It was this piece of evidence that helped prosecutors decide to charge Reader with the murder. A senior officer involved in the investigation now says they never believed Reader took part in the attack. The source said: "There was never any evidence that was the case and he was cleared." A second police source said Reader did not have a "violent bone in his body" and was in the wrong place at the wrong time.

Murphy stuck to his training and waited by the front gate watching his targets. Later, asked by Noye's defence barrister why he didn't go to help his friend, he said: "It didn't occur to me. I knew that control would be organising for other officers to go in, far better equipped than I was." The first on the scene were Flying Squad detectives Detective Constables David Manning, 38, and John Childs, 39, who had been in an unmarked car on the drive of the house opposite Hollywood Cottage. The gates to the property had been left open after Reader's arrival, allowing the officers to speed to their colleague's aid. Manning said he found Fordham lying on his back with the dogs pulling his clothes. Noye stood over him with a shotgun. They jumped out and Manning approached Noye holding his warrant card, shouting: "I am a police officer." Noye pointed the gun at him and shouted: "Fuck off or I will do you as well." He was also alleged to have said: "Old Bill or no, he had no business being here."

Manning replied: "Put the gun down and get those dogs away from the officer." But the animals then began to attack. Undeterred, the brave officer ignored them and the gun pointing at him and went to Fordham, who muttered: "He's done me. He's stabbed me." Childs, who was standing behind the car, said the dogs were "totally terrifying" adding: "They were jumping, biting my trousers, crowding me, snarling and barking. They were very ferocious." The detective got past the beasts and radioed for an ambulance. Manning gave CPR while Fordham's life ebbed away as he lay on the icy mud.

When he was told that the policeman was dying, Noye said: "He should not have been on my property. I hope he dies." He added after his arrest: "You know how he was dressed, what would you have done? Your governors are going to be in a lot of trouble letting a man come in alone."

Fordham was taken to Queen Mary's Hospital in Sidcup, where he was pronounced dead at 8.20pm.

The pathologist found the next day that all 10 wounds were inflicted by a single-edged blade about one-centimetre wide and seven-centimetres long. The two that killed him both penetrated the heart and it was only Fordham's fitness and strength that kept him alive for so long after the attack. Added to that was the fact the knife had penetrated the left side of his heart where the largest muscle is situated. This acted to keep the wound compressed and therefore reduced the blood loss. The prosecution stated that the wounds suggested some had been inflicted while Fordham had been still, implying he was held down by a second person. This coupled with the lack of defence wounds on the dead man further contributed to Reader being charged with the murder.

After the attack, Reader had escaped by jumping over Noye's neighbours' fences and leaving his car behind. He managed to get to the A20 and hitch a lift – from two Kent detectives who were on the look-out for him. Spotting the wanted man by the side of the road, Detective Sergeant Barry McAllister pulled up his unmarked car and his colleague, Detective Constable Paul Gladstone, wound down the passenger-side window.

"Is there any chance of a lift to London?" asked Reader. "Yes, get in," said Gladstone and let him in the back of the car. As they pulled away McAllister told

Reader who they were and asked him where he had been. "The pub," said Reader, gesturing to the Gamecock Arms a few yards down the road. "Where were you before that?" came the next question, to which Reader responded with another question: "What's this all about?"

McAllister said: "We're looking for a man in connection with a serious incident tonight. Where did you come from before the Gamecock?" Reader ignored the question and was then ordered to put his hands on top of the front passenger seat before being handcuffed. He was taken to the car park of another pub, where he was told he was being arrested on suspicion of assaulting a police officer, to which he replied: "What? You must be joking."

Reader, Noye and his wife were taken to Swanley Police Station, where they were held overnight. They were all then transferred to Dartford as a battle raged between Kent Police and the Met for control over the murder investigation. The death had occurred on Kent's patch but the Met had been investigating the suspects over the Brink's-Mat gold.

CHAPTER 9

Feeling the Heat

The cell door slammed shut and Reader collapsed onto the dirty mattress. His mind was racing as he stared at the breeze-block wall of Dartford Police Station. The cell was 10-feet long and six-feet wide, and Reader knew that he could be spending the rest of his life in one just like this if he failed to give a clear account of what he had seen at Hollywood Cottage. He needed to persuade detectives he had nothing to do with the attack. But Reader was also bound by the criminal code never to "grass" and could not try to extricate himself by placing all of the blame on Noye. If he told the truth he could implicate his friend, but if he stayed silent he may implicate himself.

As Reader lay alone in the dark, he was haunted by the image of a young man. Wearing a roll-neck jumper, his blond hair was combed back and a cigarette hung from his lower lip. Reader had seen the black-and-white picture of Derek Bentley many times in the press after he was hanged for the murder of a policeman in 1953. Bentley, aged 19 but with the mental age of an 11-year-old, had accompanied "fast-talking tearaway" Christopher Craig,

16, on a burglary. It culminated in the fatal shooting of Sidney Miles, a Croydon policeman and father-of-two. Reader was 13 at the time of the case and, as a young thief, it had made a huge impression on him. Bentley went to the gallows in Wandsworth prison despite the fact he had taken no part in the shooting. Craig was too young to be hanged and was instead detained at Her Majesty's Pleasure. Reader wondered if he would also end up being convicted of a murder he had not taken part in.

Also swirling around in his head were the events that had led up to Fordham's death. Reader would later tell friends of his regret at spending that Saturday morning out shopping with Lyn which resulted in him missing his rendezvous with Noye at the Beaverwood Club. If he had made it to the meeting he would never have been caught up in the whole mess. Though detectives would later admit Reader had nothing to do with the attack, in the days after the dreadful killing they would seize on any potential evidence implicating him.

The killing of a police officer, especially while on duty protecting the public, always elicits a huge outpouring of grief and anger from his or her colleagues. In this case, an unarmed officer and father had been savagely stabbed to death by a known criminal while working secretly on the biggest police investigation in the country. It was to be front-page news and Scotland Yard would pull out every stop to get justice for Fordham.

Within an hour of Fordham being taken to hospital,

armed Flying Squad officers had interrupted
Lyn's Saturday evening routine by bursting into 40 Winn
Road. Neighbours came into the street to watch as officers
poured out of unmarked vans to cover the front and back
of the house. Detectives immediately recovered a black
briefcase containing nearly £66,000 in bundles of £50
notes. Another £3,000 was in the kitchen and a lump of
silver-coloured metal was found, which Lyn said was hers.
Also taken were Spanish hotel brochures, an Access credit
card and an international driver's licence.

In an interview with crime reporter Duncan Campbell,
Lyn later said: "There were about 10 of them. They were
like a crowd of cowboys. One was as drunk as a sack.
They were screaming at me, 'Has your husband got a
green Cavalier?' I just screamed back at them, 'What's
this all about?' Then they got a message on their radio
that a green Cavalier was approaching and one of them
stood with a gun pointing at the front door. When they
had me in the cell they were all screaming at me and
saying that Brian was covered in blood and he'd murdered
someone. I said, 'You're a liar, you're a liar.' I've got the
clothes back now and there's not a spatter of blood."

Lyn's family had been completely unaware of Reader's
secret life of crime until his arrest over the Fordham
murder, and it was a matter of great embarrassment to
her. They had always believed in his outwardly
respectable front as a used-car dealer, though there were a
few occasions when their suspicions were raised. Reader

liked to tell a story that amused him about when Paul was around eight years old. The friend said: "The in-laws were at Brian's house and he was going out on a job. Lyn said to Paul, 'Dad's going down to his yard,' and Paul chirped up in front of everyone: 'But dad hasn't got a yard.' I think Brian managed to talk his way out of that one." Knowing he was responsible for Lyn's arrest by armed police and being locked up in a cell was hard for him to take.

Unaware of how events were unfolding, Reader had been around long enough to guess what the police would be doing. But he had no idea of the huge power struggle going on in the background as Scotland Yard attempted to wrestle control of the murder investigation away from Kent Police, who automatically had primacy. Friends of Reader would later claim it was Kent Police's involvement in the early stages of the murder probe that secured the evidence that would later clear both men. One said: "The Met wanted Kent to hand over the balaclava that John Fordham had been wearing but they steadfastly refused. If it had gone missing no one would have believed Noye when he later said that a police officer wearing a balaclava had been hiding in his bushes. But it didn't and he was able to show the jury what Fordham looked like that night, which helped his argument of self-defence."

Detective Chief Superintendent Brian Boyce, who had led the Brink's-Mat investigation, was very concerned about Noye's close links with Kent Police officers and he was furious at being excluded from the murder investigation. When the Met finally took over on the Monday morning, 36 hours after the killing, Boyce found they had allowed Noye to have a shower and change his clothes without a police officer being present. Had vital forensic evidence been lost? Concerns over the possibility of Noye corrupting the detectives on the murder probe were cemented for Boyce when the killer asked to see him alone in his cell. Boyce would later tell an Old Bailey jury that Noye offered to put £1million in a bank account "anywhere in the world".

The day after the killing, while the smaller force remained in charge of the probe, Reader was seen by Kent Detective Superintendent David Tully. The prisoner asked immediately: "Where's my wife?" He was told Lyn had been arrested and was at Gravesend Police Station. Like most professional criminals, Reader always kept his family away from his work and never spoke to Lyn about what he was up to, despite their very close marriage. He knew that knowledge could be a dangerous thing and Lyn would be safer living in ignorance. The recent kidnapping of his friend John Goodwin's wife, Shirley, had highlighted the danger the families of criminals faced from other villains.

Reader said forcefully: "I want you to know, Mr Tully, that she is a very sick woman and needs medical attention. She is due to go into hospital tomorrow for treatment." Reader explained that his beloved Lyn was a diabetic and was booked in to have an operation on her pancreas. Tully promised he would go to see her after the interview, to which Reader responded: "Thank you. She needs special food, like boiled fish, otherwise she gets ill." But Tully warned him: "At some stage you will be interviewed about the incident at Mr Noye's home on Saturday evening. You understand that you have been detained in connection with that incident?" Reader was said to have replied: "It's a very serious matter. I know a police officer has been murdered and I was told I was responsible. I want you to know, Mr Tully, that I do not know anything about it and I did not have anything to do with it." He said he would not answer any other questions without his solicitor Stanley Beller being present.

Realising Reader's love and loyalty to his wife could be exploited to put pressure on his suspect, Tully added with a hint of a threat: "You must understand that a large amount of money was found at your house when your wife was arrested and she, as well as you, will be asked to account for the possession of that money." Brian's angry reply came back: "That money is mine. It's nothing to do with my wife."

Back at Hollywood Cottage, officers were taking the house apart as they searched for evidence Reader and Noye had been handling the Brink's-Mat gold. At 4.20 on Sunday afternoon, they found it.

Hidden under a rubber mat and a tin of paint by the garage were 11 gold bars, all three inches long, one-inch high and one-inch wide, wrapped in a red-and-white cloth. Similar material had been found in Noye's Granada, along with the operating instructions for a smelting furnace and tiny fragments of gold on the boot mat. Small shavings of gold were also found in Reader's Cavalier.

A safe hidden in the floor of Noye's home contained £2,500 in new £50 notes, which had the same prefix of A 24 on their serial numbers as the notes found in Reader's house. By the time Reader and Noye were questioned by the Met on the Monday night, another £50,000 of the same batch of notes were found close to Noye's parents' home in West Kingsdown.

Reader was questioned in his cell after refusing to go to the interview room. Leading the interrogation was Detective Inspector John Walsh, who had been the officer in charge of the search of Winn Road. When Reader refused to answer, Walsh made out as if he was leaving and sure enough his prisoner began to open up a bit.

The full interview is recounted in *Bullion: Brink's-Mat, The Story of Britain's Biggest Gold Robbery* by Andrew Hogg, Jim McDougall and Robin Morgan. Reader began by asking about Lyn again, saying: "She hasn't eaten since Monday, and the doctor said that if she doesn't look after herself, she could die." When accused of not appearing to care about the fact a police officer had been killed, Reader said: "That's not true. I am concerned. I never assaulted or hurt anyone."

Walsh probed: "Then I don't understand why you

won't answer my questions." When Reader refused without seeing his lawyer, Walsh said: "Let's not play cat and mouse."

Reader said: "When my solicitor is here I will tell you everything I saw but I'll just say that I didn't assault anyone."

"I can't understand why you're prepared only to tell me partially about this," said Walsh.

"Because you'll just add it to that when you go out," replied Reader, gesturing towards notes of Detective Sergeant Russell Jones. "The officer I saw last night said you were straight down here but I've been nicked before – well, you know that – and verballed. Do you know what I mean?" Reader was referring to the practice which occurred when it was not obligatory to tape record all interviews, of detectives "fitting up" suspects by attributing to them statements they had not made.

"I understand what you are saying," said Walsh.

Reader inquired: "How do I know the same won't happen here?"

"Listen to me, let me make two things clear to you. We are very upset at the death of our colleague. It is not going to help his memory if we start verballing people. We intend to get to the truth of the events of Saturday night. Nobody is going to be threatened or verballed but our thorough investigations and minute examinations are going to reveal exactly what happened on Saturday. We are merely giving you the chance to tell your side of

Brian Reader and his young family on an unidentified beach, believed to be in Spain in the early 1970s, shortly after his gang pulled off the Baker Street burglary

OPPOSITE PAGE, CLOCKWISE FROM TOP
Brian Reader on a skiing holiday in the early 1980s

Reader as a younger man

Harry Reader, Brian's father, with his wife, Joyce, in the early 1970s

Holiday snap of Brian and Lyn Reader in the early 1980s

THIS PAGE, FROM TOP
Reader family skiing in Méribel in the early 1980s

Brian and Lyn Reader enjoying a meal in 1970

Four jailed over the £3,000,000 Sherlock Holmes bank raid

MILLIONAIRE MOLES OF BAKER STREET

Just like Conan Doyle

NO DELAY, SAYS CID CHIEF

Radio ham tuned in

CLOCKWISE FROM TOP

Police guard Le Sac leather goods shop on Baker Street. It was from the basement of this store that burglars tunnelled into the vaults of Lloyds Bank, seen in the distance, on 11 September, 1971

How the *Daily Mirror* covered the resulting trial

Officers heading the case at a press conference at Scotland Yard following the conviction of four men for the robbery in 1973. Left to right: Det Chief Insp Jack Candlish, Commander Bob Huntley, Det Chief Supt Robert Chalk

Rubbish and rubble left in the basement of Le Sac by the robbers

CLOCKWISE FROM TOP
The Security Express depot in Curtain Road, Shoreditch, London, scene of a robbery in 1983 by Terry Perkins and other gang members, who escaped with £6million. It remains Britain's biggest cash heist

Terry Perkins, who was serving 22 years for the Security Express robbery in Shoreditch when Brian Reader met him in prison. They would later collaborate on 2015's Hatton Garden burglary

Brian Reader's old friend and partner John "The Face" Goodwin

CLOCKWISE FROM TOP

The Brink's-Mat Security Depot at Heathrow, scene of a £26million gold bullion raid

Mrs Ann Fordham, the widow of John, the undercover officer who was stabbed to death, and her son, John, at a press conference after Kenneth Noye and Brian Reader were found not guilty of murder

Lyn Reader and son Paul leave the Old Bailey, London

How the *Daily Mirror* covered the Fordham verdict

CLOCKWISE FROM TOP

Brenda Noye shows her relief after the acquittal on a murder charge of her husband, Kenneth

Kenneth Noye with a black eye, photographed in police custody

Kenneth Noye's home and extensive grounds at Hollywood Cottage, West Kingsdown in Kent, scene of the stabbing of DC John Fordham in 1985

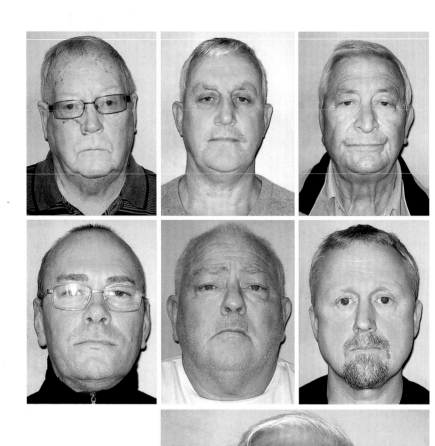

ABOVE The Hatton Garden gang
Top row, left-right: John "Kenny" Collins, 75; Danny Jones, 60; Terry Perkins, 67
Second row, left-right: Carl Wood, 58; William Lincoln, 60; and Hugh Doyle, 48

MAIN PHOTO Brian Reader, 76

(Ages at time of sentencing in 2016)

ABOVE Detective Chief Inspector Paul Johnson of the Flying Squad speaks to the media outside the safe-deposit building in Hatton Garden, central London, April 9, 2015

LEFT The *Daily Mirror*'s front-page exclusive featuring CCTV footage of the Hatton Garden burglars in action

CLOCKWISE FROM TOP

The rear yard behind Hatton Garden Safe Deposit Ltd

The front of the safe-deposit business on Hatton Garden

The Hilti DD 350 drill that was used to bore through the wall

The hole the gang drilled into the safe-deposit vault

The vault door that the burglars bypassed – to the left of it the drilled hole can be seen

Danny Jones hides his face from CCTV during the raid

A chaotic scene in the Hatton Garden basement vault, as jewellery and valuables have been snatched from safe-deposit boxes. It was estimated that £14million worth of property was stolen

Reader's London: The key locations in his criminal caree[r]

Park Avenue, Enfield
Home of Hatton Garden burglar Danny Jones

The Old Wheatsheaf
Pub car park where Hatton Garden loot was handed over

Sterling Rd, Enfiel[d]
Where Hatton Garden gan[g] planned to smelt the gol[d]

Lloyds Bank, Baker Street
Reader's gang tunnelled into the vault in 1971

Cedar Avenue, Enfield
Boxer Tiger Hrela was killed in 2005 in an unsolved gangland shooting linked to Reader's ga[ng]

Post Office, Albemarle St, Mayfair
Reader's gang stole half-a-million pounds in cash and stamps in 1969

Chingford
House where Baker Street loot was sha[red]

Cressingham Rd, Lewish[am]
Reader family home when Bria[n] was born

Winn Rd, Grove Park
Reader's family home in the 1980s

Brink's-Mat warehouse, Heathrow
A record £26m in gold bullion was stolen in 1983

Pentire, Dartford
Reader's house raided by police in May 2015

Hollywood Cottage, West Kingsdow[n]
Kenneth Noye's home where he stabbed DC John Fordham to death

See opposite

London

10 miles

Barnet · Southgate A10 · Wood Green A10 · Brent Cross · A1 · Enfield · M25 · M11 · A12 · N Circular · Stratford · A11 · A13 · North Circular · Heathrow · Hounslow · M4 · A4 · Fulham · A3 · Peckham · Balham · South Circular · Lewisham · A2 · Dartford · A20 · Croydon · Sutton · Orpington · A20 · M25 · M[25] · A232 · A23 · M25

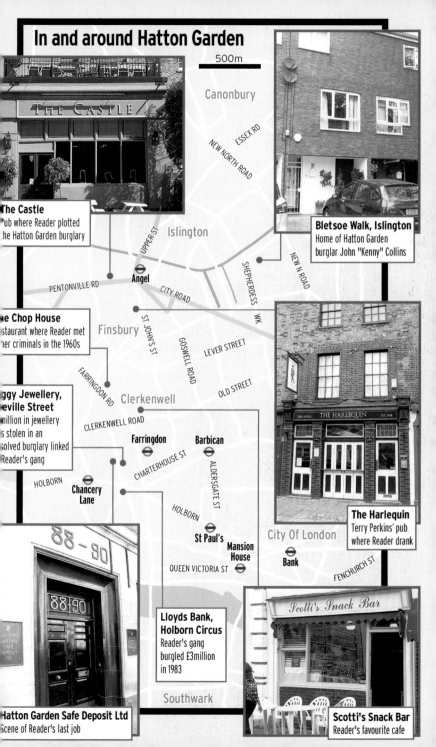

In and around Hatton Garden

500m

Canonbury

ESSEX RD

NEW NORTH ROAD

Bletsoe Walk, Islington
Home of Hatton Garden
burglar John "Kenny" Collins

Islington

UPPER ST

SHEPHERDESS

NEW N ROAD

The Castle
Pub where Reader plotted
the Hatton Garden burglary

PENTONVILLE RD

Angel

CITY ROAD

WK

The Chop House
Restaurant where Reader met
other criminals in the 1960s

Finsbury

ST JOHN'S ST

GOSWELL ROAD

LEVER STREET

FARRINGDON RD

OLD STREET

**Ziggy Jewellery,
Greville Street**
£million in jewellery
was stolen in an
unsolved burglary linked
to Reader's gang

Clerkenwell

CLERKENWELL ROAD

Farringdon

Barbican

The Harlequin
Terry Perkins' pub
where Reader drank

CHARTERHOUSE ST

ALDERSGATE ST

HOLBORN

Chancery
Lane

HOLBORN

St Paul's

Mansion
House

City Of London

QUEEN VICTORIA ST

Bank

FENCHURCH ST

88 - 90
88 90

**Lloyds Bank,
Holborn Circus**
Reader's gang
burgled £3million
in 1983

Scotti's Snack Bar
Reader's favourite cafe

Scotti's Snack Bar

Southwark

Hatton Garden Safe Deposit Ltd
Scene of Reader's last job

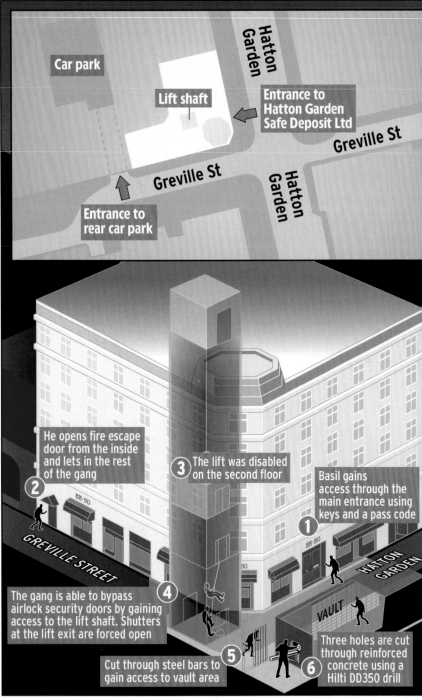

Car park

Hatton Garden

Lift shaft

Entrance to
Hatton Garden
Safe Deposit Ltd

Greville St

Greville St

Hatton Garden

Entrance to
rear car park

He opens fire escape
door from the inside
and lets in the rest
of the gang

②

③ The lift was disabled
on the second floor

Basil gains
access through the
main entrance using
keys and a pass code

①

GREVILLE STREET

88-90

88-90

HATTON GARDEN

VAULT

The gang is able to bypass
airlock security doors by gaining
access to the lift shaft. Shutters
at the lift exit are forced open

④

Cut through steel bars to
gain access to vault area

⑤

Three holes are cut
through reinforced
concrete using a
Hilti DD350 drill

⑥

Graphics by Nick Coles and Brett Die

things."

When Reader refused to talk without his lawyer, Walsh continued to chip away.

"I wasn't involved in assaulting that person," was Reader's response.

After a four-hour break, Walsh and Jones were back but this time they agreed not to take notes. This appears to have encouraged their prisoner to become more open. Everything that follows was written down by Walsh from memory afterwards.

Reader was alleged to have said: "I told you I am not violent. I saw things, heard things and did things but I am not prepared to say what until my solicitor is present."

"Did you have a knife with you on Saturday?" asked Walsh.

"I never carry a knife. I have never carried a knife in my life," came the unequivocal response.

"Did you have a knife at all on Saturday?" continued Walsh.

"No comment."

"That's an odd reply. You say you never carry a knife and happily explain that, yet you are keeping open your option about Saturday. Do I take it that you did handle a knife on Saturday?'

"No comment."

"We know exactly what you and your associates have been up to over the past months. Are you prepared to talk about that?" asked Walsh.

"When my solicitor is present."

"I don't understand why you're prepared to admit you were present at Noye's on Saturday when the police officer was killed, yet refuse to give any details of your actions."

This seemed to connect to something in Reader, who thought for a moment before continuing: "Look, I think I can trust you two. You seem all right but I don't know. A policeman has been killed and you might not want a pint of blood – you may be after two gallons."

Walsh said: "If we didn't want to get to the truth of what happened and just wanted vengeance, do you think we would be trying to persuade you to write and sign our questions and answers or make a written statement? We are determined to bring those responsible for the officer's death to court but, equally, I assure you that I would not offend John's memory by trying to implicate people who were not involved."

"I think you are all right, but I have got to be careful. I could tell you everything now and then later regret it," came the cautious response.

"I don't know how you can be surprised at anything later if you sign and agree everything now," said Walsh.

It was at this point that Reader mentioned the Derek Bentley case. "I keep thinking about that job 40 years ago, Bentley and…"

"Craig," prompted Walsh. "That's right. Look what happened there."

In an attempt to change the subject, Walsh then pulled

out the gold bars recovered from next to Noyes' garage and asked: "Do you want to tell me about this?"

Reader said with a smile: "I will tell you all about that when my solicitor is present." He then added nervously "What's in your briefcase?" Reader was worried that Walsh might have been secretly recording them.

The rules in those days allowed the police to interview suspects without their solicitors being present. Boyce enforced this as he believed it could stop the main suspects colluding. He also knew a lawyer would probably advise his client to remain silent. Noye was questioned by Detective Inspector Anthony Brightwell, Detective Inspector Bob Suckling and Detective Constable Michael Charman. Noye responded to each question with "no reply" and refused to sign the notes taken by Charman. They then continued questioning him without even taking a note.

Noye's trial on the Brink's-Mat handling charges would later hear claims that Suckling and Charman had been chosen because of their "imagination and ability to compose". Charman had allegedly got a confession from Tony White over his supposed involvement in the Brink's-Mat robbery but his conviction was quashed owing to concerns over police evidence.

Brightwell later told Noye's murder trial that he said to the suspect: "Mr Noye, you have got to face facts: you have killed a man. You have already admitted that to several officers. At some time you are going to have to give some kind of explanation." Noye replied: "You have got to believe one thing – I didn't know he was a policeman."

Suckling said: "Then tell us about it." Noye replied: "I don't want to talk to you about it. It's nothing to do with you. It's a Kent inquiry. I want to talk to someone from Kent. I have said I am not answering any questions unless my solicitor is present." He added: "I've got nothing to gain by telling you. I will give my story to the judge and jury." Noye then asked them if they knew Fordham. He was told they did and that his victim was married with three children – a 12-year-old girl and two older boys. Noye responded: "You must hate me. I have killed one of your mates and there is no way out for me. All you want to do is make sure I go to prison for the rest of my life."

Later that evening, after the interview had been completed, Kent Police Sergeant John Laker said he heard Noye call out from his cell: "Have you got a solicitor, Brian?" Reader, who was in the next door cell, replied "Yes". Noye ordered: "Don't tell them anything, Brian." Reader replied: "No, I haven't." Noye went on: "No, don't tell them anything. They don't know about the other geezer yet." Reader replied: "I don't know anything."

Brenda Noye's questioning by Detective Sergeant Kenneth O'Rourke did not yield any more information. "I don't know about anyone else," she said. "I was in the house and didn't see anything." She told them she had never heard of Brian Reader and denied stabbing

Fordham. Asked who did, she allegedly said simply: "I love my husband."

In a second interview with the same officer four hours later she said: "Look, I can't help you. My husband couldn't do such a thing." Before finishing she added: "I'm not a hard bitch like you think. My stomach is knotted up. My life is destroyed."

Tuesday morning, three days after the death, Brenda Noye was questioned for the last time by O'Rourke. She told him: "I'm not frightened of anyone. I didn't see anything. I was out after. It had all happened by then." She added: "Whatever happened to him. I didn't take any part. The dogs were making a lot of noise, so Kenny went to see. He was out for a few minutes and the dogs were still barking, so Brian went out and a bit later Kenny came running in and got his shotgun. I knew that something was wrong. I went down the drive and could see Ken and Brian standing over something. I got closer and could see it was a man. He didn't move."

Asked if she thought he was dead, she said: "I didn't know what to think. I can remember becoming hysterical and shouting. I suppose I must have thought that. I was just shouting at the two of them. I can't remember what I said." O'Rourke then asked if she knew her husband was moving gold: "Of course I did. You said yesterday. I am his wife." She later denied making these comments when she appeared as a defence witness at her husband's Old

Bailey trial.

Brenda Noye later told Duncan Campbell about her experience: "I've got to say some of the Kent Police were good. There was a policewoman outside my door and she was a very nice woman, trying to comfort me, get me to eat something. She even said: 'I'll send out and get something for you. I don't blame you for not wanting to eat the stuff they dish out here.'"

By this time, the press had been issued with details of the murder and arrests and the story had made the front pages. On Monday, January 28, the *Daily Mail* had a photograph of Fordham, stating three people had been arrested in connection with his murder. It named Noye, who was described as a "builder and haulage boss", and his wife. The story, by David Williams and Ted Oliver, claimed Fordham had been killed while trying to serve a search warrant at Noye's £1million home.

Noye's brother-in-law, Richard Wilder, told the paper: "We are shocked by this. We have no idea why the police should want to search Ken's house."

The next day, Walsh went back to Reader, who told him: "I'm sorry about what happened."

"Last Saturday was not the first time you have been to Noye's to collect gold, is it?"

"What does he say?" countered Reader.

"That's not relevant. Unfortunately, we can't separate the two incidents and offences. You and Noye were disturbed moving the gold. You were involved in transferring the proceeds from one of the largest robberies ever. You were caught in the act and I put it to you that you and Noye decided you had to kill the officer."

"I didn't agree to kill him. That's not true," said Reader.

"What did you decide?"

"I am not answering that until my solicitor is present," came the familiar response.

Again Walsh tried: "Did you at any stage touch the police officer?"

"I've told you, I didn't assault him."

"That's not my question. Did you touch him or hold him at any time?"

When Reader remained silent, Walsh asked: "Did you kick him?" When the question was ignored, Walsh took a deep breath and weighed in again: "Look, Brian, you obviously want to say more because of the way your brain keeps ticking over between every question. I can tell that you're close to saying what happened. Why do you still keep holding back if you genuinely were not concerned in the attack?"

"I am worried that you are going to do me with murder," came the reply.

"The charge that you face will depend on the facts."

Again Reader said he wanted to talk to his lawyer and this time it was Walsh's turn to ignore him.

"Where was the officer when you first saw him?"

"No comment."

"Where were you when the events leading up to his death first began?"

"Look, I was in the house."

"What happened?"

"The dogs started barking."

"Did you go out?"

"Not at first."

"What does that mean?"

"I…" Reader began.

"Did someone else go out?"

"You know what happened."

"I know some of what happened. One of the men went out of the house. Was it you?"

"No."

"So it was Noye?"

"You know it was."

"Did you go to follow him?"

"No comment."

"Why did he go out?"

"You know."

"You joined Noye in the garden, didn't you?"

"I didn't join him."

"What does that mean?"

"I went out, but I didn't join him."

"Did you see the officer at that stage?"

"No comment."

Walsh asked: "What went through your mind when you realised that the police officer had seen you?"

"I don't know. Things just happened."

"What things happened?"

"No comment."

"Where was Mrs Noye at this time?"

"What does she say?"

"That doesn't concern you. I am interested in anything you and Noye said to each other in the garden."

Reader refused to respond and was asked: "Did Noye tell you that he was going to assault the officer?"

Again Reader said "no comment" and again the detective ploughed on regardless: "That's an odd answer, isn't it? If it's a 'no' surely that can't cause you any problems?"

But the prisoner wasn't being drawn and instead requested his solicitor.

"You have told how the officer was dressed. How do you know?"

"What do you mean?"

"Where did you first see him?"

Silence.

"Did you see him before he was up near the gates, lying on the ground?"

"I haven't said that I saw that."

Referring to Brenda Noye's claims, Walsh said: "I know but other people have. Police – and now, more importantly, someone connected with the house also says – that you were with Mr and Mrs Noye, standing by the officer when he was there on the ground."

"No comment."

Walsh began to turn the screw: "I've just told you, other people are starting to be more explicit than you. Your time to make up your mind is nearly here, isn't it?"

"Yes, all right, I went to see what happened, but I never stabbed him."

"Did you know at that stage he had been stabbed?"

Again Reader promised to talk only with his lawyer present.

"Did you have a knife?"

"I told you, I never carry a knife."

"Did you see or touch one?"

No reply.

"Did you have a gun? A shotgun?"

"I never had a gun."

"Did you see anyone else with a gun?"

No reply. Reader said "no" when asked if he did anything to help the dying officer.

"Why not?"

"I couldn't, could I? I just ran off."

"But you didn't just run off, did you? You moved the gold, didn't you?"

Reader told Walsh he would talk about the gold when his solicitor arrived.

"Why did you run off and not take your car?"

"I knew what had happened. I couldn't drive out, could I?"

Then Walsh moved to what he knew to be the suspect's

weak spot, his loyalty to Lyn.

"She has been asked about a briefcase full of money found in your house."

"That's mine."

"So she says. Where does it come from?" When no answer came, Walsh continued: "Your wife says you have taken large sums of money home before recently. What's that all about?"

"Look, it's nothing to do with her. She never even knew how much was there."

"She says the same but she does say she knew it was not honest money."

Again Reader said he would talk when his lawyer arrived.

Asked about the lump of silver Lyn had, he said: "That's just a bit of jewellery from a bad assay. I've had it a while. It's only got a small gold content. It's only worth about £40."

"Is it the residue of smelt?"

"Yes."

"Where is the smelter for the gold you've been dealing in?" Reader laughed and said: "I don't know where it is."

When Reader continued to refuse to answer questions the interview was ended.

Boyce then visited him and showed him three knives, which Reader said he had never seen. Unlike Noye, the prisoner agreed to give the police samples of his hair, blood and saliva. The second time the police chief saw him with his solicitor, he said: "I don't wish to say anything."

On Tuesday evening, Reader and Noye were charged with the murder of John Fordham. Reader said calmly: "I'm innocent of that charge," while Noye shouted: "No." Brenda Noye was also charged with murder, perhaps in an effort to exhort extra pressure on her husband.

The three appeared at Dartford Magistrates' Court that Friday where they were remanded in custody.

The case against Brenda Noye was dropped four months later at a hearing at Lambeth Magistrates' Court in south London. Reader had also tried to have the case against him dropped. But, nearly three decades after appearing in the dock at the Old Bailey in his youth, he was due back in Britain's most famous court building, along with Noye, accused of murdering a policeman.

CHAPTER 10

Back in the Dock

The day after he was charged with Fordham's murder, Brian Reader was interviewed about his involvement in handling the Brink's-Mat gold. Like Noye, his main concern was the murder charge because if convicted it would mean an automatic life sentence with a huge minimum tariff. When Reader refused to comment, he was quizzed once more by Detective Inspector John Walsh at Orpington Police Station.

Again he said he would not talk if it was written down. As revealed in *Bullion: Brink's-Mat, The Story of Britain's Biggest Gold Robbery* (by Andrew Hogg, Jim McDougall and Robin Morgan), here are the exchanges…

"You know what you know and that's it," Reader said.

Walsh responded: "Brian, we want to find out the extent of your involvement. That could range from Mr Big to a relatively minor involvement."

Reader replied: "Look, you know I'm not Mr Big. Don't talk silly. You know what I've done and I'll have to answer for that."

Acting Detective Chief Superintendent Brian Boyce

then intervened to touch a raw nerve – Reader's family. The police chief said he would not oppose Lyn being granted bail when a judge came to decide if she should continue to be detained.

"She doesn't know anything about it," Reader snapped.

"She's well-trained, isn't she?" asked Walsh.

"She's not well-trained. I never involve her in what I'm up to," came the angry reply.

Trying to defuse the situation, Walsh said: "Let's go back to square one for a minute. Do we still agree that you were conveying stolen gold for Noye to the Hatton Garden contacts?"

"That's it and that's all I've ever done. I wish I could put the clock back," came Reader's rueful reply.

"I cannot see how it can harm your case to specify how you became involved and how many times you've done the run. I'm not asking you to implicate or name other people if you don't want to, just to put on record your full involvement, particularly if it's relatively minor, as you claim."

The mention of naming names immediately brought the double-crossing Mickey "Skinny" Gervaise to Reader's mind. He had spent the last six years on the run and fighting court cases because Gervaise had implicated him in the Piaget watch burglary in Birmingham.

Reader said: "Mr Walsh, I'd never name anyone. I got involved with a supergrass named Gervaise. He was a good friend of mine and he ruined my life by turning supergrass. I'd have never got involved in this if it hadn't been for him." The thought of Gervaise made Reader clam up completely and he refused to elaborate any further, only saying: "You know my involvement. I just took the gold to town and that's it."

The following day the routine began again, this time with Reader denying he knew Micky McAvoy and Brian Robinson, two of the men who pulled off the actual Brink's-Mat robbery.

"Does this gold come from the robbery they were arrested for?"

"I can't understand you. Of course it does," allegedly came the reply.

Asked if the gold recovered from Noye's home had been smelted with other metal, Reader said: "All that gold is pure. I don't know what you mean."

"So the only purpose of smelting it was to change its appearance so it couldn't be identified. Really it was just melted. Is that what you're saying?"

"Well, that's what I thought."

Reader, along with Noye, was finally charged with handling the Brink's-Mat gold on the Friday, nearly a week after the death of Fordham.

The interview ended when Walsh asked: "You've told us that you do not know where the gold is being smelted. Can you explain why our scientists tell me that there are traces of gold smelt on the wing of your Vauxhall?"

Feeling he was being framed, for the first time Reader

lost his cool and shouted: "That's it. You're stitching me up." It was later stated in court that the only traces of gold in his car were on his boot mat.

Walsh said: "Calm down, Brian. We're not stitching anyone up. I gather you're saying you've been nowhere near a smelter. Could anyone have done so, using your car?"

But Reader had made up his mind: "No, that's it. You're stitching me up. I'm not saying any more." He was charged with plotting to handle gold bullion and stolen cash. The case would be dealt with after the murder trial.

It would be 10 months before Brian Reader and Kenneth Noye would appear before a jury on the murder charge in the oak-panelled splendour of Court One at the Old Bailey. It was the same courtroom that had seen the Krays and Lord Haw-Haw convicted. This case would provide as much drama as any it had seen before. Due to Noye's wealth and criminal standing and Reader's previous history of involvement in jury interference, the police were worried the men would attempt to nobble the seven men and five women chosen to try them. The judge, Mr Justice Caulfield, took the unusual decision of giving the jurors 24-hour police protection and surveillance on all telephone calls to their homes.

The Flying Squad's concerns about the defendants interfering with justice were heightened when Reader's old friend and partner, John "The Face" Goodwin, turned up in the public gallery. Just three years earlier, Goodwin had been convicted and then cleared on appeal of nobbling the jury hearing Mickey Gervaise's supergrass evidence when eight jurors were offered up to £1,000 to find him and Reader innocent.

Day one of the trial saw the prosecution's opening, where an outline of the whole case against the defendants was given to the jury. It was halted when Noye's brilliant and expensive QC, John Mathew, objected to an image of Hollywood Cottage being used as it was taken in daylight. Justice Caulfield agreed that the jury should see the place during the night as it was when the alleged murder took place, and so later that evening they were taken down the A20 to the spot where Noye killed Fordham. Behind the three limousines carrying the 12 jury members was Noye in a green prison van followed by a police Range Rover. Reader had decided to stay in his cell.

As the rain poured off Justice Caulfield's bowler hat, he led an odd procession squelching through the muddy garden. Noye was handcuffed to a policeman. The jury and lawyers were followed by the court clerk and shorthand writer. They were shown around the grounds of the house. It was the first time Noye had been back since the fateful night and he was closely watched by a 30-strong press pack who noted every "cough and spit" of proceedings. The scene became even more surreal when Brenda Noye appeared at the window of the house with her two sons, waving at her husband before bringing him a pair of his wellington boots and a raincoat.

Back at the Old Bailey the next day Nicholas Purnell QC for the prosecution told the jury that Reader and Noye's involvement in the network selling the Brink's-Mat gold showed "how high were the stakes". This could provide "a motive for the killing of a detective officer as a last desperate attempt by these two men to cover up the operation being conducted at Hollywood Cottage". But Purnell had known before the trial that he was up against it. Noye's defence was to admit that he had stabbed Fordham but claim he did so in self-defence. He alleged that the officer had hit him in the face first. He would also say that, along with Reader, he had been illegally dealing in gold but would deny it was from the Brink's-Mat robbery. The two men still had to face a trial over the handling of the gold, so the prosecution could not tell the Fordham jury everything about their alleged involvement in Brink's-Mat so as not to prejudice the second case.

As the murder trial wore on it became clear to the assembled press pack that the millionaire's decision to employ the best – and one of the most expensive – defence barristers in the country had been worth the investment. Mathew had come up with the idea of mocking up a picture for the jury of how Fordham would have looked to Noye as he emerged from the darkness of the shrubbery that night, using a model dressed in a balaclava and camouflage clothing. The QC told the court the sight would have "struck terror in the bravest of us", adding that his client's reaction had been "shocked terror. He froze, literally froze, terrified with fear. The next moment he received a blow in the face, in the left eye – he doesn't know with what, but he sprang to life, thinking in a flash that he had been struck with some kind of weapon and, having seen that apparition, he assumed that someone seen like that in his grounds at night would be armed. He thought he had seconds to live, he thought his end had come, and in a blind panic stabbed and stabbed."

Mathew also emphasised the bruising to Noye's left eye, which was clearly visible in photographs taken by his wife immediately after the incident. The prosecution were unable to prove either way how he had got the injury and could not accuse Noye of inflicting it on himself without evidence. Purnell did put before the jury evidence from a police sergeant who had accompanied Noye at Bromley Police Station three days after the killing. He asked: "Did he attack you then?" The officer said the reply was: "No, but what do you do when you are confronted like that?"

Mathew also cast doubt on the evidence given by Murphy, asking why he had not identified himself in the vital moments when Noye approached his colleague. The detective told the court: "I knew control would be organising other officers to go in."

Reader did not give any evidence at all during the trial as is every defendant's right under English law. He knew he could only be found guilty if Noye was and then only if the jury found he had helped in the attack with the intention of killing Fordham. His barrister, Edward Lyons

QC, said there was no evidence he had ever been on the scene when the officer was stabbed.

It took the jury 12 hours and 37 minutes to find both Noye and Reader not guilty of murdering DC John Fordham. They had accepted the killing had been committed in self-defence and the prosecution had not given them an option of finding the pair guilty of manslaughter. There were cheers from their wives, Lyn and Brenda, in the public gallery. Noye, then aged 37, stood up and told the jury: "Thank you very much. God bless you. Thank you for proving my innocence because that's what I am, not guilty." Reader added: "Thank you for proving my innocence." But Noye's mask fell immediately. As he walked back to the cells the thug sneered at the Flying Squad officers in the back of the court and mouthed abuse at them.

Outside the Old Bailey, Reader's angry son Paul, then aged 21, said: "We are very happy. The whole thing was a complete fit-up."

A delighted Brenda Noye told reporters: "I feel marvellous. I just want to get home to my children and start smiling again. I am deeply, deeply sorry for the Fordham family but the death is down to others." She said her husband felt the same way, adding: "He would say to Mrs Fordham that he was not responsible for what happened and it was the fault of other people." Later her solicitor Ray Burrough added: "She would ask you to consider the unfortunate Mrs Fordham and her children at this time, for whom she has great sympathy. She feels the responsibility for Mr Fordham's death is on the shoulders of others and not her husband."

It was left to John Dellow and Brian Worth, assistant and deputy assistant Met Police commissioners, to defend the undercover operation that had culminated in John Fordham's death. Mr Dellow said: "I am satisfied the operation was as professional and properly conducted as could be with the evidence before me." Praising DC Fordham, he added: "His professionalism was his hallmark. He was engaged in many other operations against very dangerous professional criminals. He always faced his duties and there are many citizens alive in London today who owe their lives to John Fordham."

Hours after the verdict Ann Fordham, the officer's 38-year-old widow, told a press conference at Scotland Yard that she disagreed with the jury's decision. The New Zealander had fled from the court in tears earlier that day after the not guilty verdicts. Supported by her son, John, 22, she said: "It has been a traumatic ordeal, not just for me and my family but my husband's family and relatives." She rejected a message of sympathy from Brenda Noye, saying softly, "Not accepted", and made clear her feelings with the words: "Justice has not been done. It has not."

Reader now faced trials for not only the Brink's-Mat gold but also the burglary allegations he had been facing when he went on "his toes" in 1982. In March 1986, he was back at the Old Bailey, where he was accused of stealing over a million pounds' worth of gold and watches in raids in Birmingham and London in the late 1970s. The jury acquitted him of what trial Judge Michael Argyle described as the "rather stale" allegations.

But he was jailed for two years after pleading guilty to fleeing to Spain to avoid the earlier trial. As outlined in Chapter 6, he had been due to appear at the Old Bailey in 1982, when he dropped off his cash sureties in court and walked out saying "he was going to park his car". As far as we know Reader was not seen again by the police until his arrest at Noye's home. Judge Argyle rejected a claim from defence barrister Michael Self QC that Reader should have been dealt with under the Bail Act, which would have meant a maximum of a year in jail. The judge also ordered that he had to pay the costs, saying: "We have heard on a previous occasion that there is plenty of money and £60,000 was found in his possession."

A year-and-a-half after his arrest, Reader was taken in a prison van to the Old Bailey for trial over his handling of the Brink's-Mat gold. This time he was in Court 14 and with him in the dock were Noye; the two alleged London connections, Tommy Adams, then 25, and Hatton Garden jeweller Matteo Constantino, 66; Michael Lawson, 37, from Kent; the West Country link Terence Patch, 41; and Garth Chappell, 42. Michael Corkery QC for the prosecution said the plot was controlled by Noye, who had come up with a simple plan to sell on the gold.

He said: "Noye's answer to the problem smacks of simplicity." He decided to re-smelt the gold so the serial numbers were removed and dispose of it in small parcels on the legitimate gold market. Mr Corkery told the jury: "It was decided to provide bogus documents to provide an honest background to the stolen gold."

After being cleared of murder five months earlier, Noye appeared confident that he would again get the better of the police and prosecution. The 14 defence barristers shared his optimism as they felt the Flying Squad had not produced a case to show a direct link between the stolen gold and their clients. Once again Noye had the mercurial John Mathew QC on his side. Mathew attacked the Flying Squad officers who had interviewed his client, accusing Detective Inspector Bob Suckling of "verballing" him. Noye had not been allowed to have a solicitor so Suckling could be given the opportunity to invent his answers, came the excoriating claim.

He said that after almost an hour of interviewing Noye without writing a word, Suckling and a second detective had produced 26 pages of verbatim notes. Mathew told the jury in his closing speech that these were the fruits of the detective's "practised imagination" and his evidence was so embarrassing for the prosecution "that uniquely not one single question was put to Mr Noye about that interrogation in cross-examination, no doubt for fear that fallacies and falsehoods so obviously told by that witness would have been made even more apparent." He said the two detectives chosen to interview Noye had got the job "because of their imagination and ability to compose".

But Noye had problems and therefore so did Reader as the fate of the two men were interlinked just as they had been in the Fordham trial. Noye had to explain to the jury why he had eleven kilos of gold on his property and account for the small matter of nearly £3million that had been paid in to various offshore accounts. His approach was to admit that he was a crook but deny he was a crook with links to the Brink's-Mat robbery. He spent two days in the witness box saying he had been a professional gold smuggler for the previous four years, during which he had made a profit of around £1million a year. He had organised gold runs from Rwanda, Kuwait and Brazil to Holland, from where he had brought it to the UK by ferry in Tupperware boxes. This he was selling to Reader, described in court as his "vigorous right-hand man", for him to pass on to dealers in Hatton Garden. Chappell and Patch, who operated Scadlynn in Bristol, said they had bought more than £10million in gold from Hatton Garden dealer Constantino, who in turn told police that all he supplied was dodgy paperwork.

The defence appeared to be winning the battle until, with the trial already under way, the prosecution decided to allow Customs investigators to look at the vast amounts of paperwork that had been assembled by the police. There had traditionally been, and still is in some quarters, a level of distrust between the police and Customs officials, with the latter believing that corruption was endemic in the former. It meant communication between the two organisations was poor. So it came as little surprise to Flying Squad officers when they found Customs were already on to Scadlynn by the time their surveillance work had uncovered the link in January 1985. Customs left the Yard to the Brink's-Mat case and concentrated only on the alleged VAT fraud the gang had also been perpetrating. Now with things looking bad at the Bailey, the Customs investigators were brought on board in a last-ditch attempt to save the case.

Sure enough, when they combined all of the documents, the Customs teams were able to show a pattern of gold dealing that could be tied to the missing Brink's-Mat bullion but had been missed by the police. An unnamed defence lawyer was quoted in *The Guardian* after the trial: "Until this stage it had not been difficult to pick large holes in the prosecution case, which we felt had not been well-prepared. Once the Customs investigators, who had previously only been interested in the alleged VAT fraud, got involved in the handling charge they pulled it out the fire for the police."

Following an 11-week trial, the jury took 36 hours of deliberation to find Reader, Noye and Chappell guilty of conspiring to handle gold stolen from the record-breaking robbery. Noye's mask of respectability fell away as soon as the verdicts were announced and he screamed at the jury: "I hope you die of cancer." Furious Reader said: "You have made one terrible mistake. You have got to live with that for the rest of your life."

Reader's son Paul was arrested for contempt of court when he scuffled with police and shouted at the 12-strong panel: "You have been fucking fixed up." A fracas broke out in the courtroom and Brenda Noye joined in with: "Never has such an injustice been done. There is no fucking justice in this trial." Outside court a weeping Lyn Reader told reporters: "It's not true, it's not true. There has been a terrible injustice." Cleared of handling the Brink's-Mat gold were Lawson, Adams, Constantino and Patch. Reader, Noye, Chappell and Constantino were all found guilty of the VAT charge.

Reader and Noye were back before Judge Richard Lowry the next day for sentencing. Noye apologised for his outburst, saying it had been made in the "heat of the moment". He was jailed for 14 years. Reader was given nine years. Lyn was reported to have shouted to her husband: "I will wait for you, Brian," while Brenda Noye called: "I love you, darling." Noye replied, "I love you too," and blew her a kiss.

Lyn later denied making the comment. She told former *Guardian* crime reporter Duncan Campbell for his book *That Was Business, This Is Personal*: "I think if I'd actually said, 'I'll wait for you, darling,' Brian would have jumped out the dock and punched me on the nose."

Reader was led to the cells knowing he had already served a year-and-a-half in jail. If he kept his head down he could be back home in less than five more. But, for Reader, as one door closed it seemed another always opened. It was during the next period of his life that he would meet the men who would help him pull off his most astonishing crime yet.

CHAPTER 11

A New Team

Craning his neck up at the red-brick walls topped with gleaming barbed wire, Brian Reader knew there was no point fighting the system. By the time he arrived at Parkhurst Prison on the Isle of Wight, Reader had become used to the oppressive hopelessness of life on the inside. The stench of stale tobacco and sweat, the permanent undercurrent of boredom mixed with seething anger that occasionally exploded into violence. Reader had never liked any sort of institution or authority and had spent his entire adult life up until this point existing outside of the "system". After leaving the army he had relied on his wits and hard work to provide for his family. Never had he claimed a benefit or asked for help from the government. Never had he worked for another man or company. Reader had enjoyed more freedom than most people experience in a lifetime. But now, approaching 50, having travelled the world and become used to some of the finer things in life, he was locked up in a cell for most of the day in a high-security jail and forced to slop out.

It was Friday, July 25, 1986, when Reader arrived at

the Victorian prison that would be his home for the coming few years. He had already spent 18 months on remand in London as he awaited the two trials. If he kept his head down he would be out in less than five years, having served two thirds of his sentence. Reader had experienced worse growing up during the war, when food was hard to come by and he would shiver through the winter nights. In prison you could read and you were fed. Reader would use his time to educate himself further and develop his circle of criminal contacts. Most of his gang had been arrested or fled the country in the wake of the Gervaise and Brink's-Mat trials. Reader knew he would need a new team when he eventually went back to work. He still had big plans.

The first he met was Terry Perkins. Brought up in Edmonton, north London, Perkins was serving 22 years for a huge robbery. Born in 1948 to George and Lizzy, the powerfully built youngster had been a good amateur boxer and trained at the New Enterprise Gym in Tottenham, north London. Perkins' family were carpet fitters and he would often spend childhood summers picking hops in the Kent countryside with his siblings and the mother he was very close to. When Reader met him, Perkins was 37 years old and had never done a burglary in his life, having spent his criminal career as an armed robber working with the likes of north London blagger Billy Hickson and notorious villain John Knight. He was allegedly a friend of legendary supergrass Roy Garner who, as outlined in Chapter Six, had been one of Britain's most prolific police informers during the 1970s. Garner was finally jailed in 1989 for 22 years over a plot to smuggle 400 kilos of Colombian cocaine into the UK. There is no suggestion Perkins was ever a police informant. An underworld source said: "Most people hated Garner. So much so that when he was in the nick he had to have a minder. But Perkins really liked him and would always defend him, despite the fact we all knew he was a rat." Garner's prison minder had been Pat Tate, a violent cocaine addict and dealer who died aged 37 in the infamous Range Rover murders in a country lane in Rettendon, Essex, in December 1995, along with his boyhood friend Tony Tucker, 38, and their gopher Craig Rolfe, 27.

Perkins had been convicted for the robbery at the Security Express depot in Shoreditch, east London, over the Easter bank holiday weekend in 1983, when the gang escaped with £6million. It remains the biggest cash robbery in British history and is likely, with the rise of cashless payments and changes to the banking industry, to stay that way.

The heist had been planned and carried out by Knight of the well-known East End crime family. John's brother, Ronnie, was famous for his on-off relationship with actress Barbara Windsor. The glamorous pair had been photographed with the Krays at their Soho nightclub El Morocco in the 1960s and remained an item even as her career in the *Carry On* films flourished. Perkins was a teenager when he first befriended the Knight family. He was initially closest to the younger brother, David, who was stabbed to death by an Italian bouncer named Alfredo Zomparelli in 1970 at a West End nightclub.

The Security Express raid was well over a year in the planning. John Knight told how he was having breakfast in a cafe one Monday morning when he idly watched a Security Express van unloading bags of coins into a bank as it opened. Knight reckoned that the van was unlikely to have been loaded up with bags of silver that morning and that it had probably been full of cash all weekend. It was a tempting target. He tracked down the firm's main depot in Shoreditch, now a fashionable and expensive area of London.

Knight surveyed the four-storey depot, known to locals as Fort Knox, before breaking into a derelict office block next door. Once inside, he unscrewed the lock on a door that led outside onto a quiet alleyway. He paid a visit to a friendly locksmith who made him a new key for it. He gave all the team their own copies of the key and they watched the depot closely for months to work out every minute detail of how it worked – the layout, the security arrangements and the movement of the guards.

Knight later revealed he had a mole, a retired Security Express employee, who he met in a pub a few months before the job. An underworld source has now revealed this man was a retired police officer who had been in charge of security at the depot. He later committed suicide. The mole – who was never caught – talked Knight through the plans of the depot. He explained what each button in the control room did and the intricacies of the CCTV system. He pinpointed a weakness behind the Security Express defences – the security guard's morning cuppa. The routine involved a first guard on day duty taking over from the nightman and then leaving the security of the control room to walk across the locked-up yard to a hatch on the external wall. This would contain a pint left by the milkman. "Once you are in that backdoor, the building is yours," the mole told Knight.

The insider revealed another piece of information that Knight was to exploit. Staff were told not to resist if their lives were threatened. Knight would later reward the mole by stuffing £10,000 in a brown envelope through his door.

Knight watched as the lone guard walked across the yard every morning to collect a pint of milk. He also worked out that there was a blind spot on the CCTV camera trained on the yard. One corner, where some dustbins were standing, was not covered. The team tested this by climbing over the wall, running to the corner and back to prove that no alarm was raised. On the night of the raid, Knight, Perkins and the rest of the team, climbed over the wall at 3.30am. They hid until the morning, when a security guard walked across the yard to collect a pint of milk from the hatch in the wall.

One shouted: "Keep your head on the fucking floor! Look down!" The security guard did as he was told as something cold and metallic was pressed against his face. "Do what you're told and you won't get hurt."

One by one, more guards were overpowered and tied up as they arrived for work. Knight had done his homework and the team knew most of the guards by name. One of the gang put on a bad Irish accent. The guards were forced to open the vault after one terrified man was doused in petrol and threatened with being set alight. To their astonishment, the gang found between 30 and 40 metal cages stuffed with cash. It took Knight, Perkins and two others three days to count the loot. After paying off everyone who assisted in the planning and aftermath of the raid, the eight men on the job ended up with around £400,000 each.

Perkins wasn't the brains behind Security Express but he was a key and trusted member of the team – and one of the reasons why they got caught. He was a wealthy man owning a substantial property empire in north London and had just one conviction to his name, for drink driving. He seemed a safe pair of hands. The heist instantly generated a blaze of publicity, which only intensified once the Knights were in the frame. Much of the gang fled to Spain, which at that time remained beyond the reach of British justice.

John Knight tried to keep his head down and wait for the storm to blow over. Unfortunately for him, others on the raid didn't take the same precautions and this should have been a warning to Reader to steer well clear. Police surveillance teams spotted Perkins socialising with another of the robbers, Billy Hickson, and drinking in a pub in Dalston a short distance from the depot. A few months after the raid, Perkins turned up at the offices of his accountant, Robert Young, with £50,000 in used notes stuffed in the pockets of an anorak. Perkins and Hickson also stashed much of their cash in bank accounts in Jersey, travelling together to the island to deposit the cash – another huge and unnecessary risk. They were caught, John Knight believed, because they were spending too much time together after the raid.

Perkins was spotted driving Ronnie Knight's old two-tone blue Granada. It was registered to a bodywork repair outfit in Southgate owned by Knight and run by Alan Opiola, who would later confess to his role in laundering the cash and provide the evidence that jailed many of the gang.

When Perkins was arrested, police found £10,000 in his house in Enfield. They also found a hole in the floor under a wardrobe, which they felt was likely to be used for storing the cash. His wife Jacqueline was arrested too, for money laundering.

John Knight was also arrested, along with key members of the team. Ronnie had already fled to Spain, where he had stashed £100,000 of John's share of the proceeds through contacts in the Costa del Sol. Ronnie finally ended his tempestuous relationship with Barbara Windsor and started a new life in a beautiful Spanish villa with his mistress Sue Haylock.

The trial, in 1985, took its toll on Perkins, then aged 37 but already suffering from heart trouble and a doctor was called to the Old Bailey when he had a turn. He was jailed, along with John Knight, for 22 years. The judge called them "evil ruthless men" and made them criminally bankrupt. Police had only traced £2million of the missing £6.2million and the judge complained that: "The powers I have to extract the ill-gotten gains are most limited." The maximum penalty for Perkins or Knight failing to pay any fines or compensation orders against them was another 12 months in jail. "That is derisory when one examines the large sums concerned," said the judge.

Jacqueline was cleared of money laundering and as she left the dock she kissed Terry on the lips and whispered "good luck". The criminal bankruptcy meant all their properties were sold. Knight lost his pride and joy, a large and remote country house called High Trees in Wheathampstead, Hertfordshire. For Perkins, it was the end of his property empire. The law eventually caught up with Ronnie Knight too. After years in the newspaper spotlight, he agreed to return home for a cash payment from *The Sun*. The money that was left after legal fees went to Sue Haylock. Ronnie pleaded guilty to handling stolen goods and was sentenced to seven years in jail. Judge

Gerald Gordon told him: "Clearly, I don't know what your precise role was but… you benefited by an enormous amount and not one penny has been recovered."

Reader and Perkins became firm friends in Parkhurst and began to discuss working together when they got out. Perkins realised there was good money to be made doing burglaries and he vowed never to go back into armed robbery, knowing another conviction would probably mean spending the rest of his life in jail. The two men were joined in March 1989 by John "Kenny" Collins, who had been jailed for nine years for the £300,000 robbery of a jeweller's in Ealing. Though Collins always admitted to friends that he had taken possession of the stolen gear, he denied being on the actual raid. Collins is described by one friend as an "Arthur Daley" character who "knows everyone" in London. He was two years younger than Reader and had met Perkins when he was a kid at the same gym in Tottenham, where he had also been a promising boxer.

Collins came from Irish stock but was brought up in Clyde Circus, north London. A Spurs fan and dog lover, he was a "sociable bloke who likes a drink". One underworld source said: "He is fearless but comes across as very nice. He's a very kind bloke and a good conversationalist." Another source said: "If you talked to Kenny in the pub you'd think he was a decent guy. He's got a lot of money, which he's made mainly out of illegal cigarettes and vodka from Eastern Europe. But he's a dumbhead and tells everyone his business. I remember when he was dealing in fake pound coins and he went around telling people he needed to get a bigger truck because of the weight of the coins. That's just asking for trouble." As one criminal associate was later to put it: "He can't keep a fucking secret."

Collins was not a specialist burglar and had a string of convictions for offences, such as handling stolen goods, fraud and robbery. Like Reader, his first conviction came when he was eleven years old. In 1951, Collins was given a probation order for theft and was eventually sent to borstal aged 17 for stealing bicycles and loitering with intent. A string of prison sentences followed between 1961 and 1978 for warehouse-breaking, robbery and handling stolen goods – namely 31 dresses and two skirts. Baker Street or Brink's-Mat it wasn't. But, despite the gulf in their criminal pedigrees, Reader got on well with him. Collins had experienced his fair share of tragedy in his life. His brother, Patsy, a roadie for rock band Deep Purple in the 1960s and 70s, died in Jakarta, Indonesia, in December 1976 after mysteriously falling six storeys down a hotel lift shaft as the band prepared to play in front of 100,000 fans. Patsy was a much-loved character on the British music scene and guitarist Tommy Bolin's bodyguard. He fell through central heating pipes and water ducts, landing in the basement of the hotel. But it didn't kill him instantly and he crawled out, got into a minibus outside the hotel and just murmured "hospital, hospital" before passing away. This was a story Collins would later share with Reader and Perkins over a pint of Guinness.

When Reader finally got out of jail in 1991, he was 52 years old and life had changed drastically. Lyn had moved the family to a spacious detached home called Pentire in Dartford, south east London. The house was shielded from the busy road by overgrown trees and bushes, which prevented prying eyes getting any view of the building. Lyn had done her best to make it a home, even without her husband. Framed family photographs lined the walls and windowsills. Reader's three grandchildren would often visit with their dad Paul, who lived a couple of miles away. It was a huge relief to be back home and Reader vowed to make the most of his freedom with Lyn. In May 1992, he took her to see their favourite singer, Frank Sinatra, at the Royal Albert Hall in what would turn out to be Ol'Blue Eyes' last appearance in the UK. A friend said: "Sinatra was his favourite and, though Brian couldn't sing to save his life, he loved listening to music. He would often tell us about how great that concert was."

Reader soon settled back into his daily routine of buying a copy of his newspaper of choice, *The Independent*, from the newsagent across the road. The left-leaning publication reflected Reader's politics. Growing up in the heavily unionised docks on south east London in the 1950s, most people he knew read the staunchly Labour *Daily Mirror*. Reader had been a supporter of the party all his life and among his heroes was Tony Benn, whose career he had followed throughout Benn's 47 years as a Labour MP.

Neighbours would later describe Reader as a quiet man who would always say hello. Every Monday morning he would head into London and see his old mates at Scotti's cafe on Clerkenwell Green. Soon, ideas for bits of work started forming in his head. But the world had moved on in the six years Reader had been in jail. CCTV was beginning to be far more widely used by businesses and local authorities, while improvements in lock and burglar alarm technology had made things more difficult for thieves. Forensic science was also developing fast and in 1988 Colin Pitchfork had become the first person in the UK to be convicted using DNA evidence when he was jailed for the rape and murder of two girls in Leicestershire. Reader realised he would need the help of a younger man who understood the new digital world if he wanted to continue working.

In October 1995, with only months left of his 22-year sentence, Perkins absconded while on day release from Springhill open prison. It was the headstrong act of a man prone to making decisions he would later regret. Perkins had begun a relationship with an Irish pub landlady 20 years his junior and couldn't face returning to prison. Over the next few years he would live in the flat above the Harlequin pub in Islington, north London. Reader and Collins would join him on Friday nights for a lock-in when they would chat about old times and make plans for the future.

One ageing villain who would also go down there said: "We would have a meet up every Friday. Perkins was on the run but still ran the pub openly. It has a well in the cellar that would be a good place to hide stolen gear. Perkins was there for several years, up until he got nicked and returned to prison in 2011. He was on his toes and running the pub with a woman from Ireland. The police caught up with him and he went back for about another year to finish his bird from the 1983 job. Brian would be in there [in the pub] with Kenny Collins. It was a great laugh with everyone telling stories about the jobs they'd done." Another source said: "They meet-up every Friday night. It was almost like going to church. They are such funny guys and not at all as they have been portrayed in the media. You would think they are just scumbags. But they are very entertaining characters. They didn't act like gangsters or anything like that. You wouldn't know they were top criminals. But you did know they pushed the boundaries." Hugh Doyle, a sociable Irishman in his early 30s, was a trusted friend of Kenny's and he would join the group for a pint after finishing work for a printing firm around the corner from the pub.

It was around this time, in the mid-1990s, that Reader was introduced to armed robber and career criminal Danny Jones. Jones had been jailed for seven years in 1989 and it was during this time, while in Maidstone prison, that he had been given a cell next to Reader's old mentor

Billy Barrett. Jones also got to know a leading burglar who had run with a gang from Clerkenwell that rivalled Reader's group in the 1960s and 70s. It was this man, who cannot be named for legal reasons, who taught Jones that burglary was a far better pursuit than armed robbery. There were higher rewards and less jail time if you were caught.

A teetotal fitness fanatic, Jones was also from Tottenham and a lifelong Spurs fan. Seventeen years younger than Reader, he is described by a gang insider as a compulsive liar and Walter Mitty character. Not the smartest, he is "as strong as an ox" and addicted to working out. One criminal source described Jones' strength: "He grabbed me around the chest once for a laugh and I couldn't breath. He could have killed me easily, just needed an extra little squeeze. He's a fitness nut. He doesn't drink or smoke and does endurance running in the desert. Did one in the Sahara, bloody mad if you ask me. He needed to be controlled, that's why he should have been in the army."

Another friend described Jones as a "show-off" who walked up a street in Enfield on his hands to demonstrate his fitness. He had convictions including burglary, theft, robbery and handling stolen goods, which meant he had spent much of his adult life in prison. Jones was so institutionalised that he referred to evenings after 5pm at his substantial detached home in Enfield as "bang-up" and would refuse to receive visitors or take phone calls. In the garish surroundings, where the large wooden staircase was adorned with a carved skull, he would not sleep in bed with his partner, Valerie. He preferred to dress in a Tommy Cooper-style fez and his mother's dressing gown, before bedding down for the night in a sleeping bag on his bedroom floor. He used to urinate in a bottle because of his obsession with the army and the SAS and talked to his wire-haired terrier Rocket as if he were human. A source said: "Jones tells his wife everything and that is a big concern. You never tell your wife anything about bits of work because you never know what she might do if you fall out. You would be with him and he'd be on his phone to her telling her where he was and who he was meeting. What an idiot."

Jones claimed to have supernatural powers and said he could read palms. He spent his evenings in his bedroom studying books and films on crime and scouring the internet for ideas. A gang source said: "He would boast and tell a lot of lies because he was trying to impress others with more experience than him. Once he went on the Underground with army gear on and told a passenger he was special forces. Danny is a compulsive liar. I'd say 99 out of a hundred stories he told me were untrue, but he has got a likeable character. He is very forceful and impatient. If you were on a bit of work the odds of it being successful would get better and better every week you were planning it but he would always want to do it that night."

Though Danny's physical strength and fitness were

things Reader needed in his team, he was not the younger gang member that he so desperately sought. That person came in the form of an individual who called himself "Basil". In his mid-30s when he was introduced to Reader by another ageing criminal not long after Reader's release, Basil was an alarm man and computer expert who had been "turned" by the man who introduced him to Reader. Prior to that, this youngest member of the gang had had no involvement in crime, the source said. He had grown up in a respectable middle-class household and his father was a law-abiding professional who passed away when he was a small child. Reader immediately recognised himself in the younger man and took him under his wing.

A gang insider said: "He's a kid who would find things out using his initiative. He's a problem solver. He would be shown how to open a door or pick a lock and then he would go away and improve on it. Basil was good with computers but if he used one it wouldn't be at his own home, he would be ten miles away on someone else's. He was always very surveillance-conscious. If you went to his house he would say, 'Let's go out,' and he would only talk on the street. Basil's got more brains than Perkins, Jones and Collins put together."

Originally from the South East of England, Basil is around six foot tall and slightly built. The last we heard, he was single and childless and living in Islington, less than a mile from Reader's stomping grounds of Hatton Garden and Clerkenwell. He is believed to have pulled off a number of burglaries over the last 20 years but is understood never to have been caught. The source added: "He got into crime in his mid-30s and he didn't need much coaching. Brian recognised his ability and brought him on board. It was obvious he had to be properly looked after. Basil was like gold dust because of what he knew and his skills."

Basil's mother is still alive and he has brothers and sisters living in the UK. The gang's hierarchy would go on to be split between Basil and Reader, the only true specialist burglars on the team, and the rest – who the source described as "labourers". The insider said: "He's very innocent in some ways and would have been vulnerable to Perkins and Jones." Of the Hatton Garden gang only Reader knew his real name. Though he did own a mobile phone nobody on the firm had a number for him.

CHAPTER 12

88-90 Hatton Garden

Brian Reader had been a regular at Scotti's Snack Bar for six decades. It was like a time capsule on Clerkenwell Green, in a corner of London that had changed a great deal during that time. The old tenement blocks that had housed Italian and Irish immigrants were long since demolished, replaced by modern loft apartments and shiny office blocks. Property prices rocketed and working-class families were replaced by wealthy professionals as central London became unaffordable for most people. But the tide of change had been resisted by Scotti's, owned by the same Italian couple, Antonio and Maria, since 1967. The old metal tea urn still steamed away on the counter, resolutely refusing to make way for a cappuccino maker. It was operated by a waitress rather than a barista or whatever the marketeers were calling waitresses these days. For Reader, there was something reassuring about the formica surfaces and ham rolls wrapped in cellophane. Most importantly for him, Scotti's was still part of a community, something Reader felt was disappearing in London.

Clerkenwell Green had a tradition for attracting plotters. Wat Tyler, the leader of the Peasants' Revolt, rested there in 1381 before meeting Richard II at Smithfield, where he was murdered by the King's men. It was on this green that Chartists, battling for all working men to be given the right to vote, met during the 1840s. Vladimir Lenin and Joseph Stalin even supped warm bitter in the local Crown and Anchor pub as they discussed revolution. On this Monday morning, in early 2014, it was hosting a new pair of underground schemers.

Reader was sitting at his usual table, at the back of the tiny cafe, opposite a middle-aged man, who would later become known around the world as Basil. They were deep in conversation. To anyone watching, the pair might have been mistaken for a father and son, having an argument about politics or football. Only their urgent and hushed tones indicated they might be talking about something more serious. This was one of their regular planning meetings, in which the pair discussed the Hatton Garden job. A gang insider said the two men sometimes had a confrontational relationship and could end up rowing about the best way to approach a problem. As the only two specialist burglars on the gang, Reader and Basil were the brains behind the operation and it was only natural they would sometimes disagree.

The source said: "Basil had a nickname for Reader. He would call him Brenda, as did a few guys who would meet him down in Clerkenwell. Don't ask me why, but Brian somehow got it because the woman in the cafe was called Brenda. Basil and Brian had a chippy relationship and would clash. Basil would come over and confide in me. He would say, 'Brenda's done so and so.' They would argue about things but they also had respect for each other."

Reader could not remember when the idea first came to him to try to hit the vault at Hatton Garden Safe Deposit Ltd. It was one of scores of jobs on a list of "possibles" he carried around in his head. This list included most of the places in London where large sums of cash, gold or jewels were kept. The underground vault at 88-90 Hatton Garden had been on his radar for at least four decades. He never stopped working following his release from prison though developments in technology and banking made things harder for him. His deteriorating health had not helped. In the mid-2000s Reader was diagnosed with prostate cancer, which doctors had been able to manage.

Cancer struck again, though, this time affecting his beloved Lyn. The lifelong heavy smoker had lung cancer and she passed away in January 2009, aged 65. It was a devastating blow. Lyn was Reader's rock and had stuck by him through the bad times as well as the good. They had an enviable marriage by any standards, even more so for a leading criminal living an unpredictable and at times chaotic life. Reader consoled himself that he had always provided for Lyn and the kids through thick and thin. His one regret was letting himself take the risks in the 1980s that had led him to jail and out of his family's life for six long years. Fear of it happening again had kept him, if not on the straight and narrow, then at least taking even greater precautions against getting caught. Now Lyn was gone, she had left a huge void in Reader's life. He needed to fill it with something and plotting a way into the vault at Hatton Garden took his mind off things, at least for a while. It was very risky but, without Lyn to come home to, perhaps he no longer had as much to lose.

The possibility only began to become real sometime around 2012 when Reader was handed the key to the front door of the building. One of his many contacts in the Garden had a box in the vault and would make regular visits. He also knew a number of jewellers renting rooms in the rest of the building and had copied one of their keys. The insider said: "The man gave it to Brian on the promise he would get a cut if it worked out but he died not long after. I won't tell you his name. He was English, had a wife and children, was in his 60s and had always been involved in jewellery. He would buy stolen jewellery and had done bits of prison over the years."

Reader and Basil then used the key to enter the building repeatedly at night in the years before the raid. The source said: "They knew the place inside out. It was easy for them to slip into the communal area and soon they had worked their way down to the basement area."

The vault at 88-90 Hatton Garden was built in 1948, when Reader was nine years old, by local jeweller George

Edward Gordon. Gordon was born in 1900 and had already had a successful career as a metallurgist. He had invented an alloy for dentists to use in fillings that wouldn't give their patients electric shocks. He opened a jewellery shop called Gordon and Company on the first floor of 88-90 in 1945. His daughter Dorrit described how her father was always looking for the next business venture: "He kept looking forward. He never stood still." When he started the business, Gordon was shocked by the lack of security on the street outside his shop. "The nearest safe deposit was in Chancery Lane," explained Dorrit. "The traders used to carry their diamonds and jewellery back home with them. It was terribly dangerous. Daddy wanted to keep the trade off the street. They used to stand in Hatton Garden with loose diamonds and jewels."

Gordon took out a lease on part of the basement and drew up plans for what his daughter believes was "the only privately owned safety deposit in the world". It cost £20,000 to build – equivalent to more than £600,000 today. A short film was made to promote the new state-of-the-art vault. "Sparkling diamonds – their value running into the millions – are giving Hatton Garden sleepless nights," said the voice-over. "To foil the thieves, Hatton Garden now has its own giant strong room… a two-foot-wide bomb-and-burglar-proof door – operated by a combination that has to be worked by at least two men – opens up a labyrinth of safes."

It was an instant success. The security was cutting-edge

at the time and changed little in the following decades. A security guard sat in the corridor outside the basement office. He let customers past a security door and grill. A second custodian was inside, who told customers to sign their names in a book. There was a lift up to the rest of the building but it only went down to the basement when the shutters were unlocked and opened up. In this office area were a number of cubby holes or booths and a telephone. Dorrit explained: "The telephone line was for security and the booths were there for our clients to use with their customers. It was an area where diamonds could be inspected and deals could be done."

Customers wanting the vault would pass through a second security door with a grill. This took them to a corridor outside the vault itself, protected by a ten-tonne door built for Gordon by Chubb. Dorrit recalls: "It was so finely balanced that you could move it with just one finger. Daddy was very proud of that door." It had two combination locks and one key and, though many will have sorely wanted to, no criminal has managed to break it open to this day. Once inside the vault, customers needed two keys to get into their safe deposit boxes – their own key and a master kept by the custodian.

The first robbery at the vault was 11 years after it opened. The circumstances are unclear and nobody was ever caught. Dorrit said: "Daddy compensated a lot of people even though he wasn't legally obliged to because he felt he had a moral responsibility. It put the family into a very bad financial position." Gordon died in 1960, leaving his wife Lily and 24-year-old daughter in charge of the struggling business.

Hatton Garden was becoming more dangerous and it needed the vault more than ever. The 1970s robbery gangs were running rampant across London and Hatton Garden was a prime target, as Dorrit and her mother were to experience first-hand. In one week at the start of August 1975, Hatton Garden and the surrounding area was robbed five times. The biggest haul by far was from the vault itself.

Lily Gordon later explained what happened to police: "On Saturday, 2 August 1975, I opened the office of my shop at about 8:40am. I was with my daughter and we took the keys to the safe deposit from the office. We both came down the stairs and Mr Newman, my custodian, and Mr Doyle, another custodian, met us at the bottom of the stairs. This is a daily routine. Mr Doyle, who holds one key, opened one lock on the door and I opened the other. We went in and locked the door.

"We took the boxes out from our safe deposit and opened the lift shutter. The grills were locked and the custodians and my daughter went upstairs in the lift with the boxes. I pulled the shutter of the lift down and locked it."

Doyle and Newman were returning back down to the vault by the stairs, as the lift could not return to the basement before 9.30am. This was another security measure to ensure there would always be a guard in place when the lift was running. Doyle told police: "As Mr Newman and myself walked downstairs, we got to about the fifth step from the bottom when I think about three men jumped out and one of them pointed what I thought looked like a sawn-off shotgun at me. One of the other men had an iron bar and was holding it above his head. The man with the gun said, 'Be quiet, be quiet.' Then one of the men started shouting, 'I've fallen down the stairs, I've fallen down the stairs.'"

Mrs Gordon, who was waiting for them thought it was Doyle's voice. "I went to the door and suddenly there was a gun pointing at me through the grill," she said. "The next thing I can remember is being on the floor in the safe. There were a lot of men wearing stockings over their heads and they were dragging men in and putting them on the floor. All I can remember clearly is that they had large white containers with lids that they were filling with boxes. I can't remember how many men there were – about 10, I think. After a time, the men came round and started to tie up our hands. I didn't see the men leave because I didn't look up. The men told us not to look up."

Doyle recalled: "When I was on the floor, one of the men went through my pockets, asking for a master key. I told him there was no master key and he took the keys I had in my hand. As I lay there, I could hear the sound of the deposit boxes being broken into. After about 30 minutes, they made myself and the others go into the safe-deposit vault, then they left. I would say there was about seven or eight robbers."

Upstairs, 39-year-old Dorrit was working in the shop. She took a call from a tricky customer wanting to speak to the manager. She buzzed the downstairs office to speak to her mother. No one answered.

So she buzzed the line in the safe-deposit vault. She later explained: "This was answered by a man with a deep Cockney-like accent. He said, 'Oh, they'll be up in a minute, dear.' I said, 'Who's that?' There was no answer. I asked again and still no answer. I became alarmed." She asked a staff member to mind the shop while she went downstairs. "I told him to call the police immediately if I did not return in five minutes," Dorrit told police.

Sitting in the family's north London flat, Dorrit – now aged 80 – chokes up as she recalls the scene that greeted her. "I came down to find mummy tied up and the vault looking like an Aladdin's Cave," she said. "They had threatened to kill me. They were never caught. It was so traumatic. I have only recently been able to talk about it."

The robbers escaped with more than £500,000 in gold and precious stones. Loss adjusters offered a £50,000 reward for information leading to the recovery of the stolen goods and the arrest and conviction of the robbers. They were never caught. The abandoned jewellery, which the robbers couldn't carry, was scooped up by police to return to its rightful owners. Some of it, embarrassingly, later went missing from Holborn Police Station.

It was a wake-up call on the Garden. If the safe-deposit vault wasn't safe, where was? In the jewellery trade press it was reported that "in some quarters there have even been suggestions that the Garden itself should be closed to traffic to make escape more difficult for villains but such a move could result in more robberies with violence as all goods entering and leaving the area would have to be carried on foot". It went on: "Other suggestions have even included the idea of encouraging all firms in Hatton Garden to contribute towards the cost of a private security force for the area." That was an idea two-and-a-half decades ahead of its time.

Once again, the vault had suffered a terrible blow to its reputation. Some customers lost faith and closed their boxes. In truth, nowhere was safe. Two years after the raid, prominent Hatton Garden diamond merchant Leo Grunhut was shot outside his Golders Green home while carrying £250,000 in diamonds.

The Gordons sold up around 1980. It was a relief to the ageing Lily Gordon and her daughter. "The safe deposit was never a good earner, to be honest," said Dorrit. "It was not profitable. I wish my father had never even thought about it, to be truthful."

The owners changed but villainous plotting went on regardless. The Bavishi family bought the vault in 2001. Two years later, the Hatton Garden safe deposit was at the epicentre of a crime that stunned the Garden. Diamond trader Philip Goldberg appeared on the scene in late

2002. He was a well-dressed man, in his 50s, wearing a suit and tie and a Homberg hat. He fitted in easily among the older members of the orthodox Jewish community. He brought diamonds to trade and, like many other regulars in the Garden, rented a safe-deposit box downstairs in 88-90 Hatton Garden. There was nothing remarkable about Goldberg – apart from the worrying fact that others knew him as Luis Ruben.

One Saturday morning in June, Goldberg/Ruben was signed into the vaults. He had rented four separate boxes by this point and so was given some considerable amount of time alone inside the vault. He emerged later with a black holdall. The contents of the holdall – £1.5million in diamonds and gems – were not discovered missing until the following Monday. The boxes he targeted appeared undamaged but had in fact been glued shut. Goldberg/ Ruben had somehow penetrated the double-lock system – one key kept by the vault owners and the other by the box holder. He too was never found, the third criminal or gang of crooks to help themselves to the riches of the vaults and get away with it scot-free in five decades.

The security measures in place at the Hatton Garden safe-deposit vault had barely changed since Reader first began to plot his way inside. Seven decades after it first opened for business, the vaults were available to customers five days a week, between the hours of 9am and 6pm. It was visited by scores of local jewellers every day. They entered the building through a large black wooden front door, which locked itself as it closed behind them. The front door was locked overnight but over the years copies of the key had been provided to more than 60 different businesses that rented office space inside. The jewellers often worked late and needed to let themselves inside out of hours.

Another glass security door had been installed inside the front door, which could be opened with a personal identification number – or PIN. The gang had no difficulty getting the code by simply looking at the keypad and seeing which numbers were more worn out.

Past the glass door and into a communal hallway were the stairs and lift shaft. After the 1975 armed robbery in the vault, the lift was prevented from going below the ground floor. Instead, visitors to the basement had to pass through another locked door to the side of the lift. Only four people had keys – the cleaner and people working for three businesses downstairs. Reader did not have a key to this door, so it was necessary for the gang to make one themselves during their night-time visits. Someone with the expertise can make a key for a lock by spraying a blank key with paint, wriggling it in the lock and then filing down the bits of the key where the paint has been rubbed off. This process is repeated until the lock opens.

CCTV systems monitored all visitors to the seven-storey block. There were five cameras trained on the main building – two on the ground floor, two on the outside courtyard and one monitoring on a flat roof outside the first floor. The safe deposit had its own CCTV system and it too had five cameras – two inside the vault, two outside and a fifth watching the entrance.

The door to the safe deposit company was alarmed. Once opened, the alarm was set to go off within 60 seconds unless someone keyed in the five-digit code.

There was one other way out of – and so into – 88-90 Hatton Garden. From the basement, a corridor led out into a sunken courtyard. A fire escape led up to ground level and out onto neighbouring Greville Street. For safety reasons, the first door to the courtyard was not locked. It was secured by two sliding bolts on the inside of the door, one at the top and one at the bottom. The second door from the fire escape to the street was locked and just two people had a key.

The gang's Friday-night boozer had switched from The Harlequin to The Castle, a short six-minute walk away on the busy Pentonville Road in Islington. Danny Jones, Terry Perkins and Kenny Collins met there on January 16, 2015. It was around this time that they were arguing about whether or not to use a flat bed truck or a van. Later secret recordings made by the police reveal Reader had won the argument with Perkins and Jones and they took a van, even though it had less room for the stolen gear.

The gang insider said that Basil had worked out how to get through an internal door of 88-90 Hatton Garden in early 2014 and planted a listening device in there over the

Easter weekend. The bug revealed the businesses remained unoccupied from the Thursday evening all the way through to the Tuesday morning. The next obstacle was getting into the actual vault. The source said the gang had brought an expert safe engineer on board, but that he was straight and got cold feet.

By this time Reader and Basil had brought Terry Perkins and Danny Jones on board. It was Jones who came up with the idea of using a diamond drill. The source said: "He was driving past some builders when he saw they were using one. Jones just piled in and started asking them loads of questions about how it worked. They realised it would be much easier to go through the wall than try to penetrate the door." Police searches of Jones' computer later showed that by May 2014, a month after Basil bugged the building, Jones' searches had become focused on a Hilti DD350 make and model of drill. The source said diamond-tipped drills were not new to Reader: "We'd known about them since 1979. Brian and me bought one that year for a job but ended up not using it."

A new barrel would have to be custom made for the drill. The standard German one was 45cm long. That would not be enough to get through the Hatton Garden vault wall. A new one, 60cm long, was ordered. The barrel came with diamond segments on the tip from Korea but the unit would have been assembled in the UK.

Experienced villain Carl Wood, 58, was invited to take part in the raid after he was vouched for by Billy Hickson, one of the Security Express team with Perkins. Wood grew up in Hackney and was jailed for four years in 1993 over a plot with two corrupt police officers. They had teamed up with crook Robert Kean in a bid to recover £600,000 owed to the villain by an underworld financier. DC Martin Morgan and DC Declan Costello organised a three-day hotel stake-out to try to catch their target. The victim faced being beaten up, bundled into a car boot and even being smuggled out of the country. But they were caught by police corruption busters who secretly filmed them at the hotel. Wood was heard bragging how he would beat the debtor with an iron bar. The line-up of the Hatton Garden gang was completed when Brian decided to let his old prison pal Kenny Collins into the plot as the lookout or "outside man". This would prove to be a fateful decision that would have dire consequences for them all.

The final piece of the jigsaw to fall in place was the alarm. Basil, the "alarm man", had been searching for the phone line which connected the system to the central control. Finally, he found it and worked out how to cut the cable without setting off the alarm. The source said: "It was very late on, maybe two or three weeks before they went, when they realised how to overcome it."

On Friday, March 10, Jones, Wood and Perkins went to Collins' house in Islington. They left their phones there so they could not be traced and all piled into Collin's Merc, driving down to Hatton Garden for a final dry run. It was two weeks before the raid.

Hatton Garden jeweller Lionel Wiffen had traded at Hatton Garden for more than 50 years. For many of those years he had been based at 88-90 and regularly used the Greville Street exit. By January 2015, Mr Wiffen had begun to feel he was being watched. He later said: "There seemed to be a lot of cars parked with people in it... looking over."

Perkins was one these suspicious-looking men. He drove down to recce Hatton Garden from his home in Enfield in his blue Citroen Saxo – with its proud number plate EN51 EUD – on several occasions. Another regular visitor was in a white Mercedes. Collins visited Hatton Garden five times in early 2015.

The plan was to get into the safe deposit down the disused section of the lift shaft. This would take them into the "air lock", the office area of Hatton Garden Safe Deposit where the alarm and CCTV was housed. During the day, it was where the two security guards worked. The lift would have to be moved out of the way onto one of the upper floors. But if it returned to the ground floor while they were climbing down, it could be catastrophic.

Police would later claim that to allay their fears, Perkins took one final huge risk. On Tuesday, March 31, diamond trader Katya Lewis was visiting clients in 88-90 Hatton Garden and pushed the button for the lift to take her to the third floor. She had visited the building many times before but this time the lift was unusually late. When it finally arrived, a 60-something-year-old man with white hair and wearing blue overalls was inside. He was surrounded by tools. Katya wondered if someone had helped him load his tools into the lift. He smiled apologetically at her because there was no room for her to get into the lift alongside him and the doors closed. The gang insider denies this was Perkins and it does seem unlikely that Reader would have allowed him to risk all his hard work with a last-minute recce during the day when he could simply do it at night. The source said: "The only ones to go in before the raid were Basil and Brian."

The next day, an electrical fault in nearby Holborn was to bring that part of the capital to a standstill. An underground explosion in one of the Victorian tunnels running under busy Kingsway ruptured an eight-inch gas main. The leaking gas caught fire and started a ferocious blaze. Smoke began to billow through vents into the busy city streets above. Flames licked upwards through manhole covers and reached 10 feet into the air. Soon, 70 firefighters were on the scene tackling the inferno. It would take them 36 hours to bring the fire under control but the chaos it caused lasted for days. 1,900 homes and businesses lost power and 5,000 people were evacuated from the area. Trials at the Royal Courts of Justice on the Strand were halted, West End theatre performances were cancelled and operations at the Great Ormond Street Hospital for children were postponed. Tourists taking to the giant London Eye ferris wheel that night could see the extent of the damage. In the patchwork blanket of street lamps and headlights below them, a vast blacked out area stretched half a mile from the River Thames northwards to Hatton Garden and beyond. The fire was a useful distraction for the gang as it would make what they were planning appear more natural.

CHAPTER 13

Knowing the Drill

Thursday April 2, 2015, was fresh and sunny. Perfect white cotton-wool clouds scurried across the blue skies over London. It was a nice day for it.

Brian Reader left home after finishing his tea and flagged down the number 96 bus on Dartford Road, outside his house. He sat anonymously in a windcheater and flat cap, just another old geezer on the bus.

The journey was at the taxpayer's expense. Like all London pensioners, Reader had a Freedom Pass, which allowed him onto every London bus or train for free. This municipal generosity began in 1973, at the same time as Reader was helping himself to the riches of the capital. Now, as then, he didn't look a gift horse in the mouth. Unlike other London pensioners, Reader's card didn't have his name on it. The card was made out to a Mr T McCarthy – the same pseudonym he'd had since the 1980s.

Reader emerged from Waterloo East station just after 6.30pm. Another bus ride, on the number 55, took him to within striking distance of Hatton Garden.

Minutes earlier, the two security guards at Hatton Garden Safe Deposit Ltd had gone through their normal evening routine. Kelvin Stockwell had worked at the vault for 20 years. Keefa Kamara, known as Ronald, had worked alongside him for the past 12 of them.

The following day was both Good Friday and the start of the Jewish Passover. That afternoon the punters, mostly local jewellers, had been queuing out the door, anxious to get their valuables to a place of safety ahead of the holiday weekend.

Together, Kelvin and Ronald locked the vault and retreated to the office, closing and locking the door and security grill behind them. Kelvin set the alarm and a second electric sliding grate was closed behind them. In the final piece of security, they locked the solid front door to the business and headed up the stairs to the communal lobby. Caretaker Carlos Cruse was waiting for them. He had already checked the basement and the courtyard beyond. All that was left to do was to shut the magnetic glass door. Then he walked out into the street. The heavy black door swung shut and automatically locked behind him. The four-day bank holiday weekend beckoned.

For others, the hard work was just about to begin. As agreed, Terry Perkins, Danny Jones and Carl Wood had switched their phones off before they left home. They had already made their way against the bank holiday traffic to Kenny Collins' house in Islington. Now the four clambered into the white van and drove westwards, into the city. The buzz of adrenaline began to fill their veins.

They picked up Reader near Farringdon and waited until their run was clear. The pubs of Holborn and Clerkenwell were overflowing that Thursday night. Office workers, shop staff, IT engineers and business people packed every available boozer to make an early start to the long weekend.

It was standing room only in The Argyle pub on the corner of Greville Street and Leather Lane. This modern pub, at the bottom of a block of flats, is just 50 yards from Hatton Garden. It used to be called the King of Diamonds and has long been a popular choice for those non-Orthodox Jewish jewellery workers who fancied a post-work tipple.

From 6pm, the pavement outside the pub and the first-floor balcony were crammed with people. By 8pm, the crowd began to thin. It is most unlikely that anyone gave a second thought to the anonymous white van that pulled up shortly after 8.25pm into Leather Lane, which runs parallel to Hatton Garden and 50 metres to the west.

Two men got out. Jones wore a dark hoodie, striped trousers, red trainers and a navy baseball cap. He also wore a high-vis vest over the top. Wood was with him. He too was in workman's clothing, with a hi-visibility waistcoat and a navy baseball cap. Wood added a white dust mask and dark gloves.

First, a quick recce. The pair walked up Greville Street to Hatton Garden where they paused for a few moments.

They then walked 100 metres up Hatton Garden, turned left onto St Cross Street, left again onto Leather Lane and completed the block. Collins, Perkins and Reader were waiting in the van for news. "Not yet," was the word.

Lionel Wiffen was working late that evening, dealing with the last of the week's customers. As the main entrance was already locked up, Wiffen met them at the Greville Street door and then showed them back out the same way once their business was done. His last customer that Thursday left at 8.30pm, just as Jones and Wood were doing their rounds. It was almost another hour before Wiffen finally left his office, locking the door, climbing the fire escape and shutting the door behind him.

Almost immediately, the gang swung into action. Basil walked along Greville Street with a hat pulled down low over a red wig and a black bag slung over his shoulder to further hide his face from prying eyes and – more importantly – any CCTV cameras.

Jones and Wood followed shortly afterwards, Jones clasping a walkie-talkie. Its partner, tuned to the same channel, was in the van. The pair stopped at the corner with Hatton Garden and waited.

Basil let himself into 88-90 through the black front door. After pausing to ensure the coast was clear, he punched in the four-digit code that opened the set of sliding doors before walking across the grey marble floor of the building's main lobby. All was silent as he produced a second key that he used to open a wooden door to the right of the main reception desk. This took him to a flight of stairs that he descended to the basement, where he turned right before sliding open the unlocked bolts on a fire door and emerged into the lower level courtyard and then back up the fire escape to Greville Street. The van was there waiting for him.

Collins stayed behind the wheel, while Reader and Perkins got out.

Reader wore a jaunty pair of stripy socks under his brown shoes and a scarf to keep out the early evening chill. Although a full decade past retirement age, he too was trying to pass off as a workman. He was wearing a yellow hard hat and a hi-visibility jacket with "GAS" written on the back. Completing the outfit were a pair of orange and cream gardening gloves to take care of any fingerprints. He quickly made his way through the door. Like the others, Perkins was dressed in dark clothing, with a hi-visibility waistcoat, a yellow hard hat and a white dust mask. He was also carrying his pills and insulin injections, enough to see him through the night. They were joined by Jones and Wood and the five men began to unload the van. From a distance, they looked the part. Up close and aged between 58 and 76, they looked like London's answer to *Last of the Summer Wine*. It was beginning to get dark but, even so, Reader's disguise in particular wouldn't take much scrutiny.

Two wheelie bins were pulled out from the back, along with bags of tools. One bin was weighed down by the Hilti drill, the other sloshed around with the water they would need to keep the drill cool. Jones and Perkins would later grumble about the amount of work they did while Reader took it easy. They lugged heavy metal joists down the stairs and into the basement.

Meanwhile, Collins impatiently shifted the van round the block to St Cross Street. He still had one box of tools left in the back. Jones ran up Leather Lane to meet him and returned with the green crate. Wood was waiting for him at the fire escape door with the last of the wheelie bins.

Minutes passed and the gang gathered in the basement lobby, yards from the vault but with a series of locked and alarmed doors standing between them and its vast riches. So far, so good.

Collins grabbed the other walkie-talkie from the van and locked the vehicle behind him. He wheezed his way back along St Cross Street to Hatton Garden, turned right and headed down towards 88-90. An elderly man, wearing a green quilted jacket, a flat cap and carrying a brown briefcase, was an unlikely figure to be seen inspecting the building. Collins raised his rheumy eyes over the six floors of windows above the vault. Good. All were in darkness.

He walked across the junction with Greville Street to number 25 opposite the vault. No doubt swearing under his breath, he fumbled with the stolen key in the lock. The minutes it took to unlock the door seemed like hours. His heart thudded inside his rib-cage. How much more excitement would it take?

Back inside 88-90, Jones and Basil climbed up three flights of stairs to the heart of the building. It was eerily yet comfortingly quiet. Hopefully it would stay this way. They were as confident as they could be that they were alone but there was no way to be 100 per cent sure the building was entirely empty. Well over a hundred people worked in more than 60 separate offices. All the lights appeared to be off but any one of them could contain a master craftsman working late to finish off an order before the Easter weekend.

On the second floor, they pushed the button to call the lift. The whirr of the machinery broke the silence and the men waited without a word. It was a simple job to disable the lift. They ripped off a sensor so that the doors remained permanently open. The noise was echoed around the corridors – if anyone was in the building this would surely bring them out to check. Basil and Jones held their breath. Silence. They then went back down the stairs, stopping on the ground floor to place a handwritten "Out of Order" sign by the lift.

The pair prised open the lift doors and clambered down the shaft, dropping eight feet to the basement level. The decades-old sliding metal shutter blocked the way into the basement, but this was forced upwards using crowbars to give them enough of a gap to slip into the pitch-dark office space beyond.

They were in. But it was a critical point in the job. If they triggered the alarm now, they would have just 60 second to disable it. Basil knew exactly what he had to do.

He made his way by torchlight to the cupboard beneath the stairs. It was exactly as described and relatively easy to disable. An old-fashioned phone line ran from the box. Basil found the grey cable and cut it. Again, silence. Just the sound of his breathing. He snapped off the GPS aerial attached to the alarm. This was the wireless back-up to the alarm but it would now have a significantly reduced range.

Next, Basil turned his attention to getting the rest of the gang inside. They were getting increasingly nervous as they waited in the corridor. He crossed the room to a desk and peered underneath. There was an electrical box that operated the security grill. He lifted the cover and snipped the power cables inside. Without any power, the gate was disabled. It opened by simply pushing down on a foot lever. Helped by Wood on the other side, they smashed through the wooden door, breaking the lock.

Shortly after midnight and almost three hours after entering the building, the whole gang was finally inside the safe deposit office. But they were about to come within a hair's breadth of being caught red-handed.

At 18 minutes past midnight, the alarm managed to send an SMS alert to the company that monitored it 24 hours a day. Opening the door had improved the mobile signal to the panel under the stairs – only marginally, but enough.

Southern Monitoring rang Alok Bavishi, the younger of the Bavishi brothers, who ran Hatton Garden Safe Deposit Ltd while his brother and father were out of the country. Alok lived in Harrow, a dozen miles north-west of the vault in the suburbs. He was a good hour's drive away. Alok rang security guard Ronald at home in Uxbridge. Ronald took the call but explained that the trains had stopped running. He was even further from Hatton Garden, nearly 20 miles to the West, near Heathrow airport and the M25, and didn't have a car. Next Alok tried his most senior guard Kelvin on his mobile. It went to voicemail but within minutes Kelvin rang back. It was half past midnight but Kelvin agreed to make his way in from London's Docklands in the East. Alok made himself ready to jump into his car and head into town to join him. The alarm call would have immediately notified the police and he hoped to be in time to meet the officers on the street outside. The company had a policy that, in situations like this, staff would not go into the vault alone. This way there would be two of them and the police would be a reassuring back-up.

But the police never came. The Met received the alarm call but graded it "no response required".

It was an uncanny echo of events more than four decades earlier – the Baker Street raid of 1971. Both times, police had by a stroke of luck – good or bad, depending on your perspective – been alerted to two of the biggest crimes of each century. Then, in 1971, it was the recordings of the amateur radio ham. This time it was the last gasp of a fatally wounded burglar alarm. Then, the police response was found wanting. This time, there was no police response at all.

Inside the vault, things were moving quickly. The gang had smashed past the second door and used an angle grinder to cut through the bars on the second security gate. Jones bent four bars upwards leaving enough room to get to the other side.

Within the confines of the basement rooms, the atmosphere was intense. Choking plumes of dust filled the corridors and got everywhere, in their eyes, ears, noses, hair.

Above them, the last pubs would be closing and most drinkers long gone. But there would be occasional passers-by and what about the residents in the flats above? Wood popped out through the courtyard and up the fire escape. He paused and listened. There was no one. Of course not, it was 10 minutes to one. Collins had their backs. It was now a race against time to get into the vault by morning. Almost half the night had gone already.

Collins had none of this adrenaline. It was well past his bedtime. He tried to focus on the two streets that he could see from his vantage point upstairs in number 25. The shorter of the two, Greville Street, ran off to the left, to The Argyle. The other, Hatton Garden itself, continued 300 metres north to the busy Clerkenwell Road, one of the main routes out of central London. It would be full of taxis and night buses heading east, taking people home at the end of a night out. Home to bed. Collins closed his eyes, battling against sleep. He lost.

Collins was sleeping like a baby when Kelvin Stockwell arrived at Hatton Garden at 1.15am. Stockwell later described what he did next: "I got out of the car, went to the front of the building. I pushed through the doors, they was secure.

"I went round to Greville Street and I looked through the letterbox. All I could see in there, the light was on, there was a metal box on the floor and a bicycle."

He then rang his boss. "He said he was about five minutes away in a car," recalled Stockwell. "I told him the place was secure and he said you might as well go home."

While Collins slumbered, the rest of the gang worked on tirelessly, with no inkling of how closely they had just courted disaster. Modern technology had very nearly proved their undoing. Collins wasn't helping things either. Both were recurring themes that would come back to haunt them.

For now, everybody was concentrating on just two things – the drilling and the clock ticking.

In time, three perfect 18-inch columns of concrete lay on the floor of the corridor outside the vault. One full moon and two crescents. The German machine and its Korean diamonds had ground out an irregular hole in this London wall, 25cm high by 45cm wide. It was exactly as they had practised. Basil and Reader would fit through, Jones and Wood, too, with a bit of luck. Portly Perkins would have no chance. But he could keep watch outside.

Shining a torch through the hole, Reader could see the metal backs of the safe-deposit boxes on the other side. Finally, their prize was within touching distance. They were sitting on heavy metal shelving racks. They would have to be shifted.

Jones carried the piece of equipment he had bought along for this precise moment – a 10-tonne pump and hose. This hand-operated hydraulic pump cost less than £100 and had a number of uses. It was capable of exerting immense push pressure. Most commonly, it was used to reshape battered metal car chassis and body panels. But the gang had found a novel use for the red portable pump. It was to be used to help pull off the crime of the decade.

The ram was not long enough to reach from the back wall of the corridor, through the hole in the vault wall to the shelving beyond. That's where the metal joists came in. The gang placed one steel acrow prop, normally used by builders to support masonry, up against the shelving rack and placed the pump between the other end of the pole and the wall of the corridor. Slowly the pressure was increased as the steel pole began to push against the shelving.

The men were tired and tempers began to fray. Carl Wood was walking round in circles, increasingly agitated. Jones, who had convinced the others this would work, lashed out at him. "Carl, do something for fuck sake," he said.

It was no use. With a wrenching crack, the base of the pump shattered. It is a known problem that with this type of pump it had to be kept entirely straight. But that was no comfort.

The gang were as deflated as the pump itself. There was nothing to do. The air was blue with cursing.

Jones led the team out into the courtyard and up the fire escape stairs, carrying two holdalls. The rest carried up more tools and piled them up in the corridor outside the exit to Greville Street. Reader and Perkins could barely find the energy to make it up the stairs. It was 8am. The clocks had gone forward to British Summer Time the previous Sunday. A week ago they would have been hidden in the half-light. Now they stood bathed in daylight and they didn't half look a sight. Bloodshot eyes, hair caked with dust. They were more *Walking Dead* than *Sexy Beast*.

Collins emerged from number 25 looking like Marilyn Monroe in comparison. It had been a long night but he'd grabbed 40 winks. Not that he felt much better for it. The bad news had been relayed to him by walkie-talkie. They were heading home empty-handed.

Collins walked round the block to the van in St Cross Street and drove it back round to Greville Street. Reader, Perkins, Jones and Wood piled in the tools in near silence. Only when the van pulled off did they begin recounting the events of the previous 11 hours with a string of accompanying expletives.

Basil, meanwhile, had slipped out the front, bolting the doors behind him. He left the fire escape to Greville Street unlocked. If they came back for a second go — and this was by no means agreed — they could get off the street and out of sight of the neighbours quicker. Basil walked to his home less than a mile away.

The van dropped Reader with Collins at his house in Islington. Then it headed north to Wood's house in Cheshunt. Finally, it headed back south to Enfield, with Perkins and Jones.

While Reader began cleaning himself up, Collins turned on his phone and his first call was to Billy Lincoln. Lincoln was the brother of Collins' partner, Milly, and someone Collins felt he could trust. He hadn't mentioned this to the others but Lincoln was already on standby. If they hit the jackpot, Collins didn't want his share of the loot in his house for a second longer than needed. Lincoln would take care of it for him.

Lincoln had been a low-rent thief back in the day, with a string of convictions for attempted burglary, burglary and attempted theft between 1975 and 1985.

These days he was more of a wheeler-dealer and was known as "Billy the Fish" because of his weekly visits to East London's Billingsgate market, where he would buy haddock, kippers, eels and salmon to sell on to family and friends.

He wasn't in the best of health. He had a hip replacement, a knee operation, another on his achilles. His arthritis was playing him up, as he told anyone who would listen, and don't get him started on his bladder. But he had still managed to pick up a conviction for battery in 2013. He had attacked a gang of youths with a chair because they were causing trouble on his street in Bethnal Green.

That Good Friday morning, Lincoln had already been driving around the area of Collins' house in the early hours. But, as the hours ticked by, he had gone home. The phone call from Collins lasted all of ten seconds before Lincoln was back in his car and heading to Islington.

When Reader came downstairs from his shower, Lincoln was there and Collins had told him everything. That was the last straw. Reader was already minded not to go back. He borrowed Collins' phone and rang home to his son, Paul.

At least Lincoln would be good for something. Instead of heading back home with a boot full of stolen booty, Lincoln drove into the City of London with a dejected Brian Reader on the passenger seat beside him.

They passed through the district's shining office blocks, largely deserted on that religious holiday. This part of London had changed beyond recognition since Reader's early days with Bill Barrett, plotting in the Chop House.

Lincoln drove in silence under the long shadows cast by the futuristic 180m-high rocket-shaped building at 30 St Mary Axe, better known as The Gherkin. It was one of a small forest of skyscrapers flung up during the boom years of the early 2000s when the sky was the limit. The Chancellor of the Exchequer had told the country there would be no more boom and bust. Bloody idiots. Reader had seen enough booms and busts in his own career to know there was always a crash coming.

So was this what retirement felt like? There was going to be no fanfare, no party, no carriage clock or gold watch. The Audi purred over London Bridge. The rising tide was performing London's twice daily enema. Reader looked down the muddy strip of water to the distant silhouette of Tower Bridge. Always a reassuring sight.

It was just before 11.30am when Lincoln pulled over outside London Bridge Station. Reader crossed the road and swiped his way into the London Underground with his Freedom Pass. He wasn't going to risk his freedom on this one.

But others weren't going to let it go so easily. That afternoon, Jones called Wood at home in Cheshunt. They were so close to a payday they had always dreamt of. All that stood between them and a place in criminal folklore was that bloody shelf.

Negotiations continued through to the following Saturday morning. Jones again called Wood. Perkins visited Jones at home in Enfield. At some point, one of the gang must have spoken to Basil face-to-face and persuaded him to give it one more go. None of them had a phone number for him but Collins, Perkins and Jones all knew where he lived in Islington. Without Basil's keys and knowledge it would be hard to go on. Unlike Reader, he was unaware that Collins had already blabbed to others about the plot, so the youngest gang member decided to stick with it. Basil may have thought better of it if he had spoken to his mentor before making the call.

They would need fresh tools. After phoning a branch of hardware shop Machine Mart from his landline that afternoon, Collins drove Jones to Twickenham, the home of English rugby in London's leafy western suburbs. Jones went into the shop while Collins kept the car idling outside. He bought a replacement Clarke pump and hose, giving his home address and the name V Jones – which was either the name his other half Valerie would have had if they had married or a tribute to the football hardman turned actor Vinnie. Vinnie would be perfectly cast as Jones if they ever made a film out of this job.

Jones called Perkins and Wood. It was back on.

At 8pm that night, Lionel Wiffen returned to Hatton Garden with his wife. An electrician was due to visit the next day and he wanted to make sure the office was ready. When he arrived at the fire exit on Greville Street, he was shocked to find it unlocked and ajar. He later explained: "It has never been open. I crept upstairs instead of downstairs, went up to look around to see if there was anyone around. I was very nervous to go in."

He checked the door from the courtyard into the basement. It was bolted from the inside as Basil had left it.

Reassured, Wiffen and his wife were inside the office for an hour, cleaning and rearranging the furniture. They left at 9pm and Wiffen locked the fire escape behind them.

A quarter of an hour later, Jones and Wood left Bletsoe Walk, Islington, in the Mercedes with Collins behind the wheel. Ten minutes after that, it crossed Hatton Garden and stopped on Leather Lane. They walked up Greville Street to the front door, checked all was clear and returned to the Mercedes. Back to Islington again.

Shortly after 10 o'clock, the remaining gang members were back on the road and heading to Hatton Garden for one final time. The same routine. Jones and Wood loitered in Greville Street while Basil went through the front door. Wood then clocked the gate. It was locked.

This rattled all three of them. Who had locked the door? And when? What had they found inside? Was this a trap? Basil was already inside. They looked around. This time there was no one watching their backs. Wood freaked out most of all.

As Collins later put it: "His arsehole went and he thought we would never get in. I said, 'Give it another half hour. Fuck, we've done everything we can do. If we can't get in, we won't be able to get in, will we? It's simple, we won't be able to get in'."

Wood didn't give it half an hour. He walked away from the vault and the millions of pounds inside. Sure he needed the money. But he needed not to go to prison again even more. He could go to jail without getting a penny for his troubles. They all could. He never spoke to his mate Jones again.

Back in the corridor next to the vault, Jones immediately got to work with the new pump. A gang insider said they had spent the previous 36 hours thinking about how they were going to topple the steel shelving bolted to the wall. They needed to avoid cracking the hydraulic pump by using it at an angle as they had done previously. They decided to reverse the approach and put the pump directly against the shelf. The acrow prop was jammed against the wall of the corridor and the pump went between it and the shelving.

Perkins eyed the shelves: "I mean, they have got to be two-feet thick, ain't they?"

"More than that," replied Jones.

Basil and Wood were chipping in, pointing at possible weak points on the shelving. They took it in turns pumping very carefully now.

"Smash that up," urged Jones, impatiently.

They pulled a knob on the pump to release the pressure and shift the angle. The rack did not move.

"It ain't fucking come back," shouted Perkins, triumphantly. "We're in, we're in."

Jones started pumping again: "Get some more, get some more."

The pump was hissing under the strain. Jones was getting a headache. All of a sudden there was a crack.

Jones thought he had broken a second pump. But it was the screws holding the racks giving way. They were in.

They had spent years working towards this moment. It took a few seconds for the men to fully comprehend their achievement. A sudden rush of joy and relief washed over them. They were inside Aladdin's cave, packed to bursting with thousands of diamonds, hundreds of thousands of pounds in cash and a huge amount of gold. The physical and mental strain of the last 48 hours, entering the building, disabling the alarm and drilling through the wall had coiled their nerves tight. Slowly, the muscles in their shoulders began to loosen as they realised they had made it. They were in the vault.

But there were no whoops and shouts of joy. This was a professional outfit and instead they got to work efficiently and quietly. Ever eager, Jones was the first to squeeze himself through the hole while holding a torch as Basil and Perkins held his legs. It was now a race against time to open as many of the safety deposit boxes as possible before morning. Basil followed Jones through the hole and as he did so the fluorescent strip lights in the vault flickered on to reveal a room about 12-feet wide and 30-feet long. The ten foot high walls were encased with 999 shiny, steel safety-deposit boxes. Each was numbered and had two locks, one for the key of the owner and one for the box holder.

The two men immediately got to work, forcing open the boxes by smashing the doors using a crowbar.

They jemmied open 73 of the boxes, which they proceeded to ransack.

It was still dark at 5.45am when Jones emerged exhausted but elated into the courtyard. He carried the pump and climbed up the fire escape. Perkins was soon after him. The pair dragged the two bins up the wrought-iron stairs. They were weighed down with their new riches and this was no easy task.

Collins puffed his way down the stairs of 25 Hatton Garden and passed by the fire escape as he made his way down Greville Street and up Leather Lane to the van. He pulled up outside the side door.

Basil joined them after letting himself back out the front. They loaded the van and drove back east.

By 7.24am, the van was back at Collins' house. They were in the clear. Six minutes after that, Lionel Wiffen returned once again to Greville Street to let in the electrician, only to find the door open a second time. He could have stumbled upon the heist of the decade. But the gang were riding their luck. If ever there was a time to buy a lottery ticket, this was it. Except for the first time in a long time they didn't need to. They were minted.

Things began to turn nasty when it came to the cut-up. The gang insider said the normal practice was to separate stolen gear into roughly equal piles as soon as they got to a safe house. Each pile would be given a number and then the gang would draw lots out of a hat.

The members would then take their "whack" and hide it somewhere secure for a few months until it became safer to begin trying to find a market for it. During this time it was unwise to communicate with other gang members because the police would be watching. But Perkins and Jones weren't having any of it. When they began examining the jewels their expressions changed from smiles of joy to ones of lust and greed. Peering through their bifocals, they almost drooled over the cash, diamonds, rubies, sapphires, gold and silver.

It was now that the fault-line in the gang, which had always existed, began to fracture wide open. The hierarchy was split between Basil and Reader, the only true specialist burglars on the team, and the rest – who the insider described as "labourers". The two master thieves did not use violence, whereas Perkins and Jones had spent most of their lives as armed robbers. The insider said: "When they got back to Collins' house, him, Perkins and Jones took control. They said they didn't want to carve it up and go their separate ways there and then, like they should have. The three of them said to Basil: 'We're taking that,' and he hardly had anything. I warned him not to get involved with those people because that's what they'd do. Basil's never had a fight in his life, he's not that kind of person, and he was outnumbered. Brian wouldn't have stood for it. If he had been there he would have made them cut it up immediately and go their separate ways. If they'd done that they probably would have got away with it. Their greed has led to their downfall. I think it's crazy as they could have split the gear and then disappeared and not associated with each other for a while."

The source said the men had estimated they would get up to £600,000 each in cash alone. In reality it was half that. They split that up on the spot and each got around £80,000 in sterling with around another £10,000 in foreign currency. They also allowed Basil to take a lunch box-sized quantity of gold.

Collins was nervous about hiding his share of the stash and Lincoln was not happy about handling it either. Besides, he had a two-week holiday in Greece planned. Lincoln called his nephew Jon Harbinson, a licensed taxi driver from Benfleet, Essex. Lincoln decided not to explain to Harbinson what was in the bags. There was no need. But the younger man felt uncomfortable with it burning a hole in his garage.

The last bit of work is believed to have been completed by Terry Perkins. He got rid of the white van they had used. The gang insider said he had it cut up at a yard somewhere near Ponders End in north London. It has never been recovered.

CHAPTER 14

Diamond Geezers

It was 48 hours before their handiwork was discovered. Kelvin Stockwell and Ronald Kamara turned up for work as usual on Tuesday morning. They made their way down to the basement, where they were greeted with mayhem. Kelvin said: "I looked and there's a lock on that wooden door and that had been popped. There was a hole and I saw we had been burgled. On the floor was tools, cutting material. I could see the lights were on. On the second door the bars were lifted up. I went into the yard to get a signal and phoned the police. Fifteen, 20 minutes [later] they turned up. They looked through the door. We went inside. It was like a bomb had hit the place."

Once again, the trail of chaos Reader had initiated was a job for the Flying Squad. Detective Chief Inspector Paul Johnson said matter-of-factly: "It was a burglary in Hatton Garden. We knew it was going to be high-value. We decided straightaway that yes, we'd take it, get down there as soon as possible, assess it and we'd develop it from there. Within a few hours it became apparent it was a really serious crime and that it's definitely a job for us." He later explained that the Hatton Garden case was "not usually what the Flying Squad would take, per se", as the raiders weren't armed and no one was hurt. "But obviously there was the magnitude of it and the detail that the gang had gone to to get themselves in – clearly, we'd have to take it."

Talking to us some time later, Johnson said: "It stood out a mile as being unusual. In terms of the approach to it, the way they got in, the drilling. There was obviously loads and loads of planning in it and that stood out a mile and you don't see that very often. It was obviously someone who had done it before."

News of the raid soon spread. At 11.53am, diamond jeweller Thelma West was the first to reveal the news online when she tweeted: "Robbery at one of the biggest safe deposits in Hatton Garden over the Easter weekend. The loss is HUGE #diamonds."

Scotland Yard issued a statement: "At approximately 08.10hrs today, Tuesday, 7 April, police were called to a report of a burglary at a safety-deposit business at Hatton Garden, EC1. The Flying Squad is investigating and detectives are currently at the scene. It appears that heavy cutting equipment has been used to get into a vault at the address, and a number of safety-deposit boxes have been broken into. Enquiries are ongoing."

The media was all over the story. Sky News presenter Kay Burley tweeted to her 300,000 followers: "BREAKING: Police investigating robbery in Hatton Garden diamond quarter in London. Many safe deposit boxes raided over Easter."

The street outside the vault was filling up fast with anxious jewellers desperate for news. But box holders faced an agonising wait to find out if they were among the victims of what was soon being called "the biggest raid in UK history". It was rumoured that between 300 and 600 boxes could have been smashed open. Michael Miller, a jeweller from Knightsbridge, had kept £50,000 in his box, including a £3,200 watch he'd bought as a birthday present for his son. Friends of another jeweller with a half-cut aqua diamond worth £500,000 passed on the news that "he's terrified it has gone". One dealer said: "Some traders have been hit for millions. I have hundreds of thousands of pounds' worth of jewellery in there but I don't know if any's left." Mohammed Shah, a wholesaler of precious stones, spoke for them all: "Everybody wants to know what has been taken but the police are not telling us anything." To make matters worse, many of them were uninsured.

"I was sitting at home enjoying an afternoon cup of coffee, a piece of Passover cake, when I heard my children speaking of a big robbery," said a diamond dealer, who claimed he had more than £500,000 worth of diamonds in his box. "I didn't take notice because there are robberies all of the time. Then, after a half-hour, one of my children said, 'It's the Hatton Garden Safe Deposit.' I heard that and I've never felt anything like it. If you had said to me, 'Jump out of a 20-storey building onto a mattress in the street,' that's what you feel. Everything you worked for… gone!"

Another victim, Kjeld Jacobsen, said: "I have been through the door every single day, or certainly three or four times a week, for 45 years. My wife and I were sitting in the car and listening to the BBC. Just before 6.30, the last thing on the news was the fact that Hatton Garden Safe Deposit had been done and lots of the boxes had been opened. The Flying Squad phoned and said my box was opened and empty. It was quite a big part of my pension that was sitting in there, or had been sitting in there, which was now gone. I needed to see my box, which I did. Box 998, completely broken and empty. The biggest shock was to see the size of the actual hole. Honestly, only a very small, very slender person could get through that hole. It was tiny. I could only get my head and half my shoulders."

Detective Constable Jamie Day was the first Flying Squad officer on the scene. "This crime has been three years in the planning for them, but we have to hit the ground running," he said.

"Initially, I assessed from the doorway. Kelvin Stockwell, when he turned up, he walked in and forensically we didn't want to go in again. So from that doorway in the basement you can see into the premises and I could pretty much see – until forensication – all I needed to see.

"They had been broken in and there had been a

substantial attempt made in there. I could see the hole from the side profile, the drills were there and the heavy cutting equipment was there.

"We've got victims. A lot of these victims were going to be significantly financially affected."

By Wednesday morning, the newspapers were speculating that the burglars had made off with up to £60million, £100million or more. The headline in *The Sun* was "Tunnel Raiders in £200m Heist". Some were comparing the heist with the plot of *Sexy Beast*, the cult crime caper from 2000, in which Ben Kingsley's menacing gangster character Don Logan recruits Ray Winston's retired safe-cracker, Gal, for one last job – drilling into a bank's safe-deposit vault from a neighbouring swimming pool. As Ian McShane's crime boss character Teddy Bass put it: "Where there's a will, and there is a fucking will, there's a way – and there is a fucking way."

But *The Guardian*'s veteran crime writer Duncan Campbell hit the nail on the head: "As for the leisurely style of taking a long weekend to carry out the theft, the closest parallel is that of the Baker Street bank job of 1971, when a gang spent a weekend tunnelling their way into safe deposit boxes held in the vault of the local branch of Lloyds, with a lookout watching from a nearby roof-top and keeping in touch via a walkie-talkie."

Speculation about the identity of the gang soon began. The *Daily Express* suspected the gang were from Eastern

Europe and guessed their haul had already been smuggled out of the country. Campbell wrote: "Given the reputation that Eastern European criminals now have as jewel thieves, as a result of the 'Pink Panther' robberies carried out all over Europe over the past few years, supposedly by a gang of Serbs, no doubt attention will be focused eastwards now." Jason Coghlan, a former armed robber turned lawyer living on the Costa del Sol, was of the same view: "I would not be surprised if the men behind the raid were from Eastern Europe because that's where the best thieves are from these days. I would be equally unsurprised to find out that the loot had very quickly found its way out of the UK and into Europe for disbursement to more friendly places to wash hot gems and cash – which is very likely to be reinvested into the narcotics industry. That provides a pension for villains to live comfortably off for life rather than a potential headache hidden some place that it might be discovered." Everybody from former Serbian paramilitaries to Russian gangsters were in the frame.

To the real gang members, this was more than just a source of amusement. It was good news. The wider the police were casting their net, the better. Author Scott Andrew Selby discounted one of the most outlandish theories: "The Pink Panthers tend to use very fast, paramilitary violence. This seems impressive and well-planned. I think it will be local British criminals." But who? Nobody knew – but it didn't stop them taking a guess.

The Sun claimed that an unnamed black cockney known as the King of Diamonds was suspected to be on the run. It said the man, a "major-league bandit", who had stolen more than £50million in two raids on two London branches of Graff jewellers, was a serious suspect for the role of "draftsman". Former Flying Squad chief Barry Phillips said: "There are less than a handful of villains left knocking about who could have acted as the draftsman for this caper. It's inconceivable that it could have been carried out without an inside man and that makes it more likely it was a British gang, rather than foreign, because Hatton Garden is such a tight community. You've got your major firms to the north, south and east of London who might be able to assemble the required expertise. This was a very slick operation and the role of the draftsman was vital to get the detail exactly right. There simply aren't that many faces who could have done it."

There was even an outbreak of nostalgia, with *The Guardian* proclaiming the "Return of the Old-Fashioned Heist". One former armed robber from south London told the paper: "It's gone back to the old days, hasn't it? No one's been injured. No one's been shot. Everybody's happy because everybody's skint at the moment and they reckon – rightly or wrongly – that whoever's lost something can afford it."

The legend of the Hatton Garden gang was growing by the day. They were even credited with deliberately starting the electrical fire in Holborn to cover their tracks. Was this a ploy to knock out the alarm systems? Amid the breathless excitement was genuine admiration for the way they had pulled it off.

Local resident John Han, a data scientist living opposite the exit on Greville Street, said he'd heard drilling in the early hours of Good Friday. "We had been out for dinner that night for my girlfriend's birthday," he told the *Sunday Times*. "We did hear what sounded like drilling in the middle of the night but went back to sleep. I did think at the time, who the hell does drilling at this hour?" They assumed it was connected to the power cuts of the previous week.

The Met released a statement about the midnight alarm call and their failure to attend. How did that not stop the burglars in their tracks? Security man Kelvin Stockwell told local jeweller Norman Bean all about his brief trip to Hatton Garden in the early hours of Friday morning. "I went down the stairs and looked through the windows but I couldn't see anything," said Kelvin. "Why didn't you open up and have a look in?" asked Norman, the question many more would ask. Kevin shrugged and apparently replied: "I don't get paid enough."

But, once again, it was the police who got the most stick. It was like 1971 and Baker Street all over again. Scotland Yard had to admit they knew the alarm had been activated but failed to attend. "It is potentially extremely embarrassing," said the former operational head of the Flying Squad, Barry Phillips. "If they had reacted, they could have walked in to the villains doing the dirty deed." It was up to the Flying Squad to salvage the Met's battered reputation. As always with a big job, they felt the weight of history on their shoulders.

"The Sweeney?" DCI Paul Johnson told *Vanity Fair* magazine. "It has moved on. It has to move on. We haven't got a Granada or Cortina. But it's the same commitment to getting results. You've got this legacy over the years: Brink's-Mat, Millennium Dome, Graff, the Great Train Robbery from years ago. You want to make sure you perpetuate that legacy… There's a pride. We all like to wear our ties with the eagle."

Barry Phillips explained: "The Flying Squad logo of the sweeping eagle depicts 'silently they come, swiftly they go, picking off their prey and taking them off'. The Flying Squad operates against the most violent criminals that London has. They build up a reputation over many years. There isn't a major robbery that hasn't been solved by the Flying Squad."

Their forensic search of the vault yielded nothing. The copy of Forensics For Dummies that Danny Jones kept at home had come in handy. The gang had used bleach to clean up the crime scene and had worn gloves throughout. But these criminals had all cut their teeth in the 1950s, 60s and 70s. The world had moved on and so had most criminals. For good reason. The modern world contained many an elephant trap for those artists of the criminal world, the high-end burglar.

The first public breakthrough came five days after the burglary. Police had soon found that the hard drives containing the CCTV footage had been swiped. DC Day said: "The building manager was quickly able to establish there was no CCTV. He said, 'I can't see any recordings on there,' but it was immediately apparent the hard drive had been taken out of the CCTV." More proof that this was a skilled and specialist operation.

But Reader and Basil didn't realise that one camera was on a separate system. It was placed inside the fire exit passageway to Greville Street and was owned by a jewellery business called Berganza. They had trained the camera to watch over the back door to their premises. The system was triggered by movement and it had captured the comings and goings of the gang.

In a "World Exclusive", the *Daily Mirror* obtained the footage and splashed it on the front page: "The £60million Gems Heist Caught on CCTV." Reporter Russell Myers and photographer Ian Vogler had trawled through 120 hours of footage to identify six members of the gang and revealed they made two separate visits to the vault. Basil – renamed Mr Ginger – was spotted first "keeping his head down, obscuring his face from the camera". Next was "the Gent", as the *Mirror* dubbed Brian Reader, "wearing dark trousers tucked into his stripy socks

revealing a pair of smart brown shoes". Mr Strong, aka
Carl Wood, and Mr Montana – as Jones was named after
the logo on his top – were seen dragging the wheelie bins
into the building. On Sunday morning, The Old Man was
seen to "struggle to move a bin but managed to drag it
outside. The Old Man leant on the bin, struggling for
breath, as he revealed a clear shot of the side of his face."
The Old Man was Terry Perkins, a full eight years
younger than Reader.

Hours after the *Mirror* team had secured their scoop,
the Flying Squad got their hands on the same footage.
Day insists he had seen it within 24 hours of the crime
being discovered. He said: "I knew on that first day they
had come and gone twice. The difficulty was it was stored
remotely. There was no facility in there to do anything
with that footage other than burn onto a CD. I knew what
was there and then tried to speak to the owner to establish
how to download it."

Angry that the *Mirror* had got the footage first and
desperate to appear on the front foot, Scotland Yard
rushed out their own CCTV images and an appeal for
information. They only identified three burglars but they
had a better idea who they were up against.

Day said: "A lot of effort had gone into disguising faces
in that corridor. They obviously knew that camera was
there."

The burglars also missed a second CCTV camera. It
was on the second floor, owned by an independent

company, Premises 21, and it captured the moment when Basil and Jones disabled the lift.

The gang was worried the game was up and it might soon be all over. A source says that it was around this time that Basil disappeared. He was the most surveillance-conscious of the group and he became suspicious at around this time that officers were watching him. The gang insider said he does not believe claims made as late as July 2016 by the Flying Squad that they had no idea who Basil was. He said: "They know who he is and are waiting for him to come back. But I don't think they'll have much on him."

As the days passed, the gangs' names did not feature in news bulletins and the police cars they expected did not appear outside their front doors. They began to relax and once again revel in their exploits.

The rumour mill got back to work. *The Sun* reported that "Britain's most notorious crime family were hit by the Hatton Garden raiders". Underworld sources claimed the Adams family were among the victims. "The family are very well-connected in Hatton Garden," said the source. "Traditionally, firms have been wary about doing any work there because of the Adams' reputation and the fact it is their 'manor'. The word is they had gear stored at the deposit centre and have lost a fortune. They are not happy."

Former bank robber Noel "Razor" Smith told the *Mirror* after watching the CCTV footage: "They will be a crew made up of foreign nationals, likely Eastern Europeans and Israelis, who have never met and are together for this one job." *The Times* reported that the Hatton Garden heist was "inspired" by a book, the 1992 thriller *The Black Echo* by crime novelist Michael Connelly. Criminologist Richard Hoskins told the paper: "It is so similar it's extraordinary. It gets you thinking – did the thieves read the book?"

Days later, *The Times* was claiming the gang could have been behind a similar raid in Berlin two years previously. That burglary had the hallmarks of a Reader special – the criminals disguised themselves as construction workers and spent weeks digging a tunnel from a rented parking space to the vault owned by Volksbank. They then drilled through 80cm of reinforced concrete to ransack 294 safety deposit boxes and steal £8.3million in gold, silver and diamonds.

The *Daily Express* went one stage further by asking "Did £35m gems gang use a contortionist?" They reported a "theory that they copied a tactic from the movie *Ocean's Eleven*", in which "a 5ft acrobat called the Amazing Yen – played by Shaobo Qin – has a key role in a raid in the 2001 film, starring George Clooney and Brad Pitt".

The country was gripped. As the *Daily Mail* put it: "Not since Michael Caine uttered the immortal line, 'You're only supposed to blow the bloody doors off!' in the 1969 movie *The Italian Job* has a crime of this nature captured the public imagination."

Most of the blame, rightly or wrongly, was piled on the shoulders of the police. Why had they ignored the alarm? Some speculated that the burglars could have deliberately triggered false alarms to put off the police. *The Times* reported that after three false alarms, police were no longer required to attend. So could 88-90 Hatton Garden have been placed on a blacklist? The police hit back, briefing *The Times* that alarm calls had been "degraded" for years. Officers would rarely venture out unless a witness had seen suspects at work.

Former police officer Nigel Tillyard, who used to patrol Hatton Garden in the 1970s, was not impressed with this modern-day policing. "During the day, it was very busy with the hustle and bustle of a diamond market," he wrote in a letter to the *Daily Mail*. "However, at weekends and night it was a boring beat as it was deserted, but still had to be patrolled. In those days, we checked the front and rear of the premises as well as door handles as we were all aware of the repercussions should there be a break-in. If an alarm went off there would be an instant response by the beat officer and the station area car.

"With regard to the recent safe-deposit boxes robbery, the reports of an alarm being sounded, especially as it appears to be a Central station one and not being responded to by police is very worrying. If true, heads should roll ... people will lose their businesses and other valuables and it will mean a continued lack of faith in the police."

Two weeks after the raid, vault owner Mahendra
Bavishi broke his silence. He said: "To many, this robbery
is like something out of a Hollywood fiction film but to my
family it is a tragedy. It is the end of the business my son
has worked so hard to build slowly over the last seven
years. It was making a loss when he bought it and only
first made a profit last year and, even then, it was very
little. Now the business is finished. Who will trust their
valuables with us after this?" He saved much of his anger
for the police. "It is incredible that the police did not act
on this," he said. "The police knew in advance that it
would be closed over Easter so they must have realised
that nobody was meant to be in the vaults." It was the
final straw for the Bavishi family. They cut their losses and
put the firm into liquidation, the final victims of the
Hatton Garden burglary.

Meanwhile, around 25 of the 40 box holders met in
Hatton Garden to discuss their next moves. They were
told their chances of recovering their stolen items were
very slim and advised to form a committee and hire a
lawyer. Loss adjuster Rick Marchant at Marchant and
Marchant Limited was advising seven clients. One dealer
lost diamonds worth £1.3million. A pawnbroker in his late
50s had placed jewellery, watches, silverware and pens in
his deposit box. They were being held as security against
around £200,000 in loans. He would now not be able to
recover the loans. Mr Marchant told the BBC: "They
have had friends and colleagues who work in the quarter

with them, grown men, hardened dealers, in sobs, they don't know what to do because of course some haven't insured at all. These aren't extremely wealthy people, for a lot of them their livelihoods are gone. All of us might be forgiven for thinking how audacious, how clever, but what they have done is ruin the lives of many people within the Hatton Garden jewellery quarter."

On the evening of Thursday, April 23, three weeks almost to the hour after the gang began to make their way to Hatton Garden, the Flying Squad again appealed to the nation for help. They released the iconic images of the three holes Jones drilled through the wall showing the chaos left inside the ransacked vault. Detective Superintendent Craig Turner revealed that his officers had been studying thousands of hours of CCTV footage seized from the streets around Hatton Garden. "We have now completed our forensic examination of the scene. The hours of forensic work and inquiries have been vital in order to ensure we are able to exploit all investigative opportunities to their fullest extent and assist us in identifying those individuals responsible. We appreciate that this situation has been frustrating for those affected by this crime and thank those individuals for their ongoing patience and support."

DS Turner offered a £20,000 reward for information leading to the arrest and conviction of the gang. He said: "This was a particularly ambitious burglary... and has affected so many victims. We may well be misled – this is carried out by an almost *Ocean's Eleven*-type team – but in essence there are victims behind this and these are callous thieves. We are keen to hear from wives or partners of anyone who has specialist knowledge or skills that use this sort of equipment. Were they away during the Easter bank holiday weekend or have they been acting oddly since the burglary was carried out?" The Met also announced it had launched an internal investigation into why it failed to respond to the alarm. It said in a statement: "It is too early to say if the handling of the call would have had an impact on the outcome of the incident."

But it was what they did not reveal that was much more significant. "You want to keep all the cards close to your chest," Johnson later explained. The Flying Squad had set up a field office in Putney, southwest London, and 100 officers were to work on the case. The pride of the Met was once again at stake.

One of the first jobs was to hoover up all available CCTV from shops, offices and local councils before it began to be deleted or copied over. Depending on how far these burglars had travelled to carry out the job, this could mean trawling a vast area. Officers paced the streets and amassed evidence from 120 cameras. One of the younger officers in the team made the first vital spot – Kenny Collins' white Mercedes E200 with the black roof and alloy rims caught his eye. It had arrived at Hatton Garden shortly after 9pm on the Saturday night and left soon afterwards. Police were able to trace the distinctive car on the two-mile journey back. It passed through an Automatic Number Plate Recognition – or ANPR camera – on Clerkenwell Road at 9.35pm. Next it was spotted by another ANPR camera on City Road at 9.40pm, more than half-way home. Finally, it was seen on CCTV in Cropley Street, round the corner from Collins' home. The journey had ended nearby.

It wasn't long before Collins' name cropped up. He'd made little attempt to hide it. His name was on the deeds of the former council house he'd bought with his ex-wife Sheila in 1999. His criminal record showed he was an experienced criminal, if a little rusty. He'd been caught for a string of robberies in the 1960s and 70s. He was clearly a person of interest. Once again, Collins was proving a liability.

Hopes were rising at the Flying Squad that this was not a wild-goose chase. "That gave us a breakthrough," said DC Jamie Day, "because it led the CCTV officers to identify that on the second night they'd arrived in a Mercedes earlier. Because Collins was using his own vehicle, it was a Mercedes E200, very distinctive and very few of them on the road. Had a black roof, black wheels, and so even the grainy CCTV, which probably normally wouldn't be of a high evidential value, identified it and we were able to track that car."

But Day and his team are unwilling to discuss how much help they got from underworld informants. It is unlikely that it was purely CCTV that led the Flying Squad to Reader and his team. Regulations introduced to try to put a stop to the abuse of the supergrass system has made it harder for today's detectives to forge close relationships with villains. However, obtaining information from criminals remains an essential element of modern law enforcement and most successful villains have channels into the police. A gang insider said he suspected at least one person, who was close to one of the raiders, had passed information to the police.

Day's team found that the Mercedes had gone to Twickenham on the Saturday and parked outside the tool shops. Then it had gone home via the vicinity of Danny Jones' house in Enfield. The cracks in Reader's brilliantly planned job were beginning to show. They were not of his making and he was powerless to stop them.

Day told us: "The people who are very good at it are the ones who have never been caught. The longer you are in a crime scene the higher the level of risk of being caught and so I think they had considered every eventuality to overcome that.

"They did do a good job because they got in and got a load of stuff. But when they came up against something as in the cabinet not going over… if they had walked away we would probably have been in a difficult position."

Reader's gut instinct was proved right – walk away, don't get caught, there will be always be another opportunity. But the rest of the gang did not heed him.

Johnson said: "That was their vulnerability because at that point it was no longer an organised plan and they were making it up on the hoof, so they made mistakes."

Day agreed: "However much planning went into it, whether it was three years, 10 years, they have gone from that organised planning to cobbling things together on the Saturday afternoon."

"In a panic," added Johnson.

"If they were 100 per cent they would have said, 'That's it, another day,'"said Day.

Their boss, DS Turner, said: "They didn't have a contingency plan. There was a lot made at the time about the quote 'analogue criminals in a digital age' and there was a lot to be said for that comment because that's where they slipped up."

Johnson was delighted: "They've planned for three years, they've not been able to get in. It's a big payday and they've just started to take risks. They've not thought through what they're doing next. All the imagery is quite murky, the CCTV team had to get all the angles on it. So it was piecing together the jigsaw of all the different angles you can get. When they went down initially they had the white van… That was a car that they bought months ago and wasn't attributable to anybody. So they could quite safely drive down there, drive away in that on the first night, because it's never going to raise any suspicion. If anybody checked on that van, it wouldn't mean anything to anybody. On the second time they come down, what they don't know is, 'Has that van been seen? Has the burglary been discovered? Has there been a report on that?' So they couldn't come down in that van. You wait until you've got something that is concrete and tangible and you know is a good start point – which is what the Mercedes and Collins were – and then you commit your resources down that line."

It was the week after the raid, when Collins – never the sharpest tool in the box – got a new shadow. "Surveillance teams," explained Day. "They follow people around on and off for about seven or eight weeks without being compromised and that's not an easy thing to do." Johnson added: "The whole thing about surveillance is you do as little as possible. Once they start looking over their shoulder, it gets to be hard work."

Collins was a marked man and it was contagious. He could now infect every gang member he met.

The gang's old drinking buddy Hugh Doyle was the first to catch it. On Thursday, April 16, they tailed Collins to Enfield, where he met Doyle for a drink in The Moon Under Water pub. Reader was next. On Friday, he caught the train into London. He got off at Farringdon Station and strolled five minutes to Scotti's. He sat at one of the two plastic tables outside and was joined by Collins. They were photographed by police.

It was another terrible error of Reader's failing judgement. He had decided to bail out of the job halfway through. Now he wanted some of what was rightfully his.

It meant taking risks. He should be keeping his head down in Dartford. Maybe he should take a little trip somewhere, just like the old days. But he had given Collins and the others a crack at the biggest job of their lives. Hatton Garden was way out of their league. They should have been begging him to get onto it. Now he was going to have to beg them for a cut of the action.

It took the Flying Squad a couple of weeks to identify Reader from his surveillance shots. Here, at last, was a man who undoubtedly possessed the almost unique skillset to set up a job like Hatton Garden. But there was the rest of the team to catch. It was a waiting game.

The following week, Collins called Terry Perkins on his mobile phone. It did not take the police long to figure out who he was. A few hours later the pair met Jones at Ye Olde Cherry Tree Pub in Southgate, before moving on to the nearby Highlands Angus Steakhouse. Four down and two to go.

Johnson said: "Brian Reader was one of the first but it took us a while to work out who he was… until a week or two before the arrests. Our focus was on Collins and anyone else we knew who was involved. You stick with Collins, you know it's him and then it builds out from there. Don't forget, when this is going on Collins is meeting loads of people and you don't know who is significant. As it develops, three start meeting and then the three become four."

"The group were coming together," said Day. "It was now a patience game on our part and that paid off when Kenny Collins, Terence Perkins and Brian Reader met on a Friday night in the Castle public house to discuss, we say, what had taken place."

It had been a good few weeks since the last Castle get-together. They were long overdue another and there would never be one quite like this. It was four weeks almost to the minute since the three of them had been sitting inside the van, putting on their hi-vis and getting ready for the job of their lives. They were now the most-wanted criminals in the country – and also, somehow, the most revered. The week before they had starred on TV as *Crimewatch* used CCTV footage to recreate their crime. There was nobody in that pub who knew what they had just achieved. If anybody could have listened in to the three old men in the corner, they might have heard another re-construction by one of only three people in the country who knew what really happened.

Perkins regaled Reader with a blow-by-blow account of the night he had missed. Collins, of course, had heard it all before and joined in. "Boom," went an excited Perkins with a wild gesticulation of his hand, to describe the moment Jones dislodged the shelving with the pump. He explained to Reader how they had reversed the pump – "wind everything around" – for the final heave. He told how Carl lost his bottle after Wiffen locked the gate: "You know the old chap... he walked in and he panicked." Who knows what a punter at the bar would have made of this. Not a lot, probably. But the hidden police camera captured the entire show.

Back in the Flying Squad office, a lip reader was brought in to make sense of it all. Shadows, partially hidden faces and the quality of the footage made it difficult. But there was enough. When Perkins went "boom", Johnson and Day must have thought the same. They had their men. Now they had to build the case against them. "They can meet people all day long," said Johnson. But this was not going to convict anyone. The evidence was mounting up – the cars, the phone calls, the CCTV footage, the meetings. It was enough to get authorisation for Scotland Yard's Specialist Crime & Operations 11 Surveillance Command team to plant listening devices on the suspects. These bugs are only used in the UK for the terrorism and top-level organised crime. With a grin, Johnson called them the "surveillance pixies". "It is a tactic that is used in serious crime investigations and can be quite productive," explained Day. "And obviously it was very productive on this occasion." Just two of the bugging devices have been admitted to – one was placed in Collins' beloved Mercedes and the other into Perkins' little Citroën. But these two little gizmos were enough to transport the Flying Squad right into the heart of the Hatton Garden gang.

CHAPTER 15

Thick as Thieves

Six weeks after the raid, on Friday, May 15, Terry Perkins' car —which had nicknamed Beeney — became a broadcast studio and he and Danny Jones began unwittingly transmitting their every utterance to police officers.

Through the rumble of the road and the crackle of the mic, Jones spoke first: "He got the cream there, fuck me, there's a lot of rings there, Tel."

"Is there? Any value?" asked Perkins.

"Two grand, two-and-a-half grand…" replied Jones.

"Sellable?"

"Sellable, yes," said Jones. "Few of those bracelet ones, then you got the necklace with the fucking big emeralds in it, with the matching earrings."

Minutes later, Perkins piped up with something that had been bugging him. "I've been thinking, you know, how the fuck has that Bill [Lincoln] got involved? Another two people know, Bill and the taxi driver… I was thinking, who told Bill?"

"Him and Brian," replied Jones – referring to Collins.

The pair had been plotting what to do with the stolen gold. The plan was to smelt it down. But where? Perkins' daughter, Terri, had a house near his in Enfield. He had treated her and her husband to a getaway in Portugal with the cash from the raid. The truth was, he wanted her house empty for a few days. "I don't want the taxi driver at my daughter's den, no way," he said.

"Bollocks," agreed Jones.

"No fucking way," insisted Perkins.

"Fucking bollocks," repeated Jones. "Tell you what, when we going to your daughter's? Tuesday?"

"Yes," replied Perkins.

"Tuesday morning…" pondered Jones. "When does she go, your daughter?"

"Sunday night."

"Sunday night, Sunday night," muttered Jones. "Well, I'll tell you what, Tel, I'll drop that, my one, I won't bring it round in the morning, I'll bring it round of a night, Monday night or something."

"I'll meet you Monday night," agreed Perkins.

"Sensible ain't it," said Jones, "then I ain't going there with nothing."

It became clear to the eavesdropping detectives that the pair were planning to reassemble some of the loot the very next week at Perkins' daughter's house in Sterling Road. They were even discussing their whack – and how much they hoped to end up with once Collins brought the rest over.

"I tell you what, he's got a heap of gear, you know," said Jones.

"Well, he's fucking got to have otherwise we got fucking 300 grand each," agreed Perkins.

"Well, I'll tell you something and all," went on Jones. "You don't realise what you got because there are hundreds and hundreds of rings, Tel, you know what I mean? There's loads of them."

"Well, I hope we get close to the mill, don't you?" asked Perkins.

"Yes so do I," agreed Jones.

"Fucking hell, he's got to have a lot more gold then," said Perkins.

"He's got a heap of gear, Tel," insisted Jones. "Play your cards right…"

They continued to discuss what they had and how to shift it.

"I don't know how you sell the fucking pieces of Indian," said Perkins, referring to Indian jewellery stolen from the vaults.

"Throw it in the fucking pot then," said Jones.

"We'll see what happens," said Perkins, "see what we do."

"He's got a heap of gear, Tel," said Jones, back onto Collins again. "He has, on my life, Tel. Remember, I only took half a bag with me, Tel… he was definitely banged out his bag."

"The stones, where did you put them?" asked Perkins.

"With them or over the cemetery?"

Perkins knew that Jones had hidden some of his whack up at Val's family plot at Edmonton Cemetery. Jones had no intention of sharing those with Collins.

"No, leave them over the cemetery," he breezed. "We will have them, they don't need... it's only a packet like that," he gestured with his hands. "Ain't it? We will say that that's our bit."

"Yeah, like a carat?" asked Perkins. "I never looked at them," admitted Jones. "No, no, we will have them," Perkins said with finality.

Police would soon find out where yet more of the gear was. Jones had stashed it in a haversack in the loft of his brother's house. He had booby-trapped it with wires so he knew if it had been tampered with – he was not taking any chances, not even with family – and nearly got caught by another relation.

"I was round my brother's," he told Perkins. "I'm in the fucking loft, he lets me go up the loft and turn the light on, I put the lid back down. Went to get up there, all of a sudden my nephew Paul come in with his girlfriend and is saying, 'What you got up there?...' I come back down and they had fucked off."

"Oh," grunted Perkins.

The pair started worrying about Collins next. How was he going to get his gear back off Jon Harbinson, Bill Lincoln's nephew?

"He wants the taxi to go somewhere," said Perkins.

"Well, it's down to him," said Jones. "We can't just change over in the streets in taxis – we will lose the gear. You've only got to have Old Bill drive past."

"He is a fucking idiot," agreed Perkins.

"He'll go with anyone so he ain't got to move the fucking gear himself," said Jones. "He doesn't even know the geezer where the gear has gone, that geezer could go zip… you've got to know people. You're never going to know if anything has been taken out of there."

"Not in a million years," agreed Perkins. "We could have lost two million pound."

The pair had seen a TV news report that a massive diamond had been stolen from the vault. They hadn't seen anything that big. "That geezer on the telly talking bollocks about 12 carat?" pondered Perkins.

"What happens if it is here," wondered Jones.

"Fucking exactly," Perkins agreed.

"Twelve-carat diamond, Tel."

"Fucking exactly."

"You ain't going to know, are you?" said Jones.

"No."

"I don't think Kenny [Collins] would take it out," said Jones. "He's been fucked 24-7 all his life."

"He's fucked every day of the fucking week," agreed Perkins.

They pondered where the bags were now. Who had ended up with them? What if they did contain a million-pound diamond?

"I'm not being funny, Tel, someone said to me, 'Look Dan, can you look after that?' Tel, I would," said Jones.

"It's human nature, ain't it," agreed Perkins. "I'm going to think, 'What am I going to do with that?' The soppy cunt gets a 12-mil stone and fucking go and sells it for 30 quid or something!"

But they were soon distracted by the sight of a woman they passed on the pavement.

"Look at her, Tel – the bird," said Jones pointing. "We could give her a ring, couldn't we," leered Perkins.

Jones laughed.

They were soon back to daydreaming about their new-found riches.

"I'm looking for a nice peach of a car – about two grand – to ride about," mused Perkins. "I'm going to give Beeney a rest cos if they see Beeney they know it's me. If I were outside your house in that, he'd know I was there."

It was a bit late for that. They were currently being tailed by surveillance officers in shifts and were broadcasting live to the Flying Squad. Not that they were paying any attention.

"See that bird there," said Perkins, pointing. "Randy Mandy is a bit better than her – but like her."

Jones claimed to have word from a relative with a police contact that detectives thought Hatton Garden was an inside job. That was good news, if only it had been true.

Perkins agreed. "That's a good thing cos if they think it's an inside job they will not put a hundred per cent into it, cos they'll think, 'You're mugging us off, you cunts. You want us running all around London when it's fucking from inside.'"

"He said all them are thinking, 'It's one of our own,'" repeated Jones. "That's what's going around. Do you know what's fucked them up and all?"

"What?"

"Just opening 70 boxes," said Jones.

"I know."

"They cannot work it out."

"No, they can't work that out," agreed Perkins. "That is the biggest robbery that could have ever, ever been."

"Yeah."

"That will never ever happen again," said Perkins.

"No."

"The biggest robbery in the fucking world, Dan, we was on," went on Perkins, warming to his theme, "and that cunt…"

"Yeah."

"The whole fucking 12 years I've been with him… three, four bits of work… fucked every one of them," said Perkins bitterly.

"And he would have fucked this if we walked away with him," added Jones.

"Course we would have," agreed Perkins.

"If we didn't say, 'Oh, come on, we will have another

go," said Jones.

"Yeah, we would have been absolutely fucked," said Perkins. "I would have… fucking hell…"

"I would have probably gone back to fucking low-life screwing and got nicked," admitted Jones.

"Well, I would have been with you," agreed Perkins. "Any fucking thing would do me. At least what I've done, I've paid for my daughter's holiday, I've made sure they are all right, with their holidays and what not. Not all that I wanted to give 'em, but let's see what we got. Once we chop it up, we will have half a clue. You can't plan on doing anything until you know what you got, can you?"

They drove on through the city, the radio tuned to Smooth FM.

Jones broke the silence. "He must be cursing himself, that cunt."

"Who?"

"That Carl [Wood]."

"He must be thinking of committing suicide," said Perkins.

"I'm trying to put myself in his mind," said Jones. "Forget about everything – I'm him. The bloke would be sitting at the airport. I bet he is boozing now, smoking that shit now. Unless he has seen the light."

"I would not know what to do, Dan, now, if I were him," said Perkins. "I would not know what to do. I would be the horriblest cunt in the world to live with."

"I'd be absolutely devastated, I would," agreed Jones.

Perkins' thoughts turned to Reader and they made his blood boil. After all those months of work, he abandoned them. He was sitting on a goldmine with that housing development in his garden.

"This cunt," he said. "I wouldn't feel so bad because I would think, 'Fuck it, I got four-hundred grand in six months' time.' You know what I mean? You got a back-up. That's why he would never come back, the cunt. He's got his 400 grand in six months' time… I'd have spent 12 years with the cunt and I'd have [been] living indoors on a pension."

"He had a backup," agreed Jones.

"A backup! I can't get over him, the cunt. He's done me out of fucking money."

"Everything he has done, he's the master criminal," said Jones.

This wound up Perkins even more. "Please God," he began. "I have to say that, in my opinion, that… to be true… he's a cunt. He might have been years ago, but he's no value in my fucking eyes."

"Everything he has done has fucked up," piped Jones, knowing he was back on safer ground. He knew Perkins liked to blame Reader when jobs went wrong, as they sometimes did.

"He's fucked bits of work up," continued Jones.

"Think of the three bits of work," said Perkins. "Put them together."

"Million-and-a-half pound?" suggested Jones.

"You can't put a price on it," said Perkins.

He hated to admit it, but they could have stolen even more from the vault if only Brian had stuck with it. He knew more about breaking into safe-deposit boxes than the rest of them put together. His gang has smashed through nearly 300 of the bloody things in Baker Street. Jones and Basil had barely got into 70 and nearly half of them were empty. It was embarrassing.

"Tel, but you'd never got the gear out," said Jones. "The van was too small, for one."

Brian would have left even less room in the van. It was a squeeze as it was. They should have gone for the truck, as Perkins had been arguing. "He would not have it about the open back truck, would he?"

"No," agreed Jones. "Fantastic… all of it on… all in your fucking bags."

"Yes, 50 bags."

"Plus the dust bins," added Jones. "Fifty bags, oh my good god."

They chewed over that thought.

"It don't matter now though, Tel," said Jones. They had what they had and planned to make the most of it.

"To be truthful, Dan, I want every tenner I can get. That's the fucking truth."

"Anything big, Tel, we leave in the pot."

"Yes," agreed Perkins. "I'll take it to Frank. Not all at once and I hope we get a decent fix for this, that we agree. I'm seeing him tomorrow afternoon."

"Oh, are you?" said Jones.

"Saturday, yeah. The reason I'm seeing him tomorrow afternoon is that I've got to take my little granddaughter to her dancing-acting class."

Finally, he'd be able to look after her financially. He thought about Jones and his son.

"I bet he's a bit quiet now, ain't he now?" he asked Jones.

"Oh, very quiet, he got all that going on…"

"I bet he is a bit more respectful now," Perkins went on. "He thought I was past it, that will show him who is past it."

"Fuck no," said Jones.

"They are wrong," said Perkins. "They got to swallow their words, ain't they. Swallow their words now."

"Tell you what," said Jones, changing subject. "I wonder what he would do now, Basil?"

"Think of what he has got at the moment, right," said Perkins. "He's got that gold, some of that gold."

"Yeah."

'I don't know what it comes to," said Perkins.

"Three-hundred on the floor, Kenny said," replied Jones.

"And he's got 70, weren't it?" added Perkins. "Just forget that he's got nothing else but that – how long's that going to last him?"

"Forever, Tel," answered Jones. "That will last him right through. He goes for the cheapest gaffs."

"That foreign money he fucking won will probably last him 10 years," added Perkins.

"Do you know what, I don't want to be paranoid or nothing, but you know all those fifty-pound notes, they were all new, weren't they, Tel?"

"Yeah, they looked new," said Perkins. "I found them."

"Brand new."

"Did that come out of one box," wondered Perkins.

"Yeah," said Jones, smirking. "I'll tell you what he lost shall I? £1.6million worth of gold he lost, plus £70,000 in notes. He's lost a chunk, that cunt there."

"I feel a bit sorry, don't you?" asked Perkins, in a rare display of sympathy for his victims.

"Give it back to him," laughed Jones. "They are all getting together now to sue the police. I'll tell you what, it's left a mystery, that bit of work. There's 70 boxes. They'll think straightaway, 'They have gone in there for one thing only.' I would."

"Yeah," said Perkins.

"I'd say," Jones went on, "you got blackmail paperwork there on someone high profile, or there was something like… fucking… a mental bit of of jewellery there. You would have found it, if you would have done it all."

"Oh, you would have done," agreed Perkins.

"It would have been the biggest headache ever in your life, Tel," said Jones, trying to convince himself it was lucky they hadn't found it. "Yeah, you would have to move away and take drugs or something, to get back to normality."

"You would have," agreed Perkins.

They were listening to the radio but heard another sound – a siren.

"And there's the police again, they keep pulling people," said Perkins. "The fucking Old Bill."

Jones recalled something a young family member had told him. "I said, 'What is it?' He said, 'Fit it in your car… it's a little black box… it will go bip bip bip .. Old Bill 20 feet away from you, plain clothes… anything. They use Tetra radio."

"Fuck me." Perkins liked the sound of that.

"So if they come on you within half-a-mile, that goes bip bip bip… as soon as they get closer, it gets louder and louder," explained Jones. "It's a good tool, ain't it?"

Who would have thought it? Here they were, two of the most wanted criminals in Western Europe, driving through Enfield in a Citroen Saxo. Jones looked at the man in the driving seat, enviously. Thanks to this one job, they had all moved up through the criminal hierarchy. But Perkins would always be several rungs above him.

"Just think, in your lifetime, Tel, you have seen enough money… fucking hell!"

Perkins smiled. "Six-million pounds out of there, fuck me," he said, recalling what they found in that Security Express depot back in 1983. It seemed like a lifetime ago. Now, thanks to this, he wasn't just a one-hit wonder.

"The biggest cash robbery in history at the time, and

now the biggest [in the] history in the fucking world, that's what they are saying," said Jones. "And if you listen to the Master, you walk away."

"And what are the odds, what fucking odds?" said Perkins.

"What a book you could write, fucking hell?" said Jones.

Would anyone believe it, though? At their age?

"And I know I thought I am fucking different," said Perkins. "Sixty-seven. Fucking 20 pills a day. Think of it – three injections. I had it all with me, my injections."

"You never," said Jones, looking over at the man nine years his senior. He probably hoped he would be in better shape in nine years' time.

"Course," said Perkins. "I had to take them in there for three days."

"And you've got Carl, who's been on massive bits of work, screaming like a fucking pig," said Jones. His mate had embarrassed him.

"Yeah, if I don't take the insulin for three days," Perkins went on, ignoring him, "you'da had to carry me out in a wheelie bin!"

As Terry Perkins and Danny Jones drove around London, slating their so-called friends and colleagues, it was Collins' turn for some criticism next.

"Ken, you only sat up the fucking room and fell asleep," exclaimed Jones. "You never done no graft, you were invited on it."

The idea that Collins was getting an equal share for falling asleep still rankled with him.

"You guarantee Kenny has told them all about it, every mortal thing," added Perkins, thinking again about Lincoln and Harbinson. An unnecessary risk.

"Don't matter now," Jones tried to reassure him.

"No," agreed Perkins. "Anyone who grassed me like that, you know what I would say… 'He was with us.'"

"Yes," said Jones.

"He was fucking with us," continued Perkins. "I'd say, 'You want to grass us, to be in nick, come on, you can be on the food boat, you cunt.'"

The afternoon wore on, yet the pair couldn't help themselves. Their thoughts drifted back to that weekend in the vault.

"When you think about it, we must have been crackers," said Perkins. "We got to be stone crackers."

"Well, Brian must have thought so," admitted Jones, "and Carl. They went didn't they? I thought, 'You saucy cunt.'"

They discussed giving Carl Wood some money, even though he was a "fucking yellow cunt".

Back at Flying Squad HQ, Detective Constable Jamie Day "spent hours and hours" transcribing these ramblings.

To anyone else, it would have sounded like the random

rantings of a pair of old geezers long past their glory days. Out-takes, maybe, of a Danny Dyer movie that ended up on a cutting-room floor, or a bad episode of Minder. A few decades earlier, Perkins and Jones could have been the inspiration for Peter Cook and Dudley Moore's x-rated Derek and Clive sketches. Everyone, it appeared, was a "cunt", apart from Perkins and Jones themselves. And some poor so-and-so now had to put in the time to unravel their London dialect and slang. A lawyer, with his tongue half in his cheek, would later compare the labour put into deciphering their conversations to the work done over the centuries by Shakespearean scholars. But it was worth it. As DCI Paul Johnson put it, "For all of us, it was obviously a gold mine of evidence and information as to what they were up to."

Perkins and Jones might as well have signed confessions. But Reader – the "master" as they called him – was only implicated thanks to these two. Johnson needed something that would stand up in court. Although it has never been confirmed, sources have claimed that Reader was bugged too. He did not have a vehicle and so listening devices are likely to have been planted in his house and garden. But nothing of evidential value ever came from them. Was that down to Reader's savvy and natural sense of self-preservation? Or did he have no one to brag to and little to brag about? Either way, the police needed to keep building their case.

It was a Friday so, as per usual, they ended up in The Castle pub in Islington. Collins drove them there, where they met Reader. After a few drinks and dinner at the Delhi Grill in nearby Chapel Market, Collins dropped Reader at Angel Tube Station. Next, he deposited Perkins and Jones where they had parked Perkins' Saxo. Shortly after 10pm, the pair were heading north to Enfield and chewed over the evening's conversation. The fallout from the job and the quarrelling over the loot was continuing. If anything it was getting worse.

Collins could "go and fuck himself". He'd have to get the bags back from the taxi driver himself.

"You got money for nothing, mate. You sat up there and fell asleep," said Jones.

"And Basil come over and woke you up and embarrassed ya," finished Perkins.

"So don't make it out that you are the hierarchy on the firm cos you're not," added Jones. His final word on Kenny is damning: "Kenny is a wombat thick old cunt."

Basil was still owed some loot but would have to join them at Perkins' daughter's house next week if he wanted any of it. "I'd say to Basil you have got to come and get it, you cunt bollocks," was how Perkins put it. "You ever seen a shambles like it? Fucking cunts, cunts… I am beginning to fucking hate them, I am."

"All fucking idiots," agreed Jones. "That Brian, he didn't half give me the hump then. I said, 'Stop being fucking silly.'"

"He is fucked now," said Perkins. "He can't tell us nothing."

"He's not getting a penny out of me," said Jones. "Not a fucking bit."

"No, no, Kenny'll give him some money," said Perkins. "Nothing he can tell me… fuck all… my little granddaughter… she is having it."

"Yeah, fuck him, fuck his daughter, fuck his will, fuck Kenny, fuck them," ranted Jones.

"Never bought a drink at the pub," raged Perkins. "That's his intention there, you know. Never buys fuck-all."

"I won't be over here no more," said Jones, looking out the window into the street lights of Islington.

"No, I won't," agreed Perkins. "I don't like this fucking area. It's finished, over, specially if we sort the gear out by then. That's it, innit."

"Done."

"Take your gear," began Perkins.

"Go and get nicked selling it in Hatton Garden," finished Jones.

Next week would be dicey. The riskiest part of the job since the break-in itself.

"If someone comes to pull you, no comment," said Perkins. "We are arresting you for the Hatton Garden. No comment, I'll say, 'You what, you dopey cunt? I can't even fucking walk.'"

"We will go, 'It's him,'" said Jones, meaning Collins presumably. "It's the first thing you say, it's bollocks."

Perkins recalled what he said 30 years ago, when he was pulled in for Security Express. "I said, 'You're fucking joking, inch'ya?' I said, 'The only fucking way I got my money is buying and selling houses... no comment, no comment.'"

"But it's all changed now," said Jones. "That goes against you now in your defence. But if you know they've got something serious, then you say, 'No comment.'"

Inevitably, they got back onto Reader. "Argumentative, that old cunt, still argues," said Jones. "He knows he ain't getting a dollar."

"He knows it now," agreed Perkins. "If he don't, he is a cunt. He's still hanging on though, ain't he?"

"Yeah, he ain't got nothing else," said Jones. "He ain't got no friends no more. He's got the Monday club, all day yesterday."

"The Monday club... sitting down there with that Bruce in the café," said Perkins. "Blackie goes there, sits in that café, talks about all their yesterdays."

"Ponce, sitting there doing nothing," said Jones. "He's only going to be a ponce up there, Tel."

"Course he is."

"Nothing else," said Jones. "Never going to work again... I really want to have a go at him but I've got to stop myself. Really want to hit him and say, 'Toughen up, you fucking prick. That's what you are. You lost all the fucking work. You bottle out at the last minute."

"I'm going to tell him about the three bits of work," said Perkins, bitterly. "I fucking gotta tell him, I can't help it. I am going to say, 'You fucked every one of them up, Brian, and the last one you walked away from… you gave up being a thief ten years ago, you cunt."

Perkins was just getting going. "If we had took any notice of you, we would have walked away from it as well. We had no other bit of work and in three months' time you would have got £400,000 for your house. That's how much you were fucking worried about it. And that is the fucking truth."

"He never took nothing out, did he, Tel," interrupted Jones.

"Fuck all," agreed Perkins. "He carried one thing in there, he diddley'd and doddley'd about, and then it was all in. He's not a thief."

"He was a thief 40 years ago," said Jones. "They never took no chances, had it all their own way. Like all them thieves then. All that… fucking… all his partners Millsy and all that. They weren't worth a wank. He's done nothing, the cunt. You would think he would shut up, Tel."

"You would think he would be shut up with shame but he's not ashamed of nothing," said Perkins.

"Nothing, with all that booze down him."

"He never bought a drink in the pub, did he?"

"He's a fucking know-it-all," said Jones. "That's what

he is and anything he knows he's got wrong. Every bit of fucking work we've been on, he's fucked up."

"He fucking has, we should be sitting here now…" began Perkins.

"… with half-a-billion pounds…" added Jones.

"… with chauffeur-driven Bentleys, one for every day," finished Perkins.

"And all them months and fucking years he put work in to go, 'Look, I won't be here tomorrow.' Cos he's thought, 'Them cunts, you'll never get in there,' and the simplest fucking thing – common sense – got you in."

"I wish I had a photo, Dan," said Perkins. "I know you and Basil was inside. I wish I had a photo to show me sat outside all on my own, right, doing what I had to do. To say to him, 'That's where you left me, Brian. Look. All on my own.' True, ain't it?"

In another nugget for the eavesdropping detectives, they were about to learn how Perkins and Jones planned to offload some of the stolen gear. They already had their suspicions. By tracing the movements of Perkins' Saxo in the run-up to the raid, police believed he had made at least three visits to an East London property linked to one of Britain's most feared organised crime syndicates. His contact there was a man who called himself "Frank". Pulling off a job as big as Hatton Garden created its own problems. You just ended up paying more to the fence – he knows you can afford it and you need to get shot of the stolen goods. Everyone is taking an extra risk as the police are crawling all over the place.

"I'll tell you what to do," said Jones. "I want to see how you'd get on with Frank… let him talk on your level first, right, then I'll say, 'Right, I might as well fuck off now, you got to look after him.' You know what I mean? I'll say, 'Could you keep the gold for a week?'"

"Yeah, I'd suppose he would do that," agreed Perkins. "I'm going to melt my good gold down… the Indian, the 18, that could be my pension if I could get half an idea of what's there, you know what I mean. Any shit he don't want we will have."

"Like last time he threw all them fucking stones away," recalled Jones. "I put 'em in a big tin, I got a tin like that that high." He gestured with his hands, Perkins took his eyes off the road. "Fucking idiot cunt," he said.

"Ahhhhh, they're fucking shit, what they worth?" said Jones, mimicking Frank.

"Is it an act, though?" asked Perkins.

"Oh, I don't know," Jones went on still in character. "Know what I mean? Tommy, he never used to do that."

They claimed former Brink's-Mat suspect Tommy Adams had been approached about fencing some of the Hatton Garden gear. "He don't want it, that Tommy Adams," Jones told Perkins.

Frank was the man. As Perkins put it: "Any shit I'll give to Frank, but I want to give him a bit of cream as well, do you know what I mean?"

Perkins also revealed he had sold him jewellery stolen in a previous burglary he had done with Reader. Jones said: "There's a lot of rings there though, Tel. So I'm just looking at them…"

Perkins replied: "More rings than that out of that other gaff you know."

Jones said: "What one? Oh yeah, more rings."

Perkins responded: "The very first thing I done with Brian. Oh, fucking trays of the cunts."

Jones asked: "And who did you sell the parcel to?"

"He sold some and I sold some to Frank."

It is likely that the "other gaff" referred to by Perkins was Giggy jewellers, a Hatton Garden shop that had been burgled in 2004. The raiders made off with £2million in gold and diamonds and at the time of writing had not been caught. Some of the Hatton Garden gang were among the prime suspects after £250,000 worth of the stolen gear later turned up at the East London property where Perkins visited Frank.

A team of professional thieves entered the Giggy shop on Friday, November 27, 2004. Like the 2015 burglary at the safe-deposit vault 50 yards away, the raiders had a key to the front door and went in on two nights over a weekend. Other striking similarities between the two crimes include the fact that the thieves made a hole in an internal wall to access the jewels and disabled the security system using similar methods. The data recorded on the shop's alarm later showed the gang did not leave the premises at 8 Greville Street until 2.30am on the Sunday morning. Among the hundreds of diamond necklaces and rings taken was a five-carat sparkler worth around £70,000 alone. CCTV picked up the image of at least one white van leaving the area at around this time but it was never traced.

Unlike the Hatton Garden Safe Deposit burglary, the Giggy crime did not make front-page news. In fact, it made no headlines at all at the time, not even in the local paper. Instead of Scotland Yard's specialist team of Flying Squad detectives and the Met's finest forensic examiners who swarmed over the 2015 burglary, the owner of Giggy had to make do with a local sergeant from Kentish Town Police Station and a single crime-scene investigator. By the time the Giggy burglary took place, Reader, Perkins and Basil had been working together for some time, according to one source.

Four months after the Giggy burglary, Bruno "Tiger" Hrela, 33, was gunned down by a hitman following a suspected disagreement over the stolen jewels. Tiger, a boxer and father of two, was shot in the neck and left temple after getting out of his car on Cedar Avenue, Enfield, north London, just before 9pm on March 5, 2005. The dumdum bullets expanded on impact, killing him almost instantly. A retired detective claimed the hit was among eight underworld executions linked to Frank's organised crime gang that have been covered up by corrupt police.

A short time later, a gangster approached a person close to Tiger and demanded menacingly: "Where's the jewellery?" At the same time an anonymous caller contacted the police to say that Tiger had been involved in selling drugs and high-value jewellery for the same man. Metropolitan Police intelligence reports detailed how another person close to Tiger had seen him shortly before his death with "jewellery caked in diamonds". After the murder, police found a diamond in a box in a loft hatch above his bedroom.

Around three weeks after losing his only son, Tiger's father's business was burgled. Bruno Hrela, 76, was one of Britain's top safe engineers and owned a company selling high-end strong boxes and locks to customers, including the Royal Family and Premiership footballers. The raid on his warehouse in Bow, east London, saw around £1million worth of his gear go missing, including 1,000 safes. Mr Hrela believed the burglary was linked to his son's murder.

When police found some of the Giggy haul in 2006 at the East London property linked to Frank they also recovered some of Mr Hrela's stolen safes. In a remarkable coincidence, he had been called to the crime scene by the Met. They had employed him for decades to help detectives get through locked doors, into strong rooms and seemingly impenetrable safes. Mr Hrela immediately recognised a number of the safes as being among those stolen from him in the Bow burglary shortly after Tiger's murder. He said: "We think the theft and the murder were linked. The police were covering something, it wasn't right."

Three men were charged with handling the goods. But the case was dropped over claims that three investigating detectives were corrupt. The officers were exonerated following a £3million probe and successfully sued Scotland Yard. Then in November 2015, one of the three former suspects was arrested again, this time on suspicion of plotting to handle the jewels from the Hatton Garden raid earlier that year. The 53-year-old remained on police bail at the time of writing. Tiger's murder was also under review by the Met's Special Casework Investigations Team following work by the authors.

Like Kenneth Noye's fatal attack on John Fordham, Tiger's execution served as a reminder that the list of victims of high-value burglaries and robberies does not always end with the owners of the stolen goods. It is also a reminder that Scotland Yard corruption, a theme running through Reader's career, remains a problem.

CHAPTER 16

End of the Road

The next day was Saturday and Terry Perkins drove his daughter, Terri, to the airport for the start of her holiday – paid for by the unfortunate jewellers of Hatton Garden. It was only fair, reasoned Perkins. He'd told Jones the previous day that one of his daughters had gone down to the Garden and they had mugged her off with a fake diamond. They had it coming, he believed.

Next, he picked up Danny Jones as agreed. Jones was carrying a large paint pot, which he slung in the boot. "He's gonna give us a price, is he?" said Jones.

"The price is what you're gonna get given," said Perkins. "What would you say that parcel there is? Normal run of the day stuff, yeah?"

"Yeah, some nice little bits there," replied Jones. "You know what I mean, it's all sellable gear."

"If it's all like that, what he's got, I tell you what we gotta look for, another bit of work."

First, they had to see what they had. "Kenny [Collins] don't know where that gear is," said Perkins.

"I thought Bill's [Bill Lincoln] house, didn't you?"

"So did I, yeah."

"Yeah but he said Bill's gone away," said Jones.

"But Bill give it to someone else."

"Shouldn't have done that, mate."

"Kenny don't know where that gear is," said Perkins.

"He's a cunt."

"Bill knows where it is."

"That's no fucking good. It ain't his gear, is it?" said Jones.

Perkins pulled into a parking space in Sterling Road, Enfield. Terri's house in this typical London terraced street was a two-up, two-down – number 24. Jones fetched his paint pot from the back and they went into the house. To any curious neighbour, he looked like a decorator going in to spruce the place up while the family were away. The inside of that paint pot, however, looked like a pirate's treasure chest.

This was what the police, who were watching from the street outside, were waiting for. The recordings were all well and good. But, as Johnson said, "You have to say to yourself, what would happen if we lost this [evidence]? We've still got to have a case without it. You've still got to work your way through everything else and make sure you've got enough to corroborate what they're saying. If you don't, they would have an option of saying that, 'We're just a bunch of elderly fantasists who were talking a lot of old nonsense in the car.' So we've got to prove that that's not the case." They had to catch them with the goods and it looked like they would soon get their chance.

On Monday morning, Perkins drove Jones to Collins' house. They tried to call him but couldn't get through. They filled the minutes, once again, with endless chatter about what they had got, what it was worth, how they were going to get rid of it.

They waited for Collins. How was he going to get his gear back and would they have to get involved?

"I'm not looking after Basil's gear," said Perkins.

"We don't want it around us," agreed Jones. "That means he has got to come all the way over again and do a double journey."

"We got two weeks there, then we want it all out," said Perkins.

"Want it all out this week, Tel," said Jones. "Funny fucker is Kenny."

"Kenny is."

"Yeah."

"Hundred per cent."

"I remember, you said it," said Jones. "Remember? 'Watch him,' you said. He wants it all his own way. Does it all clever you know, I'll tell ya."

Perkins thought for the thousandth time about who was looking after those three bags of loot. "Err… what's his name, Bill – probably give him the cream and kept the shit."

"No, don't be silly, Tel."

"No, but what I am saying is, too much of hurry-up, it

was," said Perkins.

"Oh yeah."

"Do you know what I mean?" Perkins went on. "You don't do that. You sort out your parcels and, say, what's left, you give him that. You don't, fucking, yeah, yeah, yeah… that is not the way to do things."

"No."

They looked out of the window. It was the start of the week and people were getting back onto the treadmill of their ordinary lives. Delivery drivers, mums with pushchairs returning from school, office workers.

"I don't want to see Brian no more, Tel," said Jones.

"I do," said Perkins. "To tell him. I want to see him once, to say, 'That's it, Brian… I told you that I want to wait to see what I've got. And what I've got is very, very disappointing. Down to you. So, mate, you ain't on."

He had made his mind up. Neither Reader nor Wood were going to get a penny from this job. Not from him at least. "Both as bad as one another."

"Both arseholes went," agreed Jones. "In our world, you either stay or you go."

"You stay or you go," agreed Perkins. "Fucking end of story."

They started debating whether Reader was having nightmares about abandoning the job.

"I hope he fucking suffers," spat Jones. "Fucking wanker, regardless of his age. He looked defeated just when he sat in that chair."

"Yeah, he did."

"I said to him the other day," went on Jones, only too happy to belittle Reader to make Perkins — and himself — look bigger, "you're 40 years behind, Brian. You can see what a selfish man he's been, can't you?"

"I'm out of date, I'm behind," said Perkins, "but I know it and I admit it. He don't, does he?"

Reader had given them his massive payday but they did not want to give him a shred of credit. For Jones, the bar for success was pretty low — "Enough money to pay the bills next week."

"What I wanted out of this was, I wanted…" began Perkins.

"Give your kids a house each?" interrupted Jones.

"Yeah, which is out of the window now," said Perkins. "And I like to get another flat out in Portugal for sixty grand to rent out for the business thing."

"Good money would it make, Tel?" asked Jones.

"Mate, yeah, in the season you get monkey [£500] a week for it," said Perkins. "You wouldn't make any money to live on but you'd make, say, five or six grand a year. It pays all your exes and all your holiday and that."

He'd be in Portugal soon enough, once the matters were straightened out. Where was Collins? They needed to arrange this handover.

"I don't want the cab driver to see it's me," said Jones. He was referring to John Harbinson, Bill Lincoln's nephew, who was unwittingly looking after Collins' share of the loot. "Get Bill to pick the parcel up the way he took it away then and bring it back to here."

"Yeah."

"Put it in your motor, drive it over, exactly what I done yesterday," said Jones. "Went and picked it up drove 40 miles with it. He's the one who has had the biggest cut out of us all."

"He fucking has, Dan, he has."

"Sat in a room…" said Jones.

"With the less risk," added Perkins.

"He could never ever get nicked in a million fucking years," said Jones.

"Never done no running about."

"Fuck all, fuck all, and has the cheek to swap money over," said Jones. "It's the badness in him, that's the unprofessionalism… he could have gone and got a bag a day him from his house."

"Yeah."

"He's never going to get a tug round here, Tel," said Jones.

"No"

Finally, Collins joined them. He spoke to Hugh Doyle, whose role – police later insisted – was to help them hand over the loot. It was all fixed up. They would do the handover at Doyle's workshop in Enfield the next day. He ran a plumbing business next to the Old Wheatsheaf. It was minutes from the homes of both Perkins and Jones.

They drove off.

"If he thought of his place yesterday, why didn't he… drive over there Sunday?" pondered Perkins. "Lovely day. He ain't got a fucking brain, has he?"

"He's starting to forget, the cunt," said Jones.

"Yeah, take it into his house," suggested Perkins. "Get the cab driver to pull up."

"Pretend like you're going on holiday," said Jones.

"We don't want a stick up now do we?" said Perkins.

Perkins had known Doyle from the pub for years but neither man was happy that he had been dragged into this.

"Another one who knows, Hughie. He's a cunt," said Perkins. "Don't fucking leave them bags with Hughie."

"He knows he's a complete cunt," agreed Jones.

"He does," said Perkins. "They all know he is." And later, "Yes, he don't want Hughie to see us really… cos he's going to tumble, Hughie… he might think he's bought the gear… depending on what he tells him… and if he has left that more longer than 10 minutes Hughie will have something out of it."

"Yeah, you've got to treat everyone as an enemy," said Jones.

"You fucking have, Dan."

"Nice day for dropping gear off though, innit."

"Yeah."

They headed up towards Enfield in convoy, Perkins

driving the Saxo and Collins his Mercedes.

"He is behind us, he's following us," said Perkins, checking his mirror.

"That stinking dog in the motor, scratched the fuck, all the seats have gone," said Jones.

"Cunt, ain't he?"

"I'd go and buy a little cheap motor – Volvo – and a nice back for the dog," said Jones.

"I'd get rid of the dog."

Jones laughed, "What, fuck the dog off?"

"I wouldn't let him in that fucking motor that's for sure."

As they drove into Enfield, the cars went their separate ways. It had been decided that Perkins and Jones would get some lunch. Collins drove on to meet with Doyle at his workshop, where Lincoln and Harbinson had been told to join them.

When he arrived, he turned the radio off and opened the car door. Dempsey, the dog, started whining.

Doyle met him and said through the door, "Dempsey all right there for a few minutes? Can you tell me what you need, cos we have options?"

After a quick chat, Collins decided that the pub car park would work fine. It was tucked round the corner, off the road. They could pull the two vehicles in there – his Merc and Harbinson's taxi – and do what they needed to do. But they didn't call him "wombat thick" for nothing.

Not only was he still driving the same car he had used to recce Hatton Garden and buy the tools in Twickenham, he was about to make yet another blunder. If Collins had looked up, he would have seen he was on CCTV.

The plan was becoming clear to the watching and listening police. Johnson said: "Now the reason they wanted to do it in that area is because they didn't want to do a boot-to-boot in the street. Because, if they did a boot-to-boot in the street, it would potentially look like a drugs deal to a passing police officer or a member of the public. They could lose everything that they have worked for for three years over a simple error like that. So they wanted to use that car park area because it gave them some degree of privacy. They didn't realise it was covered by a camera. They didn't know that we were following them."

Neither did Perkins and Jones who were having their lunch at the nearby Painter's Café in Enfield. Back at Jones' house, they put the bins out. Later on that afternoon, Collins phoned Lincoln to give him details of the handover point. Everything was set.

There was rain forecast for Tuesday but it started out dry. Hopefully, this was a good sign. Jones decided to wear a pair of shorts. Summer was on its way and he had reason to feel it was going to be a good one. Collins picked up Jones on his way up north through Enfield. He told him about the car park next to Doyle's workshop. They didn't even need Doyle's permission to use it, he explained. "As it happens, I didn't know it until I went to see it… we could have just drove round there, took it out and put it in the boot of the car. We wouldn't have needed that but you don't know what eyes are about do you. You don't want someone thinking we're doing a drugs changeover or something." Collins peered over at Jones, "It looks like you've come off holiday innit, shorts on and that."

"Yeah, but at least it ain't pissed down with rain all day," Jones answered.

To pass the time on their journey to the pub, Jones regaled Collins with the story of the time he was pulled over by the police on the very road they were heading down.

"I ain't got no licence, have I. I said, 'Look, I've been right down on life'… I had my rucksack in the back, the army rucksack what I run with, and he went, 'What you got that big bag for?' I went, 'I'm in the army.' He went, 'The Army?… fucking, put it there, mate, and fuck off… get your mate to pick the car up, all right?' I went, 'Cheers!'"

"There's the Old Wheatsheaf," said Collins. They had arrived.

Lincoln had got there just over 10 minutes earlier and was sitting in his car in the road outside reading a newspaper. Jones and Collins joined him. They walked into the car park with Dempsey following them, wagging his tail. There was a brief conversation with Doyle and he left his workshop minutes later in his van followed by his wife in another car. The coast was clear. Lincoln called Harbinson while Collins shifted the Merc into the pub car park. The men loitered for three minutes or so, until Harbinson's taxi – a Mercedes Vito van – arrived. Lincoln talked to him through the window, while Jones and Collins stood by the boot. Harbinson got out and slid open the door to the back. Jones grabbed one black holdall from inside, while Lincoln removed a second. They were placed in the boot of Collins' Mercedes. Lincoln then removed a third smaller bag from the taxi and put it with the others. They then went their separate ways in the three different vehicles.

Collins and Jones drove five minutes to Sterling Road. Perkins was already in his daughter's house. He brought the rest of his whack over that morning in a carrier bag. Finally, they would be able to forget about Bill and the taxi driver and Hughie and god knows who else. Perkins had a small smelting pot for melting down the gold and diamond-testing equipment along with tools for separating the two. They would soon know once and for all whether they had got that million pounds each that they had been dreaming of.

Johnson and his team were in a similar state of calm excitement. This was the culmination of their six-week, round-the-clock investigation. They would catch them red-handed. Johnson said: "We had weeks of surveillance showing the principals meeting up, we had the audio recordings saying what they had done and how they were going to do it, and eventually we had some property coming out of the woodwork. So, at that point, we had sufficient there. There would be no reason to delay the arrests any longer. So that was why we made the decision at that point to go in."

Officers were poised across three police forces to lift the entire gang. Well, not quite the entire gang. Basil was still out of the picture. Maybe he would never show up again. Jones and Perkins had suggested he was already abroad. But Johnson didn't want to wait any longer. Once they began to melt that gold down, the job of identifying it as stolen and returning it to the victims would become harder, maybe impossible. It had gone up the chain of command. "I was sitting in my office with our lawyer and our press officers and staff officer, getting text message updates and it was very gripping," said his boss Commander Peter Spindler.

They sprang into action. In Enfield, in Cheshunt, in Dartford, more than 200 officers, some in riot gear, stormed 12 addresses. Perkins, Jones and Collins were around Terri's dining table, smelting machine at the ready, when a battering ram came through the door, followed by dozens of officers in riot gear and flameproof protective clothing. Super-fit Jones tried to make a break for it. He ran out of the back, scattering diamonds as he went, but found there was nowhere to go. For Perkins and Collins, their days of trying to leg it were long behind them.

Lincoln's Audi was forced to a halt on the A10 heading back into central London by unmarked police cars. Officers smashed open the side window with a baton and pulled him out onto the ground. In the intervening moments, he had been leaning across the car. Officers found a torn-up pile of paper which, once reassembled, had the handwritten name of the Old Wheatsheaf pub. His bladder, never up to much at the best of times, deserted him. He had to ask to take a leak on the verge at the side of the A10 and then, back at the police station, Lincoln wet himself. Doyle and Wood were arrested at their homes, along with Perkins' son-in-law, Bren Walters, who police suspected of handling some of the stolen goods.

Thirty miles away, officers arrived at Pentire and arrested Reader, along with his son, Paul. Neighbour Kevin Watson, said: "It was just after 10 o'clock. About three vans full of police turned up. There were maybe 20 or more officers. They surrounded the property, entered and shouted, 'Police! Police!' It was quite orderly and peaceful. They brought the younger man out handcuffed and put him in a van. Fifteen minutes later they brought out the older guy, who seemed to be struggling a bit health-wise. He was holding his chest."

At 76, Reader was the oldest suspect the Flying Squad officers had arrested. Detective Superintendent Craig Turner said: "That's old. You've normally hung up your boots by then."

CHAPTER 17

A Dying Breed

Commander Peter Spindler couldn't hide a sense of triumph – and relief: "These detectives have done their utmost to bring justice to the victims of this callous crime. They've worked tirelessly and relentlessly." His officers searched all the addresses. The evidence began to pile up. Gold and gems, clothing from the raid, dust masks. In Reader's house they found the scarf that had been caught on CCTV as he went into the Hatton Garden vault.

The first suspect to be identified in the press had the most fleeting role in the raid – Hugh Doyle. *Mirror* photographer Ian Vogler was stopping in the Enfield branch of Costa Coffee when he heard plain-clothes officers on a neighbouring table complaining about their long and boring shift. He tailed them to Doyle's home in Riverside Gardens. Photos of Doyle sat astride his Associated Response-branded motorbike were soon published, along with knowing references to his pilot's licence. The media had little to go on and this was the first face they could link to the raid. Had Doyle flown the stolen loot abroad? For the *Daily Star*, he was "rich jetsetter Hugh Doyle" and the paper printed pictures "revealing the Irishman's pricey passions, including a plane and a swanky yacht".

Next to be named was Reader, accompanied – bafflingly – by an old black-and-white photograph of somebody else entirely.

At Danny Jones' house, forensics officers emerged carrying a distinct orange Hilti drill box. His partner, Val Hart, later told friends that this was "all for show". She'd had the box for years and used to stand on it to change lightbulbs.

In custody, the gang pretended they did not even know one another.

Perkins was asked, "What was your role in this burglary?" "No comment," was the answer, just as he had practised in the car with Jones.

"What specialist skillset have you got which made you valuable on this job?"

"No comment."

"Were you the driller?"

"No comment."

"Were you the person that could de-activate the lift shaft?"

"No comment."

"The alarm systems?"

"No comment."

Police told Collins, "Now, your role – wasn't it – was to

be the driver and the look-out."

"No comment."

"You were in communication with the people that were down in the vault via handheld radios, weren't you?"

"No comment."

Jones remembered what Perkins had told him.

"We know that the vault wasn't accessed on the first night."

"No comment."

"So what went wrong?"

"No comment."

"Was it you that messed up?"

A slight change in tone from Jones but still, "No comment."

"It was your role, wasn't it, to get through the hole?"

"No comment."

Reader, utterly deflated, didn't even bother with those two words.

He was shown the CCTV footage he had already seen in the *Mirror*.

"This is 10.09pm on the second of April, so this is the Thursday evening at the start of the offence. There is one male in this image and he has got a hard hat and he has got 'Gas' on the back of his high-visibility jerkin. Mr Reader, is that you?"

Silence.

"Tell me if it isn't you."

More silence.

Detective Chief Inspector Paul Johnson said: "They're old, experienced criminals, obviously, so the drill if you're an older criminal is not to say anything, keep your mouth shut, and just see what opportunities there are to get out of it." The opportunities were slim, non-existent for some. The main suspects were played segments of the covert recordings. After hearing evidence against him, Collins did not even bother asking for bail. "Collins said, 'I'd rather have a cup of tea,'" recalled Johnson. "He knew he was never going to get bail."

Later that night, the eight were charged with conspiracy to burgle and remanded in custody. The following morning, they were taken to Westminster Magistrates' Court in no less than four marked security vans, two men in each vehicle, accompanied by armed officers. Unmarked police cars were at the head and tail of the convoy. Two more armed-response vehicles were waiting at the side entrance to the court.

They faced a world that was stunned, more than anything else, by their ages. The line-up was: Brian Reader, aged 76; his son, Paul, 50; John Collins 74; Hugh Doyle, the "baby" of the group at 48; Carl Wood, 58; Terry Perkins, 67; William Lincoln, 59; and Danny Jones, 58. As *The Times* headlined it: "With a combined age of 490, the eight jewel heist suspects shuffled into court." It went on: "They shuffled into the courtroom looking more like a casting call for *Last of the Summer Wine* than a gang alleged to have been involved in one of the most audacious raids in decades." *The Sun* went with: "Grandad Theft Auto", adding it was "more *Dad's Army* than *Ocean's Eleven*".

Collins struggled to understand when he was told by the court clerk to confirm his name and address. After no response, the clerk repeated: "Just your name, sir!" There was a pause before he complained: "I can't hear." The clerk tried again: "Do you have an address? Somewhere where you live?" Paul Reader, standing next to him behind the glass screen in the dock repeated the question for him. Members of the Reader family waved to Paul and his father from the public gallery. Reader acknowledged them with a nod of his head.

Prosecutor Edmund Hall hardly needed to tell the judge that the case was "a notorious one which has been the subject of much media attention". It was not every day that the top brass of the Flying Squad, including Detective Superintendent Craig Turner and Detective Chief Inspector Paul Johnson sat in his court.

Their second court appearance, two weeks later, was via video link from Belmarsh Prison. The gang joked about "being on telly" before Terry Perkins invited Judge Alistair McCreath and the rest of Southwark Crown Court to "come down to Belmarsh and we can have a cup of tea". The judge lost patience when a message said, "your conference will end in two minutes". "Oh, for Heaven's sake," he said before remanding the men in custody.

Behind the camaraderie and the banter, they were not much enjoying their new home. They were put on the specialist high-security unit at Belmarsh, Britain's only prison within a prison, reserved for the most dangerous offenders.

An official inspection in 2013 had described the conditions within the unit as bleak and oppressive, with a highly restrictive regime. In most prisons, the category A prisoners were kept with others, to give them a taste of "normal" life inside. Not at Belmarsh.

It had been inspected again three months earlier and an official report had questioned whether it should even be kept open.

The unit had recently been refurbished but the overall environment – especially the shower areas – remained poor: "The upper spurs had sufficient natural light, but lower spurs were much darker. Outside exercise areas remained caged and austere… Since our previous visit, prisoners from the unit had been allowed to play football outside on one occasion and it was unclear why they could not do so more regularly."

This was the world the Hatton Garden gang now called home. They shared it with notorious murderers, like cop killer David Bieber, and infamous Islamic extremists. One radical preacher – who cannot be named for legal reasons – was accused of inciting British Muslims to join terror group ISIS and he rubbed shoulders with the ageing gang.

After he was bailed he told of his unlikely friendship with Reader.

The radical cleric said: "He was the most interesting one in there. I has a good few interesting conversations with him. He follows Richard Dawkins' brand of philosophy. I ended up giving him a signed copy of a book about the Quran and wrote inside 'May Allah guide you to the truth'. Our relationship was very cordial. I think there is a general understanding and empathy between us with regard to the oppressiveness of the regime in Belmarsh.

"I'm surprised that a case that is basically about theft ends up with people being held in a high-security unit in Belmarsh. They are old guys and many of them are ill. They should be held in hospital not in an HSU."

For three weeks, they were kept together. Then they were split into two groups. They were "on the book", which meant their every movement recorded. They were kept in isolation for much of the time and their association time was limited.

It was a tough regime, much worse for Reader than his previous experience of jail in the 1980s. In September, he, Perkins, Jones and Collins bowed to the inevitable and pleaded guilty to conspiracy to commit burglary. By doing so early on, they could expect some credit from the judge. A third off their maximum sentence of ten years, in all likelihood. But it did not get them out of Belmarsh.

Five months in, Patsy Adams, brother of crime figures

Terry and Tommy, joined them. He had been extradited from Holland on suspicion of murder. It relieved the tedium for a few days.

But Jones had decided to take matters into his own hands in dramatic fashion. He began writing to Martin Brunt, the highly respected crime correspondent for Sky News. He began by complaining about the decision to keep the gang in a high-security prison. "Let me tell you, *Dad's Army* are like super sportsman compared with this gang. Run… they can barely walk. One has cancer, he's 70, another heart condition, 68, another, 75, can't remember his name. Sixty-year-old with two new hips and knees." Jones revealed that none had been allowed visitors for weeks and that he had written to the Archbishop of Canterbury begging for help. "The reply was he couldn't help me but will pray for me in his next church service," wrote Jones. "He also said sorry you got yourself mixed up in the Hatton Garden heist. And finished off by saying just being famous must now seem like a pretty poor reward. Best wishes, Lambeth Palace."

In a follow-up letter he got down to business, asking Brunt for his help in getting an important message to the media. "I've instructed my solicitor… to tell the police Flying Squad that I want to give back my share of [the] Hatton Garden burglary, they said it's in motion," he wrote. "I now understand that the police said that the prison Belmarsh won't release me to the police. What a load of bull. The police can't want it back, as I'm the only person in the world to no [sic] where it is, deep down. I want to do the right thing and give it back."

Jones went on: "They are trying to make me look a bad person. I'm trying my best to put things right and for some reason they don't want me to give it back. If I don't get the chance to go out under armed escort, I hope some poor sod who's having it hard out there with his or her family find the lot and have a nice life, as you never know, Martin, people do find things, don't they?… You would have thought the police would have jumped with joy, but for some reason which I don't know, they are not that interested. They took that sex killer Levi [Bellfield] a few years ago, he showed the police where he killed those women. So, there you go, Martin, a sex killer and there's me, a 58-year-old burnt-out burglar. Maybe they think I'm going to get [a] hit squad to get me out. My God, how stupid."

In another letter, he wrote: "I haven't heard from the police concerning the stuff I want to give back. I'm just waiting for the police to take me out giving them back part of the stolen goods. They won't let me know if they [are] coming to take me out. Security reasons. They better hurry up, we don't want anyone finding it, do we?"

Jones was to get his chance but, before the trip, detectives did their own bit of digging. They had known for months that Jones had stashed some of his gear at a cemetery. Graves of members of Val's family were found at Edmonton Cemetery. When officers lifted the marble slab at the grave of her father, Sidney James Hart, on October 8, they found two bags of precious stones. Under tight security, Jones was taken to the same cemetery a week later. But he led the officers to another spot entirely and pointed to the grave of Val's brother. Bemused officers retrieved a smaller stash and Jones assured them that was it. "There's no other outstanding property. That is all I had," he fibbed.

In a follow-up letter to Brunt, Jones continued the act, insisting he was a reformed character. "Knowing I'm going to prison for a long time, all I want to do is let my two sons no [sic] I'm trying to change for the best," he wrote.

"I no [sic] I've done wrong. I'm not crying Martin, I did it. I can't talk for other people, only for myself and whatever I get on judgement day I will stand tall, but I want to make amends to all my loved ones and show I'm trying to change. I no [sic] it seems a bit late in my life, but I'm trying."

Jones' lawyer Mark Davies argued that this was not an attempt to further cut any prison sentence. "It's ultimately a matter for the judge," he said, "but he can't go beyond a reduction of a third, so the return of his share is likely to have a minimum or no effect on his sentence."

But if Jones had managed to convince everyone that he had finally grown out of a lifetime of compulsively lying, he might just be able to escape a confiscation order. All the while, leaving himself a nice little nest egg to enjoy on his release. Like the rest of the gang, he knew he was likely to serve barely three years before being let out on licence.

In early November, nearly six months after Paul Reader's arrest, the Crown Prosecution Service finally accepted that he had nothing to do with his father's criminal enterprise. The six months took its toll. Paul had been sick since suffering an aneurism in 2013 and had problems with his kidneys too. When he was taken to hospital from Belmarsh, it was in the company of 10 armed officers and a police helicopter. "When I was first arrested, I didn't even bother to ask for a lawyer," he told crime reporter Duncan Campbell on his eventual release. "I even asked, 'What is this about?' I was dreading the interview, thinking it would be old-style, like *Life on Mars*, but it wasn't like that at all. I think they were graduates."

The next month, the trial of the four who had not pleaded guilty – Wood, Lincoln, Harbinson and Doyle – began at Woolwich Crown Court, a stone's throw from Belmarsh. It was supposed to last six weeks.

Wood was the only man from the actual raid in the dock. He could not have looked less like a member of the criminal underworld. The 58-year-old had grown a luxuriant beard and wore a pair of spectacles perched on the end of his nose. Behind them, his sharp eyes surveyed the press benches, the rows of eminent lawyers and the 12 jury members who held his fate in their hands. Wood's dress code for the trial was provincial librarian – smart trousers, shirts and v-necked sweaters. Of the man who had plotted, two decades earlier, to "smash" a gangland rival so viciously that he "ain't going home", there was no trace.

His lawyer told the court that Wood had health problems and no particular skills that he could bring to the party. He did not appear to be at any of the planning meetings and much of the evidence against him – logs of phone calls with Danny Jones – was circumstantial. When his phone "went dark" on April 1, the day before the burglary, Wood claimed this was because it had been stolen by a drug addict. He did not report it to police and never saw it again. Wood told the court he was at home in Cheshunt all through that bank holiday weekend. His wife Paula took to the dock to back him up, giving him an alibi. Danny Jones was invited to a family BBQ that weekend, the court heard, but never turned up. Of the burglary, all Wood knew was what Jones had told him – hints that he was working on a massive job that he would hear about in due course on TV.

Over three days, the jury listened to the covert police tapes. There were barely suppressed smiles as Perkins and Jones did themselves up like a pair of kippers. The air in court three turned blue with swearing. The judge questioned whether this could be relied on as evidence. Was it just the "unguarded gossip of a couple of thieves"? One lawyer went further. It was "a mixture of Alf Garnett and Michael Caine with none of the charm".

Wood must have been wincing inside as he heard his friend Jones belittle him behind his back to Perkins. Wood was a "cunt", Wood was "screaming like a fucking pig", Wood's "arsehole fell out". But he got his revenge days later. From the dock, Wood entertained the court with tales of his eccentric friend. "Eccentric to extremes," Wood said. "Everyone who knew Danny would say he was mad. He would go to bed in his mother's dressing gown with a fez on. He would sleep in a sleeping bag in his bedroom on the floor and go to the toilet in a bottle. He's got a big thing about the army. He's eccentric." Jones would talk to his white-haired terrier dog Rocket as if it were human, said Wood. "He slept on his own with his dog Rocket. He would read palms, tell people he could read their fortune. He was a bit of a Walter Mitty."

Lincoln sat next to Wood in the dock. He appeared older than his 60 years and took regular toilet breaks. The court heard all about his weak bladder, his lawyers saw to that. Lincoln claimed he was buying fish while the raid was taking place. The court heard that a mobile linked to Lincoln was used early the following morning at around 4.40am in East India Dock, close to Billingsgate Fish Market.

His lawyer pointed out: "Friday the third of April is Good Friday. You can take it from me that a lot of fish, I suggest, is sold on Good Friday."

It was thanks to Lincoln that the court had a lesson in "schmeissing" – a Yiddish term for the treatment where men are beaten with a large soapy brush. Lincoln was a regular at the Georgian Porchester Spa, a Turkish Baths in Westminster, where he was known as "Billy the Fish", because he used to turn up with salmon from the fish market to sell to his fellow bathers.

But some of his schmeissing companions had noticed that Billy had become more generous with the fish after his holiday in Greece. Lincoln and his friend, the political and sports columnist Matthew Norman, had been discussing the upcoming general election campaign. "That Ed Miliband, he's fucking useless," ventured Lincoln. "The Tories will win, no question. If they don't, I'll buy you lunch."

Norman later wrote: "A few days after the election, he strode up to my lounger. 'There you go,' he said, handing over a bag. 'I was dahn Billingsgate this morning and picked you out a Dover sole.' It was enormous and I asked what I owed him. 'Don't be a muppet,' said Billy. 'It's a gift.' I thanked him, and congratulated him on his election-forecasting skills. An hour later in the steam room, I mentioned the sole to a third party. 'Yeah, Billy's suddenly come over dead generous,' said this character. 'He keeps buying all the boys drinks and snacks. Never seen him so chipper.' He was nicked the following day."

That detail was never heard in court. Instead, his mate James Creighton, known as 'Jimmy two baths' because of his habit of schmeissing twice, stood up in court to back up Lincoln's story. He did not drop Reader off at London

Bridge, as the police claimed. He was heading to Borough Market for more wheeling and dealing. He visited Collins on the Sunday morning to talk to his sister and collect some euros to take on holiday to Greece. He saw three bags containing the loot and asked Collins, "Has she chucked you out?" Collins, he claimed, told him it was old tat and asked him to look after it for him. He passed it on to his nephew, John Harbinson. Neither man knew what it contained.

Harbinson sat next to his uncle. He admitted taking the bags but did not look inside. He realised he had been caught up in criminality only when it was too late and the others were arrested. He tried to delete information from his satnav about his journeys into London to meet the gang but failed.

Doyle sat alone at the other end of the dock, driving each day from Enfield in his Associated Response van and wearing his company T-shirt. He listened intently to the case, taking notes. He admitted he was drinking buddies with key gang members and that he had given Collins – "a real Arthur Daley character" – a key to a padlock on his office. But he insisted he was not part of their plans. "I had no knowledge of what was taking place. It was a public car park covered by CCTV. No way in a million years was this a good place to do something this stupid." Did he know they were serious criminals? "I didn't know any specifics about their past," he insisted. "I didn't know it was anything about serious crime. It was 15 years ago, so I can't remember any specifics, but they were just funny."

Doyle had struck up friendships with many in the court, offering his services as a plumber and tales of life inside Belmarsh before he finally got bail a week before the trial when a more serious burglary charge was dropped. He'd read *God Is Not Great* by the great atheist Christopher Hitchens in jail, in training for debates with those fellow prisoners who were more in the Al Qaeda camp. He trained his body too, getting fit with help from more experienced inmates who taught him how to exercise in the confines of a cell. It must have been torture for a born workaholic. His Irish aunt's reaction in response to the news that he had been arrested on suspicion of involvement in the Hatton Garden heist was, "How would he have time?"

Centre of attention in the court was an exact replica of the 25cm by 45cm hole Wood had helped to drill through the vault wall. Made from polystyrene, it was recreated from a survey using lasers by a specialist team. The prosecutor Philip Evans told the court: "I must point out – it says it's for visual purposes only. Do not attempt to climb inside."

But even the lawyers ended up with a degree of professional respect for the gang. Barrister Philip Sinclair told the *Daily Mail*: "Like a lot of people, I think, I do have a grudging admiration for the way they did it and when they did it, at their time of life. I know some of them have got very shady pasts indeed. But this particular heist, no one was hurt in it, no one was even scared. They did not confront anybody within the building."

On January 14, the jury returned their verdicts. Harbinson was cleared. The rest were guilty. There were a few people in court who could not help but feel sorry for Doyle. But the police were cock-a-hoop. After nine months and 5,000 exhibits, they had recovered £3.7million and got their men. There was humble pie too. "It is quite clear the police should have attended," Detective Superintendent Craig Turner conceded. Processes would be reviewed.

Once again, Hatton Garden was splashed all over the front page. Reader's illustrious and so far largely hidden criminal career began to emerge. Everyone knew about Brink's-Mat and Fordham. The authors of this book revealed his links to Baker Street in the *Daily Mirror* while Paul Lashmar filed the same story for *The Independent*. The *Mirror* headlined the story, "The £150m Wadfather," after adding together all the hauls on all the jobs it had linked him to.

Professor Dick Hobbs said: "Hatton Garden triggered something in people's minds. I've been interviewed by French TV, American TV… an Australian TV company flew a whole crew over to speak to me. People are fascinated. It has everything. It has the ring of Old London about it. The way they overcame their ailments

added a level of comedy to it. And then you have the idea
of them coming out of retirement for one last job. Even if it
isn't true – it sounds like something Hollywood would
make up. In this case it is very misleading. The police
today see crime in terms of cases. Who is Brian Reader?
He did Brink's-Mat and then he did this."

Even after the conviction, the speculation continued.
There had been rumours circulating in the underworld for
months that the gang had been grassed up by a "moll", a
jilted girlfriend of one of the men. There was no evidence
for this – if anything it all pointed to cock-up, rather than
conspiracy – but it still made the front page of one
newspaper.

An even more outlandish theory surfaced. The Adams
organised crime syndicate had orchestrated the break-in
to steal the contents of one particular box. The box
contained evidence linking them to an unsolved murder.
The owner of the box was Brink's-Mat launderer John
"Goldfinger" Palmer. Palmer had been gunned down in
his Essex garden not long after the raid. This was the
Adams gang too, apparently, making doubly sure that
Palmer could not incriminate them. The gang had asked
the Adams family for permission to do the job and they
had insisted on Basil being their man on the job. He was
now in Panama with the missing £10million.

It made for great reading but was sadly untrue. Anyone
who had listened through three days of probe material
knew Basil did not have the lion's share of the loot.

Tommy Adams "didn't want" anything from Hatton Garden. The gang had amused themselves with the idea that people thought they were targeting a single box.

Professor Dick Hobbs said: "It was never about asking permission. The Krays were perhaps the only people who did that. Crime families are still there but they have gone into property and other things. They don't have manors any more. Nobody can control it. It's a free-for-all and it has been for a very long time. The notion of territory – it's redundant, it's fantasy. The world doesn't work like that anymore. The neighbourhood crime family? What neighbourhood?" The gang insider who knows Basil said: "The claim that he was working for the Adams family is complete bollocks. He's never met them in his life. The idea that Brian would go and tell others of his plans is ridiculous."

But for the families of the gang, this was not just harmless fun. Somebody could get hurt. And they were facing financial ruin. Mark Jenner, who runs a forensic accountancy firm in North Yorkshire, told the *Daily Mail* that the burglars could be stripped of "practically everything". He added: "In the eyes of the law they will each have the 'benefit' of up to £20million, or whatever is agreed was stolen. Everything they own, and anything they could own in the future, could be taken from them." It made no difference how houses had been bought or when. Under the draconian Proceeds of Crime Act, any "available assets" could be seized. Reader's mini-property empire in Dartford, worth up to £1.8 million, was in jeopardy. As he had only recently transferred it to his daughter, Joanne, the police were eyeing it up. He might have got nothing from the Hatton Garden raid he had engineered but he could still end up losing the lot.

They had gambled just about everything and lost. The smart young criminals, like Reader had been in his youth, had moved into cybercrime.

Security expert Simon Atkinson told the *Daily Telegraph*: "Hatton Garden was like something from the 1980s. Generally criminals default to methods that they're comfortable with and that physical presence, the physical drilling, is redolent of an earlier generation who are less technologically sophisticated." But Jim Stickley, who is a legit burglar – a professional "penetration tester" for banks and other institutions – spoke for most when he said, "I still think the physical heist is way cooler. It makes for much better movies. It's not very exciting to watch a guy sit at a computer and type away for several hours. But the reality is that typing is far less risky and will pay off just as well." For Dick Hobbs, the Hatton Garden heist had everything: "When there's no violence, that's when people can indulge their imagination and fantasise that they might do it themselves." The Hatton Garden gang were, literally, a dying breed.

In prison, Reader's health was deteriorating. He was being taken out of jail under armed guard to get treatment for his prostate cancer at King's College Hospital in

Camberwell, south east London. Tracy Kerr, a witness who snapped him outside the hospital in Camberwell, South London, said: "He looked like any other sick, old man in a wheelchair but was surrounded by police. Some had what looked like machine guns."

The following month, six days before his 77th birthday, he suffered a fall in Belmarsh. He had had a second stroke. To the disgust of his family, Reader had no medical treatment for two days. By the time he was rushed to Queen Elizabeth Hospital in Woolwich, Reader was in a critical condition and fighting for his life. A video emerged of him being wheeled through the hospital in a bed by medical staff, accompanied by three heavily armed police officers and three prison guards. One witness said: "Why on Earth does a sick, old man like that need to have armed policemen? Do they really think he's going to try and escape? He looked unconscious to me." Even now, the authorities were taking no chances. The witness added: "He also had a heavy chain wrapped round his arm and connected to a pole on the bed. It was sad and pathetic." His lawyer Hesham Puri objected and said: "We accept there must be some security around him but that level is quite inappropriate. He is very ill and this is not helping him get better. We've asked for the security to be reduced but had no response from the police."

He was in no fit state to be sentenced just a fortnight later. The other six – Perkins, Jones, Collins, Wood, Lincoln and Doyle – stood in the dock together for the

first time since that memorable appearance at
Westminster Magistrates' Court 10 months previously.
Over the next two days, their barristers did their best for
them. It meant trying to pin as much of the blame as
possible on the missing Basil.

Perkins' lawyer accepted he was a ringleader but not
the mastermind of the plot. He told the judge, "He accepts
he was an enthusiastic member of the team but not
someone who might be described as an architect of this
audacious enterprise. Basil had the keys to the building.
Basil was the man who was able to educate the other
conspirators of the workings of Hatton Garden – where
the alarms were, what the difficulties were, how best to go
about it and so on."

Jones had gone further. The cemetery episode had
stung him badly. The police – quite accurately – had
managed to portray him as utterly untrustworthy even as
he was trying to pretend that he was finally going straight.
Lying came as naturally to Jones as breathing, so he had
written another letter to Sky's Martin Brunt in which he
tried to turn the tables. Basil was a rogue ex-cop, he
claimed – that would teach them for trying to stitch him
up. "I can say that someone told me he was an ex-
policeman who got into security by the guy who
introduced him to me," he wrote. "He said Basil heard
about me from a close friend on the police force as I was
arrested for a similar raid in Bond Street in 2010. Basil
was the brains, as I was recruited by him. He let me in on

the night of the burglary, he hid keys and codes throughout the building." Amid the fibs, there were some truths: "I saw Basil about four times throughout. He came and went. I don't know nothing about him, where he lives. I wasn't interested," he said. Even if he did know his whereabouts, Jones admitted he would not reveal it as "it's not a done thing where I come from".

In court, Jones went even further. He tried to claim that the second larger stash at Edmonton Cemetery had been planted there by Basil. Let's stop to ponder that for a moment. Jones, facing a court that was increasingly viewing him with suspicion, was now claiming that ultra-cautious Basil, the man the police had tried and failed to catch during six weeks of surveillance, the man who had managed to hide from CCTV, the man who none of them had phoned or met, had decided to hide his loot at the grave of Jones' partner's dead father. His lawyer did his best: "His position for the record is that he was not aware or responsible for the other plot. The man known as Basil, who has absconded, was aware of the other plot."

Prosecutor Philip Evans wanted the judge to tear up the sentencing guidelines and look beyond the 10-year jail sentence that all assumed would be the limit. He told the judge: "It is clear that this was a plan of the utmost sophistication, that was many years in the planning. It was designed to achieve the maximum possible return for the minimum possible risk and, the prosecution submit, plainly fits within the broad band of the worst type of this offence which comes before the Court, particularly bearing in mind the low maximum sentence." He argued that it was "contrary to the interests of justice to follow the relevant sentencing guideline" and added that it was "appropriate to take the maximum sentence as a starting point".

He asked Judge Christopher Kinch QC to slap a life-long Criminal Behaviour Order on each gang member. The 62-year-old judge peered across the court through the glass at the six men in front of him. Perkins and Collins were older than he was. They should have been on a golf course or with their grandchildren or – looking at wheezing Collins, who needed help with his hearing aid – a care home. Instead, he was being asked to protect the public from these miscreants by requiring them to surrender their passports, tell the police of their mobile phone numbers and ban them from having possession of any valuable pieces of jewellery.

He told them to stand up. "The burglary of the Hatton Garden Safe Deposit vault in April 2015 has been labelled by many – including some defendants and advocates in this case – as the biggest burglary in English legal history," he told them. "Whether that assertion is capable of proof, I do not know. However, it is clear that the burglary at the heart of this case stands in a class of its own in the scale of the ambition, the detail of the planning, the level of preparation and the organisation of the team carrying it out and in terms of the value of the property stolen."

He told Perkins, Jones and Collins he was jailing them
for seven years each. "Thank you, judge," said Jones,
delighted he hadn't been punished for his lies. Perkins said,
"Thank you, sir". Lincoln also got seven years. Wood
ended up with six. That was the conspiracy to burgle dealt
with and it only left Doyle, guilty of concealing, converting
or transferring criminal property. He was jailed for 21
months, suspended for two years. Wood patted him on the
back telling him, "Well done". Judge Kinch said, "Thank
you very much, gentlemen. You can go down". They
waved, blew kisses and gave the thumbs up to friends and
family as they filed out of the dock. Doyle shook each man
by the hand as they passed. Before the door closed behind
them, the courtroom echoed to the sound of raucous
cheering from the five jailed men. Professor Dick Hobbs
said: "When this gang go into regular prison they will be
welcomed like heroes by the other inmates. It would be
like that scene in *The Italian Job* when everyone is out of
the cells and banging Michael Caine out of prison."

Doyle looked red in the face and close to tears. On his
way into court that morning he had tweeted a picture of
his Associated Response van with the caption: "On
Woolwich ferry on way to court, last day of 37 days in
court, let's hope I don't have to walk plank!!" Ever the
optimist, he had begun to use the whole ordeal as an
advertising opportunity, managing to crack a joke in
another tweet: "Forget A rated prison – have you got a G
rated boiler? £400 cashback for new boiler."

Outside court, Doyle said: "I'm happy and relieved, I just need to catch my breath. I feel sorry for the victims. Now I'm going to focus on my business and my family. I just want to spend some time with my family now and I've got boilers to fit in north London." He'd made some new friends over the previous two months. He was to be the guest of honour at the launch of a new book by veteran journalist Duncan Campbell about his career as a crime reporter, called *We'll All Be Murdered in Our Beds!*

Once again, Scotland Yard tried to remind the nation, like disappointed schoolteachers, that the Hatton Garden burglary was nothing to be admired. Detective Superintendent Craig Turner said: "There will be some out there who have sympathy for these men believing this crime to be a bold heist where no one got hurt. The truth is these men were career criminals who didn't give a moment's thought for the people they were stealing from. For many of the victims these safety-deposit boxes represented their livelihood. They put their most valuable property into the vault to keep safe during the bank holiday weekend, only to see it cruelly snatched away."

Could a crime like Hatton Garden ever happen again? DCI Paul Johnson will never say never: "They never cease to surprise us, do they? We would have never seen this coming. You always have these good jobs and you think that's the end of that, and then another one pops up a few years later. There's always somebody there with the will and the guile who will have a go if they think the money's there."

The Flying Squad had got their men. All apart from one. Basil was believed to be the youngest of the gang and he represented the next generation of master thief who is at home with modern technology. One detective had described Reader and his team as "analogue criminals in a digital world". This cannot be said of Basil, who had used electronic bugs and computer technology to pull off the raid. He had been one step ahead of the police and had "gone on his toes" soon after the Flying Squad began their surveillance operation.

The gang insider said he thinks Basil left the country using his real name. He said: "The police will be watching his house and his sister and brother but he won't go back or be in touch. He'll probably come back in a couple of years and hand himself in. The police won't have much on him and he will have a better chance of avoiding conviction now all the rest have been sentenced and have no reason to help the police.

"There were around half-a-dozen people who know him as Basil and who knew where he lived. Jones, Perkins, Reader and two others. One of those is a big gambler and I think he could have told the police. I am sure the police know who he is. They must do because too many people knew where he lived and in my experience the police get to find out these things. I think back to how many grasses I've known in the past."

The source refused to say where he thinks Basil has

gone. "He used to talk about one country in particular. He told me a funny story about a beautiful woman he met who came from this place and he would say he was going to visit one day. He could well have gone there. He can disappear because he has money."

That left only Reader's fate hanging in the balance. For a while, it looked like he might never be sentenced. His barrister James Scobie QC said the pensioner was too ill to even appear via video-link from the high-security prison where he was being held. He told the court, "He had what turned out to be a second fall in Belmarsh prison, which resulted in him being left for two days without proper care and then ultimately ending up in a critical care unit at Woolwich hospital, having had a stroke. We suspect the prognosis for him, long term, is poor... It may well be that he does not have many more months to live, the court should be made aware of that."

But Reader once again confounded expectations. Two weeks later, on Monday, March 21, 2016, his tired face appeared on the video-link screens at Court 3, Woolwich Crown Court. Sitting in a wheelchair, wearing a short-sleeved T-shirt and glasses, he looked every one of his 77 years. The court heard more about his health problems – the strokes, the cancer, loss of hearing, his failing sight and the fact he now needed daily help with simple tasks like showering.

Judge Kinch did not ask Reader to stand up: "Mr Reader, you pleaded guilty to involvement in a conspiracy to burgle the Hatton Garden Safe Deposit vault, said by many to be the biggest burglary in English legal history and it was a burglary that involved the most detailed and intricate planning and preparation. I am satisfied that you were rightly described as one of the ringleaders. I don't place you above the other conspirators and I don't place any great weight on the nickname 'the Master', which at the time of the police recordings may have been used with a degree of irony."

Reader might have permitted himself a smile at that. As if those muppets were capable of irony. But he remained deadpan. The judge added: "It is clear there are a range of medical problems, some of them serious and potentially very serious indeed." He sentenced Reader to six years in jail. He'd be out in two. If he lived that long. Reader nodded. The screen went black.

Epilogue

The balding, grey-haired grandfather was a well-known character on the affluent street where he had lived for forty years. Sprightly for his age, he trimmed hedges for some neighbours, including a banker and BBC executive, just to keep himself fit. On Easter Sunday, April 5, 2015, the spring afternoon sunshine occasionally burst through the high clouds to bathe the old man's front garden in a warm glow, illuminating the neat rows of daffodils like nuggets of gold in the dark soil. A tall, slim figure in his mid-50s lifted the latch on the wrought-iron gate and wearily trod up the path, as he had done many times before. He carried a small rucksack on his right shoulder, over which he gave a quick glance. All was quiet on the tree-lined street, so he climbed the six steps to the house. The visitor knew the Victorian door with stained-glass panelling would only be secured by the mortice lock because the old man had been fixing the latch for months. Disassembling locks and playing with them gave him satisfaction. His friend doubted there had been much wrong with the mechanism in the first place.

ONE LAST JOB

The visitor knocked and after a short pause the door opened. Two keen blue eyes peered up out of the hallway. The old man stood back without saying a word to let his guest in. Though he didn't look particularly surprised to see his friend, the host had not been expecting him that day. But the rule was no phones, so his visits were always unannounced. The younger man was about six-foot tall with slightly hunched shoulders and his mousey hair was greying in places. He would soon become known across the world as the only master thief to pull off the £14million Hatton Garden heist and get away with it. But at that moment, the man who called himself Basil was secure in the knowledge the police would not be aware of his work for another day-and-a-half. He had not slept for about the same period and was in need of counsel from his more experienced friend, who welcomed him using his real name.

"Tea or coffee?" asked the host as he picked up the kettle. The kitchen was at the back of the house, with French doors looking out onto the old man's manicured lawn, which was scattered with pink petals from a blossoming cherry tree. "Coffee please." Basil was well spoken, with an accent that sounded like the product of a middle-class upbringing in the home counties. He slumped onto a stool and the story of the previous three nights began pouring out of him. How he had entered the Hatton Garden Safety Deposit company using his own keys on the Thursday evening, how he had been forced to leave the building to go and wake up "outside man" Kenny Collins after he fell asleep, how they had been unable to get in and returned without Reader, how he had managed to squeeze through the small hole, along with Danny Jones, and prise open around 70 boxes. And finally how Jones and Terry Perkins had turned nasty on him and refused to hand over his share when they had all returned to Collins' council flat in Islington for the "cut-up".

Basil had only been given around £100,000 worth of gold and £80,000 in cash. He said: "They've taken all the rest of the gear. What do you think I should do? Do you think I'll get anything more?" The old man responded with brutal honesty: "You won't get a dollar more from them. They're greedy bastards and you can't trust them." He was articulating what Basil already knew deep down, but he somehow needed to hear it from someone he respected and trusted. "I know where Kenny walks his dog every morning so I'm going to wait for him there and confront him about it," he said half-heartedly, before wearily getting to his feet.

The old man showed him to the door. It would be the last time he would see his friend for a long time, maybe forever. Basil would disappear like a ghost. Even if Scotland Yard did catch him, would they ever have the evidence to jail him?

Acknowledgements

We owe thanks to many people without whom this book would never have been written.

A large debt of gratitude goes to one person in particular, who must remain anonymous for obvious reasons, who patiently spent dozens of hours talking to us. We thank other members of the London underworld for their help. Also a big thank you to the retired detective who got the ball rolling. We are deeply grateful to many other former and serving detectives and thank all of those who we mention by name as well as those quoted anonymously.

We want to give special recognition to the work of other journalists. The book includes information that has been gathered from books, press cuttings and the news wires written by scores of reporters over six decades. With savage cuts currently seeing a huge reduction in the number of journalists actually going out to cover stories, it will be increasingly difficult for future generations to chronicle the lives of people like Brian Reader. Beware – you get what you pay for.

Huge thanks are owed to our two historical advisors, Dr Paul Lashmar and Professor Dick Hobbs for their time and wisdom.

We are grateful to all the team at the Daily Mirror and Mirror Books for their help and professionalism: Fergus McKenna, Jo Sollis, Robin Jarossi, Paula Scott, Julie Adams, Aidan McGurran, Ivor Game, Ian Vogler, Russell Myers, Angela Wormald, Piers Eady, Dean Rousewell, Nick Coles and Brett Dietrich.

Finally, we would like to thank Sunday Mirror editor Gary Jones for coming up with the idea of writing this book, our news editor Tom Carlin and editor-in-chief Lloyd Embley for their support, and associate editor Paul Henderson for all of his advice and encouragement.

Index of Names

INDEX

Also by Mirror Books

Anni Dewani: A Father's Story

The full, frank and ultimately heartbreaking account of Anni Dewani's life from childhood through to the conclusion of the trial of her husband Shrien in Cape Town, four years after her murder.

Written by London-based journalist Shekhar Bhatia and told from the perspective of Anni's father, Vinod Hindocha, this is the extraordinary story of how one family has coped with seeing their hopes for their daughter's future being so cruelly extinguished. How they tried to live with, and through, the aftermath, their efforts to see justice done and ultimately their attempts to reconcile themselves with the court's verdict and a future without their beautiful daughter, Anni.

Illustrated with exclusive personal pictures from the Hindocha family, Shekhar Bhatia was invited by Anni Dewani's family to write a book about her life and death and has been given full access to all materials, friends and family members.

Mirror Books

Also by Mirror Books

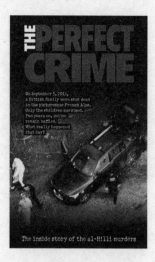

The Perfect Crime

By Tom Parry

When 25 shots from a semi-automatic pistol rang out across the Alpine woodland high above Lake Annecy, there was nobody to raise the alarm. In a car, in a lay-by, were the bloodied bodies of British computer engineer, Saad al-Hilli, his wife, Iqbal, and her mother, Suhaila. Nearby, on the road, lay the corpse of French cyclist, Sylvain Mollier. Saad's eldest daughter, Zainab, seven, had been shot, pistol-whipped and left for dead. Cowering underneath her mum Iqbal's skirt in the back seat was Zainab's little sister, Zeena – the only one of the six people left unharmed. Was this a professional assassin's error, or a humane gesture by someone who knew the girls? The motorcycle-riding killer disappeared. Was he hired by an underworld contact to take out Saad and his family? Was he paid by the Iraqi-born engineer's jealous brother, Zaid? Was he a Mossad agent under orders to assassinate an Israeli enemy? Or were the al-Hillis just holidaymakers in the wrong place at the wrong time when a French cyclist was murdered?

Mirror Books